Sociology and the Jesus Movement

Sociology and the Jesus Movement

by
Richard A. Horsley

Crossroad ◊ New York

1989

The Crossroad Publishing Company
370 Lexington Avenue, New York, NY 10017

Printed in the United States of America

Library of Congress Cataloging-in-Publication Data

HORSLEY, RICHARD A.
  Sociology and the Jesus movement / by Richard A. Horsley.
  Includes bibliographical references.
  ISBN 0-8245-0992-7
  1. Sociology, Christian–History–Early church, ca. 30–600.
  2. Sociology, Biblical. 3. Sociology, Jewish–History.
  4. Theissen, Gerd. Soziologie der Jesusbewegung. I. Title.
  BR166.H67 1989   89-38807
  306.6'701–dc20   CIP

◊ Contents

◇ Acknowledgments _____

Robert Bellah and Randy Huntsberry have been my principal mentors in sociology; I hope they are not embarrassed by my historical applications. Donna DiSciullo and Bill Locke first pointed out to me how problematic functionalism might be in application to ancient Palestine and the Jesus movement when we were reading Theissen together nearly ten years ago. Stan Stowers helped place functionalist sociology in a broad critical perspective. Burt Mack patiently read my initial gropings and offered crucial suggestions for shaping the presentation; he has also been a provocative and pushy conversation partner. Jack Elliott, Randy Huntsberry, and Andy Overman read all or parts of the draft and provided many important critical comments. Laura Whitney and Louise Mattaliano have done much to facilitate my reading and research.

◇ Introduction _____

Biblical studies has experienced a dramatic resurgence of interest in social scientific approaches in recent years. This is partly due to frustrations with traditional techniques of biblical study, which often involved painstaking poring over the meaning of Hebrew and Greek terms in dozens of biblical and extrabiblical texts. Frequently the results did not make the enterprise seem worthwhile. The texts did not somehow "come to life" after all the philological and lexicographic gymnastics. The increasing interest in social sciences was also stimulated by developments within biblical studies and allied fields such as archaeology. The dramatic discoveries of new extrabiblical evidence relevant to biblical texts forced interpreters to consider certain questions of social and historical relations. The discovery of the Dead Sea Scrolls, for example, not only provided a number of hitherto unknown texts that expressed an apocalyptic spirit provocatively similar to that in certain late-prophetic and early Christian literature; it also forced scholars to take into account the existence of a whole community of Jews that had striking similarities in orientation and practices to the earliest "Christian" communities. Biblical scholars thus began asking more concrete social questions of their sources and looked to those disciplines that had already been dealing with questions of social relations.

The recent appropriation of sociology for the study of Christian origins is also clearly a response to the burning social issues and conflicts of the last few decades. When hundreds of college and seminary students, along with older clergy and laity, were personally involved in civil rights demonstrations, it was difficult to ignore the social concerns of the prophets or to confine Jesus' proclamation of the kingdom to some call for existentialist decision about one's own individual authenticity. When thousands of students engaged in protests calling attention to their own universities' involvement in the United States' practice of political and economic violence among third world peoples, it was difficult to ignore the prophets' criticism of their monarchs' military expenditures or to miss the critique of Roman imperialism implicit in Paul's letters and the Apocalypse of John. When women enrolled in increasing numbers in theological schools, it was impossible to ignore issues such as the

1

respective images and roles of women and men in "scriptural" texts, supposedly the "word of God," that had clearly been written by men as expressions of traditional patriarchal societies. Moreover, stimulated by some of these same developments and events, new, socially critical forms of theology emerged which called biblical studies into serious engagement.

Biblical studies suddenly faced bewildering battles on two opposite fronts simultaneously. Many feminist thinkers rejected the Bible as oppressive of women, while black and Latin American theologians claimed biblical support and legitimation for their respective liberation theologies and movements. Traditionally geared toward interpretation of particular scriptural texts to make them more edifying for personal faith, biblical studies was suddenly forced to discern the social and political dimensions of those very texts. Particularly New Testament studies, so heavily influenced by Protestant theological concern with individual salvation, found itself poorly equipped to deal with the concrete realities in its own texts. The social sciences, which had themselves recently undergone considerable growth and achieved new legitimacy as instruments of social analysis in the 1950s and 1960s, seemed to offer the needed ways of approaching a broader and more socially relevant understanding of biblical history and literature.

Interest in the social concerns of biblical texts and use of sociological methods are nothing new, of course. Earlier in this century, in fact, interest in social issues and use of sociological method were strong and showing signs of sophisticated development within New Testament studies. In the United States in particular, the social gospel's concern for social justice and the early development of academic sociology converged in the Chicago School. One needs only to recall the titles of books by Shailer Mathews (*The Social Teachings of Jesus: An Essay in Christian Sociology*, 1897) or Shirley Jackson Case (*The Social Origins of Christianity*, 1923) to appreciate both the social orientation and the sociological intention already at work. Case sounds almost contemporary when he insists that early Christianity be studied "in the full light of the conditions and processes of the actual life of real people . . . within a concrete social nexus. . . ."[1] Mathews anticipates the sociology of knowledge in his insights that some of the most fundamental concepts in New Testament and nascent Christianity were rooted in the Semitic or the Hellenistic "monarchial mind."[2] During the 1930s, however, European neo-orthodoxy and its emphasis on the revelatory word of God displaced the overly optimistic social gospel in the United States, and little was done for nearly fifty years to build on the work of Case, Mathews, and others in the first third of the century.

Even in Germany some promising beginnings were made toward developing genuinely sociological methods of biblical study. In its origins form criticism was understood explicitly as a sociological method. Hermann Gunkel's concept of *Sitz im Leben* referred to the direct relationship that he looked for between the forms of oral tradition and their actual uses in social life. Although the insightful Oscar Cullmann saw immediately that New Testament form criticism required a more substantial sociological basis, both Martin Dibelius and Rudolf Bultmann, the two great pioneers of this method, understood their enterprise as explicitly sociological ("form" was a social, not an esthetic, concept!) and understood that they were dealing with popular traditions (*Kleinliteratur* from the lower strata of society).[3] Neo-orthodox theology, of course, exerted an even more dominant influence in Europe than in America. Ironically, Bultmann himself, far from developing the sociological promise of form criticism, launched into the virtually antihistorical and antisociological "demythologizing" program to make the original Christian message compatible with and palatable to the modern scientific mind. Bultmann's own highly influential theology focused narrowly on personal decision about one's own "authentic existence."

The result in New Testament studies for most of the last two generations has been a sort of "methodological docetism, as if believers had minds and spirits unconnected with their individual and corporate bodies."[4] Scriptural interpretation focused on religious ideas in its fundamental orientation toward the inner life of individuals. New Testament studies has been concerned primarily with the edification of individual religious faith and the intellectual grasp of theological truth. This seems ironic for an enterprise that deals extensively and intensively with the Synoptic Gospels, in which the main event is a political execution, or with the letters of Paul, who emphasizes not only theological truths or some transcendent spiritual life but also the absolute importance of certain political events and of social interaction in concrete communities (see especially 1 Corinthians 1–2, 10, 12–14).

Now, however, we are no longer satisfied with such an idealist individualist theological understanding of the biblical texts. We have rediscovered that biblical literature is about the problems and experiences of real people. We have discovered further that New Testament authors themselves understood the Bible as history and instruction for social relations and not only as spiritual or theological truth. Paul, for example, in contrast with some of his more intellectually inclined contemporaries, understood the stories about the passage through the Red Sea and the water from the rock in the wilderness not in terms of the spiritual salvation of the soul but as the historical experiences of earlier generations of the people of God written down to provide social-ethical warning to later generations about the importance of mutual responsibility in the community (1 Corinthians 10). In the Gospels there is little or no attention given to the salvation of individual souls and a great deal given to interpersonal and community relations, including economic matters. Story after story in the Gospels and Acts depicts serious conflict between the political authorities and Jesus or his followers. The epistles, moreover, are full of references to persecution of the early Christians and to conflicts between the leaders of the nascent movement. Once we are no longer simply looking for answers to old theological questions, we cannot help but recognize that those involved in New Testament literature, the writers and/or the actors, understood themselves as participating in world-historical events and experienced their whole lives as changed. What New Testament texts portray and express, and what New Testament studies must therefore pursue, is not so much truth as life, historical life and events.

Because the development of social scientific methods was abandoned virtually as soon as it started in New Testament studies, the field has until recently lacked adequate tools with which to deal with concrete social and historical realities and to make social and historical explanations. But new beginnings have been made, with borrowing from other academic disciplines, in the hopes that sociological and other approaches will make the life and events of New Testament literature more accessible and understandable. The social sciences, however, have meanwhile undergone an extensive and intensive development of their own as academic disciplines. Increasing specialization within fields such as sociology and anthropology and the proliferation of approaches make it impossible for students not trained specifically in such fields to have much perspective on or critical awareness of the analytical tools of social science. Biblical studies clearly is in an experimental stage and will remain so while interpreters sort out, by trial and error, what tools, models, and approaches are useful and adequate for studying New Testament history and literature. Indeed, as various approaches are applied experimentally, it will also be possible to recognize more adequately the contours of the historical materials to be interpreted.

Emergent Methodological Problems

The resurgence of interest in social issues and sociological approaches in New Testament studies has been generating momentum now for nearly two decades. The greatest productivity has occurred in the description of social facts and imagination of the social world(s) of early Christian and contemporary Jewish and pagan groups, although most such studies have not paid much attention to concrete social structures.[5] Important and increasingly sophisticated work has also been done with social theory and the use of social scientific models for interpretation of early Christian texts and social relations.[6] The social sciences have also been used to advantage in reconstructing the social history of early Christian and related groups.[7] Enough substantial studies have been published, along with numerous review essays,[8] that it is now possible to identify a number of problems that have surfaced in experimentation with others' methods.

Most fundamental perhaps is the problem of evidence. Social scientists have developed methods for study of contemporary societies for which abundant data are available. If it is not already at hand, then sociologists can conduct surveys or anthropologists can conduct a series of carefully thought out conversations with members of the social unit they are studying. For serious sociological study of New Testament history and literature there are three kinds of problems regarding evidence that must continually be faced and for which special methods of analysis may have to be developed. (a) Evidence in general for early Christianity and its Palestinian Jewish or Hellenistic-Roman context is simply scarce and fragmentary at best. Archaeological findings help, but again the gains, although steady, are minimal considering the huge gaps of evidence for life in the ancient world. (b) Available evidence does not provide much direct information of the social or "sociological" sort. Most of our evidence is from literary sources, and we can extract sociologically relevant information only by inference or by "reading between the lines" or, frankly, by speculation or "educated guessing," all the while depending heavily on comparative evidence and models. (c) Despite its scarcity—or, rather, compounding the problem of its scarcity—the available evidence is from diverse communities and social-historical contexts in the ancient Hellenistic-Roman world. If we want to maintain any pretense of being concrete in our analyses, then we must simply cease speaking of early Christianity generally, as if there ever was such a historical entity. Our evidence is sufficiently clear to indicate that the early Christian movement was diverse geographically and culturally. Sociological analysis must therefore concentrate on particular communities in particular situations insofar as possible.

Partly because of the fragmentary evidence and partly because we are dealing with ancient historical realities, there may be problems in the compatibility of modern social scientific approaches and distinctive ancient historical data.[9] The social sciences have been developed to comprehend the typical, common, and general in social behavior, even to strive for the discovery of the lawlike generalizations and to provide predictability for purposes of social control. New Testament studies and Jewish history, linked as they are, directly or indirectly, with Christian and Jewish faith, are concerned to appreciate the distinctive character of certain historical realities and/or of the origins of Christianity or rabbinic Judaism. It is interesting, to be sure, to consider that John the Baptist, Jesus of Nazareth, Paul, and other ancient Jewish prophets, popular kings, and brigand-chiefs were all "charismatic figures"—as were Elijah, Crazy Horse, Wovoka, Joan of Arc—or, for that matter, Hitler, Huey Long, and Sun Myung Moon. But what is thereby gained if we are striving for a more precise and concrete understanding of early Christian communities? The ways in which the social behavior of figures such as John, Jesus, Simon bar Giora or Theudas was determined by distinctive Jewish historical-cultural (biblical) traditions may mean that their differences with the "ideal type" of the charismatic figure are far more revealing than their conformities with it.

Most sociological methods and models have been developed in analysis of modern European or American social phenomena. There may thus be a general problem of their suitability for analysis of ancient traditional societies and social phenomena. Application of some sociological concepts and models of society to ancient Jewish and Hellenistic social phenomena may well be blatantly anachronistic and "ethnocentric."[10] For example, it was understandable that New Testament scholars might look for help from the sociology of religion, an approach with which many trained in traditional theological schools were somewhat familiar. The sociology of religion, however, was developed on the peculiar modern Western assumption that "religion" is a distinctive and even separable social institution (such as the "church"), differentiated from the political and economic dimensions of life and institutions in society (the "state" and business corporations). In ancient "biblical" societies, like most traditional societies, there was no such differentiation of the religious, political, and economic dimensions of society. Hence, to apply many of the standard concepts and assumptions of sociology of religion to Palestinian Jewish society at the time of Jesus would be anachronistic and distortive.[11] If we are genuinely interested in understanding the literary expressions and the life situation of particular ancient Jews and early Christians, then priority must be given to the historical evidence and the sociological concepts or model adapted (or even abandoned) to avoid simply projecting modern social realities back into the historical (biblical) situations.[12]

There is a similar problem with the use of comparative material and cross-cultural methods. As we have become aware of the "peril of modernizing" not only Jesus but New Testament communities as well—

reducing them to "religious communities" seeking only spiritual salvation—we have recognized how strange the early Christian movements were. We have begun to recognize that they were "revolutionary," challenging the dominant culture and ruling orders "through a powerful set of alternative values and behaviors."[13] Recognition of the strangeness of early Christian groups' mindset and behavior, however, has led to the application of concepts and generalizations based on the study of other marginal, sectarian, millenarian, and/or alienated social-religious movements. Some of the movements on which such generalizations and concepts are based, however, are radically different from early Christian groups. We might well ask how generalizations based heavily on cargo cults among relatively egalitarian Melanesian societies who had only recently faced Western imperial rule would actually apply either to Palestinian peasants with a long historical tradition of resistance to Western imperialism or to the already somewhat assimilated urbanites who joined the early Christian communities in Hellenistic cities. The cross-cultural material we use for comparisons, particularly to fill in the huge gaps of evidence for ancient Jewish and Hellenistic societies and the early Christian communities situated there should come from peoples and situations that are as similar and as broadly analogous as possible. "A good social science model for biblical interpretation . . . should derive from experiences that match what we know of the time-and-place-conditioned biblical world as closely as possible."[14] But there is a serious caveat, at least for the current situation in social scientific study of the New Testament: it is difficult to discern where any such model might be available, and it may be difficult even to find solid cross-cultural studies that meet these obviously desirable criteria. Nevertheless, we should hold out for such comparative materials and should be cautious about generalizations without a more solid comparative basis.

If would appear to go without saying that we should understand fully the methods or approaches we are adopting from social scientists and applying to our biblical subject matter. But this will in fact be difficult for most students (perhaps especially for scholars) in biblical studies. It may prove impossible ever to become more than amateur sociologists after heavy investment in the more humanistic methods of traditional biblical studies. This makes all the more important a reliance on social scientists themselves for critical assessment of the methods and models they have developed.[15]

Every bit as important as understanding the approach we are borrowing would be a critical perspective on the assumptions and the implications of that approach. Unfortunately, social scientists themselves, like other intellectuals, may not be critically aware of these assumptions and implications. We can have recourse to perspectives from the philosophy and history of science, including now social science.[16] But we cannot avoid taking responsibility ourselves for critical assessment of the presuppositions and implications of what we borrow.

A final problem evident in some of the studies using social scientific methods is the substitution of a new form of abstraction. Having been attracted to sociology and related disciplines partly because the usual philological and theological approaches were so abstract and removed from real problems of social life, interpreters may substitute the abstractions of sociological theories and models. Having become critically aware that theological agenda and concepts were determining the focal evidence and issues, they may now run the danger of allowing equally abstract sociological methods to determine their focus and selection of data. A persistent push toward concrete communities and social conflicts will be important.

Some critical responses to the use of social sciences in New Testament studies have disparaged social description as opposed to genuine sociological explanation. Surely the latter is on a higher level of sophistication and would be the ultimate goal of sociological inquiry. However, given the combination of lack of evidence with a lack of truly analogous comparative material and sociological models based on such comparative material, it may be absolutely essential to devote much more attention to reconstruction of the most pertinent ancient social structures and conflicts before we can seriously proceed to satisfactory explanation. Recognizing that even social description involves a certain projection of models, we ought to be cautious about "filling in the blanks" from comparative data and especially from borrowed sociological models. But since what evidence we have from the New Testament shows people not so much propounding new doctrines as forming new communities while locked in conflict with the dominant social institutions, we should probably focus considerable energy simply on reconstructing, insofar as possible, the fundamental social structure and the corresponding social conflicts as a context for their actions and ideas evident in New Testament literature.

Biblical interpretation should really become a two-way process of mutual criticism. Biblical studies has long espoused the ideal that the scriptural text is allowed to affect and influence the interpreter, even to call the interpreter's self-understanding into question. Anthropology apparently espouses a similar ideal: good cross-cultural methods require the interpreter to account for his/her own social location.[17] It seems difficult to determine whether and to what extent this has actually occurred and what difference it has made heretofore in either biblical or anthropological interpretations of others' cultures. We can at least allow the early Christian communities and the New Testament writings to lead us to criticize our own interests, views, and the very social scientific methods and concepts we are borrowing and applying to them.

Strategy of This Study

This study takes Gerd Theissen's *Sociology of Early Palestinian Christianity* as its starting point because it has been the most influential sociological treatment of earliest Christianity to date.[18] Theissen's study has been so influential, particularly in the United States, for a number of reasons. His presentation itself is terse, bold, concise, and provocative. It also filled, in timely fashion, a scholarly and interpretive vacuum; it was the first, and is still the only, sociological treatment of "the Jesus movement." His treatment resonates with New Testament scholars in the United States for particular reasons that we could discern via the "sociology of knowledge." Theissen happens to utilize the sociological approach (structural-functionalism) that most currently active American biblical scholars are familiar with from their own higher education. And the ideology of that sociological approach has an "elective affinity" (Max Weber) with the social location and interests of most biblical scholars, who are "middle class" and "liberals," but slipping somewhat in social status and on the defensive. Why this is so will become more evident in the critical exposition below.

In reference to the problems that have surfaced in our use of sociology in New Testament studies, Theissen's presentation holds some promise. He has recognized that early Christianity was diverse. Hence he focuses locally on the Palestinian "Jesus movement." Ostensibly, at least, he perceives that most of our evidence is nonsociological, indirect, and requires inference in order to be usable. Moreover, he understands the particular structural-functional approach that he adopts as "sociology."

Theissen's study also, however, provides a useful example (a) of how, given the scarcity of evidence, one's own presuppositions and chosen model can determine the reconstruction; (b) of how sociological abstraction can simply be substituted for the previously determinative theological abstraction; and (c) of why it is important to be critically aware of the assumptions and implications of one's approach and why it is important to allow the evidence from early Christianity critically to question one's own chosen approach.

In the most substantive and critical response to Theissen to date, John Elliott has identified some of the problems in Theissen's treatment.[19] Indeed, "too much has been attempted in too brief a space," the

conceptualization and approach are mystifying, theories are left unclari-
fied, and an overall picture of Palestinian Jewish society is obscured.
Elliott, moreover, like Bruce Malina before him, has noted some of the
principal problems with the functionalist approach. But the problems
evident in Theissen's treatment appear to be more serious than Elliott's
generous critique allows in three principal respects. Theissen has apparently not carried out a critical exegetical and historical analysis of much
of the limited data. Theissen has not so much uncovered patterns of
social structure, behavior, and tensions implicit in the sources as superimposed an abstract system of analysis and modern social patterns and
concepts onto ancient Jewish Palestine, using Gospel and other texts as
illustrations. As a result, his picture of the Jesus movement does not
appear derived from or supported by the textual data. Part I below is a
critique of Theissen's sociological reconstruction of "early Palestinian
Christianity."

Thus, Theissen's approach may not have "forged a path leading to fresh
sources of water," but wandered into a cul-de-sac, as he himself suggests.
At the conclusion of his analysis of the Jesus movement, Theissen finds
that the movement was a "failure," that it had no function in Palestinian
Jewish society. Ironically, this means that what Theissen has demon-
strated is that there is no point in pursuing any further a structural-
functional analysis of "early Palestinian Christianity." The sociological
task before us, then, is to explore some alternative approach as well as
to attend more critically to the data. Parts II and III are an attempt at an
alternative reconstruction of the social conditions and the characteristics
of the Jesus movement(s) in ancient Jewish Palestine.

The critique of Theissen's approach and presentation in Part I will be
blunt. But that is a mark of the importance of his work. Perhaps the
process I have gone through in preparing the chapters below can serve
as an illustration, and my own appreciation, of the importance of the
stimulation his work has provided. An initial reading of the book led me
to read Synoptic Gospel materials with new questions in mind, and that,
in turn, led to a section-by-section criticism of his method and reconstructions. My uneasiness with his method led me into a critical review of the
very sociology I had learned under Talcott Parsons himself (virtually the
"father" of structural-functionalist sociology), which in turn forced me to
rethink some of my own assumptions. Finally, dissatisfaction with
Theissen's overall reconstruction forced an attempt at an alternative view.
I am deeply in Theissen's debt for such stimulation. He has led many of
us to rethink a highly important branch of Christian origins.

Notes

1. Shirley Jackson Case, "Whither Historicism in Theology?" in *The Process of Religion*, ed. M. H. Krumbine (S. Mathews Festschrift; New York: Macmillan, 1933) 64.

2. Shailer Mathews, *Biblical World* 46 (1915) 212.

3. R. Bultmann, *Die Geschichte der synoptischen Tradition* (Göttingen: Vandenhoeck & Ruprecht, 1921) 4–5; M. Dibelius, *Die Formgeschichte des Evangeliums* (Tübingen: Mohr, 1919) 57.

4. R. Scroggs, "The Sociological Interpretation of the New Testament: The Present State of Research," *New Testament Studies* 26 (1979–80) 165.

5. E.g., the collection of studies in S. Safrai and M. Stern, eds., *The Jewish People in the First Century* (2 vols.; Assen: Van Gorcum, 1974, 1976); Wayne Meeks, *The First Urban Christians: The Social World of the Apostle Paul* (New Haven: Yale University Press, 1983); most such studies of the "social world" have built on and attempted to apply insights regarding the ways in which meaning is "socially constructed" derived largely from Peter Berger and Thomas Luckmann, *The Social Construction of Reality* (Garden City, NY: Doubleday, 1967).

6. E.g., John H. Elliott, *A Home for the Homeless: A Sociological Exegesis of 1 Peter, its Situation and Strategy* (Philadelphia: Fortress, 1981); John G. Gager, *Kingdom and Community: The Social World of Early Christianity* (Englewood Cliffs, NJ: Prentice-Hall, 1975); Howard Clark Kee, *Christian Origins in Sociological Perspective* (Philadelphia: Westminster, 1980); Bruce Malina, *The New Testament World: Insights from Cultural Anthropology* (Atlanta: John Knox, 1981); idem, *Christian Origins and Cultural Anthropology* (Atlanta: John Knox, 1986).

7. E.g., Elisabeth Schüssler Fiorenza, *In Memory of Her: A Feminist Theological Reconstruction of Christian Origins* (New York: Crossroad, 1983); Burton Mack, *A Myth of Innocence: Mark and Christian Origins* (Philadelphia: Fortress, 1988).

8. Among the most critically reflective on method are Jonathan Z. Smith, "Too Much Kingdom, Too Little Community," *Zygon* 13 (1978) 123–30; Robin Scroggs, "The Sociological Interpretation of the New Testament: The Present State of Research," *New Testament Studies* 26 (1979–80) 164–79; Bruce Malina, "The Social Sciences and Biblical Interpretation," *Interpretation* 37 (1982) 229–42; Stanley K. Stowers, "The Social Sciences and the Study of Early Christianity," in *Approaches to Ancient Judaism*, ed. W. S. Green (Atlanta: Scholars Press, 1985) 5:149–81; and John H. Elliott, review of W. A. Meeks, *The First Urban Christians*, in *Religious Studies Review* 11 (1985) 329–34; idem, "Social Scientific Criticism of the New Testament and its Social World: More on Methods and Models," *Semeia* 35 (1986) 1–33.

9. More generally on the relation between sociology and history as disciplines or approaches, see, e.g., Peter Burke, *Sociology and History* (London: Allen & Unwin, 1980).

10. "Meanings in history will always be perceived in terms of some social system. Depending upon the social sensitivity of the interpreter, those meanings will be either the meanings of the present day interpreter, reflecting his/her own social system (hence ethnocentric) or that of the people s/he interprets (hence based on some sort of comparative social approach" (B. Malina, "Why Interpret the Bible with the Social Sciences," *American Baptist Quarterly* 2 [1983] 128–29).

11. On the other hand, of course, insofar as the nascent Christian movement in the Hellenistic cities involved new communities that had virtually no political and economic power, perhaps we can discern here one of the historic cases in which semi-separable "religious" institutions emerged.

12. Similarly Malina, "Why Interpret the Bible," 130.

13. T. F. Best, "The Sociological Study of the New Testament: Promise and Peril of a New Discipline," *Scottish Journal of Theology* 36 (1983) 183–84.

14. Malina, "The Social Sciences and Biblical Interpretation," 240–41.

15. Ibid., 240.

16. See, e.g., Stowers, "The Social Sciences and the Study of Early Christianity."

17. Malina views this as an important infusion into biblical interpretation ("The Social Sciences and Biblical Interpretation," 38).

18. Gerd Theissen, *Soziologie der Jesusbewegung* (Munich: Kaiser, 1977; Eng. trans. Philadelphia: Fortress, 1978).

19. Elliott, "Social Scientific Criticism of the New Testament and its Social World," *Semeia* 35 (1986) 1–33.

Part I

Theissen's *Sociology of Early Palestinian Christianity*

1 ◊ A Sociology of the Jesus Movement _____

Roles, Factors, and Functions

In *Sociology of Early Palestinian Christianity,* Gerd Theissen presents in three parts a concise, lively, and provocative sociological analysis of early Palestinian Christianity as a renewal movement within Judaism: he first sketches his own distinctive reconstruction of the principal roles that constituted the movement, then explores the effects of Jewish society on the "Jesus movement," and finally explores the effects that movement had on society.[1]

Analysis of Roles: Wandering Charismatics and Their Supporters

Theissen contends that "the internal structure of the Jesus movement was determined by the interaction of three roles." The *wandering charismatics* were "the decisive spiritual authorities in the local communities," while *sympathizers* in the local communities provided indispensable material support for the wandering charismatics. Both had mutual expectations with *the Son of man,* "the bearer of revelation" who would vindicate his followers and whose expectations of them were formulated in ethical and religious commandments (7).

Wandering charismatics. As the cornerstone of his sociological reconstruction Theissen claims that "Jesus did not primarily found local communities, but called into being a movement of wandering charismatics" (8). Looking ahead, one suspects, to subsequent developments in the Hellenistic world, he asserts that while their communities of supporters "remained within the framework of Judaism," the wandering charismatics "handed on what was later to take independent form as Christianity." The absence of the earliest disciples from Jerusalem when Paul visited three years after his "conversion" is taken to mean that they "were travelling through the country, on a mission of preaching and

15

healing," as they had been commissioned to do in Mark 3:13 (9). More-over, if Paul and Barnabas were itinerant preachers, we must assume the same of the others.

Indeed, far from being marginal to the Jesus movement, the wandering charismatics "provide the social background for a good deal of the syn-optic tradition, especially the tradition of the words of Jesus" (10). Indeed, in the ethical norms of this tradition one can discern an ethos of itinerant radicalism manifested particularly in a pattern of relinquishing home, family, possessions, and protection (10–14). This direct relationship that Theissen discerns between the sayings tradition in particular and itin-erant radicalism of the wandering charismatics is more dramatically portrayed in his earlier article "Itinerant Radicalism," in which he deduces the phenomenon of the itinerants and their radicalism from analysis of the sayings tradition.[2]

According to Theissen's "analytical conclusions," the charismatic dis-ciples were called to leave their homes and lead a life of wandering in which, like the "Son of man," they would have nowhere to lay their heads (Matt 8:20). As itinerants they had no family. Indeed, they were expected to ignore the traditional demands of piety and the Torah: to "hate" father and mother (etc. Luke 14:26) and even, in one case, to refuse burial to a dead father (Matt 8:22). They justified this radical behavior, of course, by reshaping the concept of the family as those who did the will of God (Luke 9:19–21).

Correspondingly, the wandering charismatics, who traveled the roads without money, provisions, or more than one garment, criticized "riches and possessions." They warned that people could not serve both God and mammon (Luke 16:13) and, in the form of the woes against the rich and well-fed (Luke 6:24–25), "the imminent crisis in the world would overturn all earthly relationships." Like the deprived generally, they "worked off their aggression" in "vivid imaginary pictures" of "the fearful end of the rich and the good fortune of the poor in the world to come (Luke 16:19–32)" (13). Their calling involved begging, but that of "a high order, charismatic begging," in the confidence that if they sought first the kingdom of God, other things such as food and clothing would be theirs as well (Matt 6:33). The wandering charismatics also deliberately relin-quished all rights and protection, having been commanded not to resist evil, to turn the other cheek, and to go not just one mile but two (Matt 5:38–41). The analogy for the wandering charismatics can be found in the wandering Cynic philosophers, who also "led a vagabond existence and also . . . renounced home, families and possessions" (14–15).

Indeed, "the ethical radicalism of the synoptic tradition is connected with this pattern of wandering. . . . Such an ethos could only be practised and handed down with any degree of credibility by those who had been released from the everyday ties of the world. . . . It only had a chance in a movement of outsiders . . ." (15). Thus it is that both outsiders such as the sick and crippled, prostitutes', and tax collectors' "vivid eschatological expectations" of the end of the world are so prominent in the tradition. The more the charismatics "detached themselves from this world . . . the more they kept destroying this world in their mythical fantasies . . ." (15–16).

Sympathizers. The wandering charismatics were supported materially and socially by settled groups of sympathizers, who remained within "Judaism" with no intention of founding a new "church." Theissen deduces this conclusion primarily from a few references to homes of sympathizers of Jesus (Matt 8:14; Mark 14:3ff.; Luke 10:38ff.). The far more numerous references to local communities in the Hellenistic cities suggest that they were less important in Palestine than in the Hellenistic world. Not surprisingly, then, Theissen concludes that "there are very few synoptic traditions the unmistakable setting of which is the life of local communities" (18).

Theissen's two main conclusions are that the local communities "are to be understood exclusively in terms of their complementary relationship to the wandering charismatics" and that "the local communities were less radical than the wandering charismatics" (18). Indeed, the two conclusions are related: local communities' support relieved the charismatics of worry about day-to-day existence and made possible their radicalism, which in turn allowed the local communities to compromise with the world (23). In particular, the difference between the radical ethics of the charismatics and the compromise of the local communities can be seen in the three problems of regulations for behavior, the structure of authority, and the procedure for accepting and rejecting members. Those tied to family, profession, and neighbors could not possibly have acted "as freely toward the law as did the wandering preachers." Theissen in fact explains the juxtapositions of radical and more moderate norms in the Gospels (e.g., Matt 5:17–20 versus Matt 5:21ff.) in terms of the difference between the wandering charismatics and the settled communities of supporters. Moreover, the wandering charismatics exercised authority in local communities. Finally, whereas the local communities observed baptism as a rite of initiation and had procedures for expulsion (Matt 18:15ff.), baptism "had no significance for the life of the wandering charismatics" (21) and they were subject directly to the authority of God (*Didache* 11:1). An analogy to the difference between the radical ethics of the charismatics and the moderate demands of their local sympathizers can be found among the Essenes in their distinction between the extremely strict discipline maintained at Qumran and the more temperate ethos of the groups living scattered about.

The Son of man. Theissen focuses on "the Son of man" among the various christological titles because it "expresses the internal perspective of the Jesus movement and is particularly closely connected with it" (24–25). The "Son of man" sayings divide into two groups, those about the earthly Son of man and those about the future Son of man. Among the former, some take an active form in which "the Son of man transcends the norms of the world," such that he breaks the sabbath and fasting regulations and forgives sins on his own authority (Matt 12:8; 11:18–19; 9:6). Others take a passive form, in which the Son of man is rejected and is made into a sacrifice for many (Mark 9:31; 10:45). However, the Son of man will suddenly appear in the new role of "eschatological judge" to gather the elect (Mark 14:62; Matt 24:27ff.; Matt 13:41; Mark 13:27).

The parallelism between some sayings about the behavior[3] of the members of the Jesus movement and those about the Son of man, furthermore, leads Theissen to postulate a "structural homologue" between the behavior of the followers and that of the revealer. Thus, the wandering charismatics, like the revealer, both "transcend the norms of their environment" in their breaking of sabbath and fasting regulations (Mark 2:23ff.; 2:18ff.) and are homeless and persecuted (25–26). Although less attested, there is also a parallel in reference to the future glory and judgment in such sayings as that about the disciples sitting on twelve thrones "judging" the twelve tribes (Matt 19:28). The proper authority of the despised and persecuted outsiders would finally be recognized by the whole society! The itinerant preachers even "set themselves above the Son of man" in the saying about the lack of forgiveness for anyone who speaks against the Holy Spirit (Matt 12:32). An analogous "structural homologue" between the idea of the Son of man and social reality can also be seen in evidence such as Daniel 7. Indeed, the tradents of the book of Daniel, who ("themselves intent on rule") have transformed "monistic, immanent Old Testament thought into a crude dualism of ages . . . can best be conceived of among groups whose relationship to Israel as a whole was a dualistic form of life: they lived in exclusive conventicles which were clearly marked out from the contemporary environment" (29).

Early Palestinian Christianity, or "the Jesus movement," according to Theissen's reconstruction, consisted primarily of a few dozen "wandering charismatics." The bulk of the tradition of Jesus sayings, moreover, was not only transmitted by them but pertained to them in the first place; for "the ethical radicalism of the sayings tradition" could have been "practiced and spoken only under extreme conditions of life"[4] such as their Cynic-like renunciation of home, family, property, and security. Their ethical radicalism was made possible by the material and social support provided by local communities. And they "were able to interpret and come to terms with their own social situation" (27) through the figure of "the Son of man," which provided a "structural homologue" for their own situation and behavior of being simultaneously beyond the traditional social norms and socially despised and persecuted, yet confident in their own transcendent authority and future vindication.

Analysis of Factors: The Effects of Society on the Jesus Movement

In Part Two of *Sociology of Early Palestinian Christianity* Theissen analyzes "The Effects of Society on the Jesus Movement." Since we are unable to understand a total society directly "without confusing partial associations with the whole," he isolates four particular "factors" (the socio-economic, socio-ecological, socio-political, and socio-cultural) and then treats them separately (31). The analysis of the four factors is then organized rigorously according to the same steps. After describing an important "phenomenon," he looks for "analogies" in other social movements of the time (particularly "the Essenes" and "the resistance movement"), on the assumption that "the more widespread a phenomenon is in society, the more it is influenced by that society." He next investigates the attitudes expressed in texts or "intentions" from the analogous social movements. "The methodological presupposition behind this is that there cannot be any connections between social reality and spiritual phenomena of which those involved in them were not aware . . . (32)." This also makes it possible to discern that the connection between social reality and spiritual phenomena is the response of a movement to its situation as well as an effect of that situation on the movement. Having set up the situation in terms of phenomenon, analogies, and intentions, he finally proceeds to direct analysis of the hypothetical "cause" of the phenomenon.

Socio-economic factors: Ch V. "The most striking phenomenon of the Jesus movement" was "the social rootlessness of the wandering charismatics" (33). Gospel texts themselves even indicate that the disciples came from among the poverty-striken fishermen of Lake Tiberias and destitute "peasant class" of Galilee. While it becomes clear that the rootlessness was voluntary in the case of the wandering charismatics, who deliberately left their ancestral homes, his descriptions of the "analogies" emphasize the involuntary aspects. Some of the members of the Qumran community were thus "men without possessions and possibly even without homes"; "resistance fighters" were recruited from "farmers who were no longer able to pay their taxes"; and "men without means" became followers of the numerous prophets. With the abnormal increase in social rootlessness in Palestine at the time, "many lived in unconscious readiness to leave their ancestral homes" (35–36). The criticism of "both riches and possessions" by all the renewal movements, moreover, indicates that the people thus affected were aware of the social causes of their malaise (37–39).

As socio-economic "causes" of the pervasive rootlessness, Theissen lists famines, overpopulation, and particularly the progressive "concentrations of possessions" and the "struggle for the distribution of goods between the producers and those who make the profits." With the Peace of Augustus making conditions favorable for trade, the rich became richer through their profits on exports. "Perhaps the decisive reason for the explosive situation in Palestine," however, was the struggle between the Romans and the Jewish elites for the profits from taxation. Roman and Herodian taxes were felt to be oppressive, and there were "religious taxes in addition to the state ones" (40–43). The appearance of "members of the upper classes" in "many protest movements," however, suggests that the absolute extent of economic pressure is less important than "upwards and downward trends" (39–40, 45). In the Jesus movement we find both members of the new upper classes and members of the middle classes threatened with decline: farmers, fishermen, and craftsmen. "Thus the social context of the renewal movements within the Judaism of the first century AD was not so much the lowest class of all as a marginal middle class, which reacted with particular sensitivity to the upward and downward trends within society which were beginning to make themselves felt" (46).

Socio-ecological factors: Ch VI. The Jesus movement was originally located in the country, in "small and often anonymous Galilean places, and was ambivalent in its relationship to Jerusalem, which it criticized but which soon became the center of the movement. This can best be explained in terms of the conflict between city and country, which is also expressed in analogous movements of the time. The Essenes and the popular prophets went out into the wilderness and were hostile to the city. "The resistance movements were obviously based on the country areas" and attacked the Jerusalem aristocracy. As for their "intentions" or awareness, the renewal movements expressed hostility to Hellenistic cities and, while affirming the "holiness of Jerusalem," criticized the reality precisely on the basis of the idea of the holy city. The zealots even carried out thoroughgoing reforms in the Temple. The Jesus movement, however, developed an open attitude toward the Hellenistic cities, and this modified its attitude toward Jerusalem as well (50–51).

The reasons for the "conservatism of the inhabitants of Jerusalem," such that the renewal movements did not develop there, are that the Jerusalemites were economically dependent, directly and/or indirectly, on the Temple. Many were employed working on its reconstruction, and tradespeople from cattle dealers and money changers to tanners and shoemakers lived off it or from the foreign trade that arose out of religion. Jerusalemites also enjoyed certain privileges, such as remission of taxes. "The rebellious attitude of the country areas" on the other hand, can be attributed to their being harder to control, to their being border territory, and to the economic pressure being greater in the country than in the city (54–56). Whereas the tensions between the city and the countryside contributed to the failure of the Jesus movement on its first appearance in Jerusalem, the movement later became centered there, despite its initial ambivalence (56–57). Moreover, as a "universalistic Judaism open to outsiders, the Jesus movement found opportunities in the Hellenistic cities "because they could offer prospects of a resolution of the tensions between Jews and Gentiles" (58).

Socio-political factors: Ch VII. The Jesus movement was "a radical theocratic movement" which played the rule of God off against its mediators, the priestly aristocracy. The imminent rule of God it proclaimed, of course, meant the termination of all other rule, including that of the Romans and the high priests. (The two ruling groups collaborated in the execution of Jesus, though there was no reason to persecute the conciliatory, moderate Jesus movement.) Among the analogous phenomena, the prophetic movements promised a miraculous divine intervention in the form of a repetition of past acts of salvation; "the resistance movement pursued its aim of a general rebellion against the Romans over a number of generations"; and the "pacifist" Essenes fantasized a final slaughter in which, joining the heavenly hosts, they would massacre the children of darkness (60–62). All of the renewal movements expressed their theocratic "intentions" in the form of "an explicitly imminent eschatology" which entailed the end of the traditional priestly aristocratic rule as well as the alien Roman domination. Although only indirect and implicit, this was also true in the Jesus movement (62–63). The "new world" was to come during the lifetime of the first generation (Mark 9:1) and was to be centered in Palestine (Matt 8:10–11), and a small group of outsiders would become rulers in Israel (Matt 19:28). Moreover, the renewal movements expected that new priests and/ or a new, messianic king would replace the established high priesthood. The aggressive hatred of foreigners prominent in the other radical theocratic movements, however, is lacking in the Jesus movement, which was "the peace party among the renewal movements within Judaism" and which "expressly legitimated" the payment of taxes to the Romans (64).

What gave rise to the dreams of a radical theocracy was "the conflict between native and alien structures of rule" in Jewish Palestine. The Romans fluctuated in the form by which they would rule Palestine, from client king to direct rule by a governor who did not have sufficiently independent power. The Roman military presence, while small, was staffed by soldiers who, having been recruited from nearby Hellenistic cities, hated the Jews. Tensions between Jews and Gentiles in the nearby Hellenistic cities, moreover, often spilled over into predominantly Jewish territories. The "natural allies of the Romans" were the priestly aristocracy. Ironically, the Romans themselves contributed to the weakening of the high priestly rule (70). The latter also stood in considerable tension and even competition with Herodian rule or influence. The Herodians had little or no legitimacy with the people. Indeed, Herod's usurpation of power and his ensuing propaganda efforts may well have been a major stimulus to the nascent longings for a true messiah, considering the messianic pretenders that arose at his death (72–75). Thus "it proved impossible to achieve a permanent balance between the various structures of government. . . . Tensions between earthly structures of government furthered the longing for the kingdom of God" (76).

Socio-cultural factors: Ch VIII. The phenomenon of a stricter interpretation of the Torah in most Jewish renewal groups results from "the socio-cultural tensions between Jewish and Hellenistic culture," according to Theissen (77). As the role of Judaism among the nations became more problematic, there was growing uncertainty about interpretation of the Torah that gave Judaism its identity and self-awareness. The Jesus movement exhibited two tendencies, the intensification of norms, which included motivation as well as action, and the relaxation of norms. The intensification was found primarily in the social sphere, whereas the relaxation of norms pertained principally to "religious" matters such as sabbath regulations. In some respects, however, the intensification of norms dialectically became the relaxation of norms, for example, such that anger and murder were on the same level. Thus, all moral self-righteousness would appear as hypocrisy (78–80).

The "analogies" display variations on the same basic phenomenon of "the intensification of norms." "The resistance movement," unlike the Jesus movement, intensified the religious commandments such as the sole rule of God while relaxing the social commandments such as the prohibition of murder and the prohibition of slavery (in the taking of hostages). The Essenes tightened the Torah in both the religious and the social spheres, in their obsession with priestly purity and their extreme strictures regarding social behavior in their own secluded community. The Pharisees even attempted to apply intensified norms to everyday life (80–83). Theissen finds that the "intentions" of the various renewal movements can be seen in their tendencies both toward "inter-cultural segregation" and toward "intra-cultural differentiation" (84–85). Indeed, the one led directly to the other; i.e., the attempt to define what being a Jew meant led to the distinction between those who were the true Jews and those who were not and to exclusion of the latter from membership in the true Israel. "Thus the attempt to preserve the cultural identity of Judaism by intensifying the norms of the law leads to schism" (86).

The stricter interpretation of the Torah was not simply the result of a conflict between "an ethnocentric and a cosmopolitan culture," however. Both Hellenism and Judaism had universalist tendencies and claims. But, in the conflict between the two cultures, the Greeks and Romans reacted with anti-Semitic prejudice and discrimination. Ironically, when special privileges were allowed, they aroused more extensive and intensified anti-Semitism. For its part, Judaism reacted to Hellenism with xenophobia and drew in on itself (87–92). Thus threatened by a more powerful alien culture, the Jewish people underwent a severe "crisis of identity" in the first century A.D. The resultant intensification of norms simply produced divisive schisms. When the intensification of norms became the relaxation of norms, however, the result was the universalization of Judaism. "When it was recognized that even an elect remnant within Israel could not satisfy these intensified norms: all, Jews and Gentiles alike, were directed towards grace" (93). The breakthrough happened in the Jesus movement, although only with Paul were the consequences clearly drawn.

Analysis of Function: Introjecting Aggression and Controlling Conflict

In Part Three, "Analysis of Function: The Effects of the Jesus Movement on Society," Theissen proceeds "on the assumption that the Jesus movement not only emerged from a social crisis but also articulated an answer to this crisis" (97). He concentrates on only those effects "which have some reference to the objective, basic aims of society" (98). In ch IX, "The Functional Outline . . . ," he focuses on the Jesus movement's contribution to containing and overcoming aggression. Because Palestinian Jewish society had deep-seated tensions that gave rise to forms of aggression, the overcoming of society's tensions meant the overcoming of aggression. After analyzing how the Jesus movement functioned to contain aggression, Theissen then finds, in ch X, "Functional Effects," that it had virtually no effect on Palestinian Jewish society. "The vision of love and reconciliation may have been born in a society rent by crises, but it had no chances of realization here." Only in "the less tense world of the Hellenistic cities" could the "eirenic movement" have any serious "functional effect" (118).

Shifting from a sociological to a more psychological analysis, Theissen lays out four means by which the Jesus movement contained aggression: compensation, transference, reversal or "introjection," and symbolization. (1) Aggression which is made more radical by social tensions is countered by a radicalized commandment to love. The latter, in psychoanalytical terms, means that intensified aggression had turned into its opposite. "Drives which originally served aggressive ends now work in the opposite direction" (100). (2) By "transference," aggressive impulses are taken over by supernatural figures (God, the Son of man, demons), thus relieving ordinary human relationships of aggression. By substituting God or the Son of man for themselves as the subject of aggression, the wandering charismatics could call down eschatological judgment on places that rejected them (Matt 10:15). Or by transferring ultimate judgment to God, they relieved themselves of concern over aggression from others who could only kill the body (Luke 12:4–7; p. 101). In "substitution of the object," their own "aggression against the Romans seems to have been transferred to demons, as is shown by the exorcism on the coasts of Gadara (Mark 5:1ff.). . . . The way in which they are drowned in the lake along with the swine corresponds to the hostile thoughts directed against the Romans by the Jewish people" (101–2). Similarly in the exorcisms, "the demons functioned as vicarious objects of the aggression of the Jesus movement" (102).

(3) Theissen focuses most attention on the "reversal" of aggression. The Jesus movement was apparently especially successful in turning aggression back against the aggressor by introjection. "We can see introjected aggressiveness in the call to repentance and the imperatives based on intensification of norms." Jesus' use of Pilate's massacre of some Galileans as an occasion for exhortation to repentance diverts rebelliousness against the Romans to one's own guilt, a "rebellion against oneself" (103). The key to this containment of aggression by internalization for Theissen

appears to be the intensification of norms to the point that they were quite beyond the possibility of fulfillment, so that all people, pious or impious, radical or moderate, were faced with divine judgment (104). In the Sermon on the Mount, "the intensification of the commandments against killing and against adultery makes impossible demands on every man," an intensification of guilt that "makes self-righteous assessments of transgressions of norms impossible" (106). "The impossibility of fulfilling the intensified norms here becomes a pointer towards the grace of God" (105). In a series of statements of how the Jesus movement moves beyond the ascetic John the Baptist, Theissen claims that "introjected aggressiveness turned into self-acceptance on the basis of the divine love," that "the overcoming of aggression in the Jesus movement" became "a particular vision of society," or that "ethical radicalism" was transformed into "a radical proclamation of the grace of God" (105). Corresponding to the Jesus movement's introjection of its own aggressiveness it attempted, by a provocative act of defenselessness, to induce or enable those who directed aggression toward it to a voluntary acceptance of their own higher ideals. This method of dealing with aggression is reflected in the movement's christological symbols. The early Christians, rather than rebel against the Romans, accepted defeat in the repressive measure of the execution of Jesus. "The cross became the sign of salvation. It was a revelation, not of Roman guilt but of their own: Jesus had to die for our sins" (108).

(4) The christological symbolization of the Jesus movement in fact was a way of guiding and influencing the containment of aggression. As can be seen in such passages as Mark 10:45 or 1 Cor 15:3, the crucified Jesus was made into the scapegoat. He thus took over both "the aggressions of the group, their transgressions of the norm," and "the aggressiveness of the norm, the law and human conscience: the curse of the law, as Paul puts it (Gal 3:13). . . . He takes over both the aggressiveness of the drives of the Id and that of the strictness of the super-ego, backed up by the God of the law" (109).

In his final chapter Theissen addresses the question of whether the "vision of love and reconciliation" ever had a chance of realization or could "offer a constructive contribution to life in community" (111).

(1) Within the Jesus movement itself, which consisted of outsiders anyhow, the wandering charismatics had the freedom to practice even an extreme pattern of behavior. The more serious problem, how they could hope to permeate the whole society with the radical pattern—an aspiration that Theissen had not previously suggested—can be explained in terms of the movement's belief in miracles. Since "powers which foretold a complete change in the world" were at its disposal, would not ethical

extremes such as "the miracle of love" be possible also? (112).

(2) Within Palestinian Jewish society as a whole "the Jesus movement was a failure" as a renewal movement. With the increasing turbulence of the 30s and 40s, Palestinian Jewish society felt threatened and typically resorted to traditional patterns of behavior while rejecting anything alien. This diminished the chances of the Jesus movement, which "encroached on the tabus of society" and criticized the Temple and the law (112–13). Indeed, the Jesus movement was probably "forced into the role of a scapegoat," especially considering that "the Christians belonged to the peace party." The second reason why Christianity failed in Jewish Palestine, and the reason why it failed while Hillelite Pharisaism succeeded in establishing itself after the Jewish rebellion of 66–70, was its success among the Gentiles outside of Palestine.

(3) In the Hellenistic world, early Christianity had a greater chance of success. A deep-seated change in role structure took place. The wandering charismatics were replaced by a monarchical episcopate as the decisive authority by early in the second century. The ethical radicalism yielded to "a more moderate patriarchalism of love, oriented on the need for social interaction within the Christian community" between masters and slaves, men and women. The despised Son of man who is to become the judge of the world was replaced by the preexistent Son of God who humiliated himself in voluntary impoverishment (115–16). The various factors of the situation were also very different in the Hellenistic world. As opposed to the poverty of the followers of Jesus in Palestine, the Hellenistic communities at least had enough to support the Palestinian communities as well as themselves. Ecologically, a movement that began in the Palestinian countryside now took root in the Hellenistic cities. Politically the Hellenistic Christian communities were in accord with the established structures and did not continue the "radical theocratic" ideals of the Palestinian Jesus movement. The cultural changes, finally, were far-reaching, ranging from the shift from a parochial into a more universal language to the change from a renewal movement within Judaism into "an independent religion" (117–18). Thus, the less tense world of the Hellenistic cities provided a more favorable environment for the eirenic early Christianity. And the latter served the Hellenistic world's need for integration, creating a social balance between the different classes and providing internal support to the state at a time of increasing social pressure. Approaching the time of Constantine, "Christianity became more and more the social cement of the totalitarian state of late antiquity" (119).

Theissen's Project

A sociologist would immediately recognize that Theissen is pursuing a structural-functionalist approach to "early Palestinian Christianity." Functionalism was the most prominent approach in British social anthropology during the 1930s and 1940s, and (structural-) functionalism came to dominate academic sociology, particularly in the United States, during the 1950s. Although Theissen discusses his use of functionalism in certain essays,[5] he does not comment explicitly on this approach in the book. It may be useful, therefore, to those not familiar with the various sociological approaches or theories, to sketch briefly the principal features of functionalism[6] and how Theissen's treatment of the "Jesus movement" manifests them.

Structural-functional sociology focuses broadly on whole societies and "social systems" and the interaction of the whole and its component parts. It has been strongly influenced by nineteenth-century thinkers such as Comte, Spencer, and particularly Durkheim, who viewed society as a social organism to be studied in somewhat the way biology studies a natural organism. Correspondingly, from the outset Theissen conceives of his analysis in terms of a whole society, "Judaism" (or "Palestinian Jewish society") and one of its component (renewal) movements and the "reciprocal interaction" between them (1, 31, 40–43, 98). The subtitles of parts Two and Three are revealing: "The Effects of Society on the Jesus Movement," and "The Effects of the Jesus Movement on Society" (31, 97; cf. 1).

In studying the interaction of society and its component parts functionalists make a fundamental distinction between the cause and the consequence of social phenomena. "To explain a social fact it is not enough to show the *cause* on which it depends; we must also . . . show its *function* in the establishment of social order."[7] As evident in the very organization of his project, Theissen has followed the fundamental distinction between causes ("Part Two: Analysis of Factors," 31) and consequences ("Part Three: Analysis of Functions," 97).

With its macroscopic concern for society as a whole and its basic distinction between cause and function, the "central orientation of functionalism" is the interpretation of social phenomena "by establishing their consequences for larger structures in which they are implicated."[8] Such *functions*, moreover, are understood as the *objective* consequences for other parts of the society or society as a whole, regardless of the intentions of the people involved.[9] The assumption is that every part of society contributes in some way to the functioning of the whole. In this respect, structural-functional sociology remains the heir not only of Durkheim but also of British social anthropologists, through whom functionalism reached twentieth-century sociology. As articulated by its leading figures Radcliffe-Brown and Malinowski, "the 'explanation' of any belief, rule, structure, or practice was to be found either through linkages with other parts of the system . . . or in its contribution to the survival of the system and its members."[10] Although Theissen gives far more space to his analysis of factors—perhaps because he has so much material to cover under the various "factors"—his overall treatment is driving toward the analysis of function as its goal or conclusion. That analysis, moreover, is focused in good functionalist fashion on how the Jesus movement could contribute toward the order and coherence of Jewish society as a whole.

Indeed, the way Theissen has posed his analysis of function in terms of social balance and integration articulates the fundamental concern of structural-functionalism. The very concept of "functional needs" (or "requisites" or "imperatives") revolves basically around the putative needs of the social organism for *integration*.[11] Thus Theissen's opening statement on the "aims" of his sociology of the Jesus movement is vintage structural-functionalism: the function of religion (and by implication religious renewal movements) is "toward fulfilling the basic aims of a society, namely in achieving the integration of its members and overcoming conflicts through change" (2). Even more striking is Theissen's procedural statement in his preface to his section on function. "Analysis of function does not investigate all effects, but only those which have some reference to the objective, basic aims of society. When a society is involved in a crisis, its chief concern is to overcome and reduce the tensions within itself. . . . By various means the renewal movements which emerged within Judaism sought to overcome increasing tensions" (98). Thus the issue for Theissen is how the functional outline of the Jesus movement might "overcome social tensions" by "containing aggression," and whether (how) the Jesus movement with its "vision of love and reconciliation" contributed toward "social balance and integration" (97-99).

Structural-functionalism, finally, emphasizes the importance of a shared set of values and norms in regulating social interaction, maintaining integration, and thus helping society in pursuing its goals. This may be the principal reason why structural-functionalism would be attractive to theologians and other scholars dealing with religious phenomena. As Parsons, for example, explains the functioning of society, the higher order systems, the cultural order of values and norms, control the lower order "social" and "personality" systems.[12] Theissen, accordingly, makes discussion of norms, and especially their intensification, central both in the chapter on socio-cultural factors (VIII) and in Part Three on functional analysis. "The torah gave Judaism its identity." The principal way in which the Jesus movement could attempt "to renew the society from within," according to Theissen, was through the introjection of aggression by the "intensification of norms" (110, 103).

Notes

1. G. Theissen, *Sociology of Early Palestinian Christianity* (Philadelphia: Fortress, 1978). For the reader's convenience the page numbers of the references to Theissen's presentation are given in parentheses in the text, with special indication of references to other publications by Theissen.

2. G. Theissen, "Wanderradikalismus: Literatursoziologische Aspekte der Überlieferung von Worten Jesu im Urchristentum," *Zeitschrift für Theologie und Kirche* 70 (1973) 245–71; Eng. trans. "Itinerant Radicalism: The Tradition of Jesus Sayings from the Perspective of the Sociology of Literature," in *The Bible and Liberation: A Radical Religion Reader* (Berkeley: Community for Religious Research and Education, 1976) 84–93.

3. The English word "attitude" used in the translation does not adequately render the sense of Theissen's original German term *Verhalten*.

4. "Itinerant Radicalism," 86.

5. Theissen, "Theoretische Probleme religionssoziologischer Forschung und die Analyse des Urchristentums," *Neue Zeitschrift für Systematische Theologie* 16 (1974) 35–36; "Zur forschungsgeschichtlichen Einordnung der soziologischen Fragestellung," in *Studien zur Soziologie des Urchristentums* (Wissenschaftliche Untersuchungen zum Neuen Testament 19; Tübingen: Mohr, 1979) 3–34; the first essay is also reprinted in this volume, pp. 55–76.

6. See further Jonathan H. Turner, *The Structure of Sociological Theory* (rev. ed.; Homewood, IL: Dorsey, 1978); and Alvin Gouldner, *The Coming Crisis of Western Sociology* (New York: Basic Books, 1970).

7. E. Durkheim, *The Rules of Sociological Method* (1895; New York: Free Press, 1938) 97.

8. Robert K. Merton, *Social Theory and Social Structure* (New York: Free Press, 1968) 100–101.

9. For a critique of the implications and "consequences of this split, see further Stanley K. Stowers, "The Social Sciences and the Study of Early Christianity," in *Approaches to Ancient Judaism*, ed. W. S. Green (Atlanta: Scholars Press, 1985) 5:149–81.

10. W. Moore, "Functionalism," in *A History of Sociological Analysis*, ed. Tom Bottomore and Robert Nisbet (New York: Basic Books, 1978) 327; and see Merton, *Social Theory and Social Structure*, 77–80.

11. Gouldner, *Coming Crisis*, 146, 157; Turner, *Structure*, 96.

12. Cf. Gouldner, *Coming Crisis*, 140–41, 247–54; Turner, *Structure*, 43, 47, 54; George Ritzer, *Contemporary Sociological Theory* (New York: Knopf, 1983) 75.

2 ◊ Method: The Effects of Functionalism

Theissen has boldly led the way in applying sociological method to the synoptic traditions of Jesus in the context of ancient Jewish society. Not surprisingly, there are bound to be some problems inherent in attempts by New Testament scholars trained largely in textual and historical analysis to utilize sociological method developed to carry out a systematic analysis of modern society. Among the many problems entailed in one field borrowing methods and conceptual apparatus from another is that it is difficult for the borrowers to remain current in the critical discussion taking place in the field from which they are borrowing. In this case, ironically, through Theissen the application of functionalist sociology to the "Jesus movement" became influential in New Testament studies about a decade after sociologists themselves had questioned and even abandoned the method, at least in the United States. It seems timely to turn a critical eye on the method and how it affects the interpretation of "early Palestinian Christianity."

Categorization and Obfuscation

Vagueness and abstraction plague Theissen's presentation repeatedly, starting with even his working definitions. In the opening sentence of the book, Theissen writes: "Earliest Christianity began as a renewal movement within Judaism. . . ." But what is "Judaism"? Is it a "religion" (which is discussed but without definition on the next page), or does the term refer to Palestinian Jewish "society"? He proceeds as if Palestinian Jewish society could be analyzed as a self-contained whole. Yet not only was that society torn by sharp conflicts, but Roman imperial rule and Hellenistic culture intruded at nearly every crucial point. Indeed, Theissen himself finds difficulty distinguishing what are Palestinian Jewish from more general Hellenistic Jewish expressions in the sources. He never provides a more *social* definition of religion and never focuses on what "religion" might have been *concretely* in first-century Palestinian Jewish society. Similarly, in the chapter on "socio-cultural factors" (VIII),

Theissen avoids a more precise analysis of "marginal groups," giving virtually no attention to renewal movements based in the rural peasantry, in favor of his focus on the highly abstract crisis of identity in "Israel" or "Judaism."

Far more serious than the vagueness of his working definitions, however, are the more general problems of inappropriate conceptual apparatus and abstract analytical categories that bear little relation to the concrete historical realities. Indeed, such interpretative concepts and analytical categories may obfuscate rather than elucidate the Jesus movement and other social phenomena in ancient Jewish Palestine. Such problems may well be inherent in any attempt to open up a new approach to a historical field for which the sources are uneven and indirect and for which many of the questions have never before even been asked, let alone answered. Perhaps subsequent investigations can benefit from problems in Theissen's pioneering effort.

In Part One Theissen has proceeded in such formal categories (his "roles") that his sociological reconstruction has lost touch with the substance of his subject, "the Jesus movement" in Jewish Palestine in the decades following the ministry of Jesus. Four problems are immediately evident in his abstract approach.

First, despite the title "Analysis of Roles," he does not really discuss the social *role* of his "wandering charismatics," but focuses instead on their life-style or radical "ethos." He does not even pursue his own consciously chosen terms "charismatic" and "itinerant." In the field of sociology, at least since Max Weber—and, ironically, his work focused precisely on *ancient Israel*—the concept of "charisma/charismatic" denotes an unusual type of authority and one that emerges in distinctive social circumstances. Similarly, "wandering" is not an ordinary "life-style," as suggested by Theissen's own presentation. But he does not explore the ways in which his itinerants were "charismatic," and he appears to misunderstand why his charismatics were "itinerant." Ironically, a more substantive understanding of both would appear to be inherent in the only text (the "mission discourse") that directly attests any of the traits of the "itinerant radicalism": a number of disciples are commissioned to preach, heal, and exorcise demons—and that in the villages; hence they must travel. It would seem appropriate to explore the preaching and healing of the "wandering charismatics" as an integral part of their "role."

Second, Theissen conceives of "early Palestinian Christianity" as one of the "renewal movements" in "Judaism" at the time. Focusing his treatment of the Jesus movement itself on the various "roles" involved, however, leaves uninvestigated the ways in which it may have attempted to renew the society. Some of Jesus' sayings regarding the disciples themselves are highly suggestive in this regard: besides the healing and exorcism in the mission discourse, one thinks immediately of the programmatic vision of the renewal of Israel in Matt 19:28, a text that Theissen reads instead as pertaining to eschatological judgment. Moreover, because he has already decided that the more "radical" demands of the sayings tradition pertain only or primarily to the wandering charismatics, he is not led to explore the possible relevance of this material to the Jesus movement as a whole, particularly the local communities.

Third, Theissen simply divides his analysis of the Jesus movement itself, in terms of "roles," from his analysis of the movement's interaction with Jewish society, in terms of "factors." But this procedure is arbitrary and abstract, especially considering two things in particular that emerge in Theissen's own discussion of the local communities: the communities remained within Jewish society, and they apparently rejected the established institutional authorities. It seems therefore impossible even to focus on the Jesus movement by itself without taking into account its location in and interaction with the larger society.

Fourth, Theissen's analysis of the Jesus movement in terms of roles includes virtually no historical dimension at all. But sociology teaches us that people ordinarily get their ideas or models for roles and social forms from their cultural traditions. And sociological and anthropological treatments of "renewal" or "revitalistic" or "nativistic" movements emphasize the ways in which such movements draw upon and renew their traditional social forms even while adapting them to changed circumstances. If anything, Theissen's presentation seems innocent of this sociological and anthropological literature and of the interaction between people's traditions and their new circumstances that it explores.

In Part Two much of the conceptual apparatus is anachronistic and the principal analytical categories are very abstract and schematic. It is highly questionable whether interpretive terms taken from modern societies are applicable to ancient social realities. These may be particularly problematic in regard to political-economic factors because of the ways in which economic production and social-political structures have changed since Jesus' time. To what extent do concepts such as "big business" and "the real tycoons" and the production of "goods for export" (on which their income was based, 41) correspond to economic reality in ancient Palestine? Even the phrase "concentration of possessions" may be problematic. When we examine Theissen's textual references, the "resources" of the Herodian princes that "could produce goods for export" turn out to be the land, labor, and productivity of numerous villages. Ancient potentates' (kings' or high priests') right or power to claim taxes or tithes seems inappropriately described in terms of capital owned by tycoons in big business engaged in flourishing export trade. Besides the rich "upper class," moreover, Theissen imagines that there were also poverty-stricken "lower classes" and "a marginal middle class" which reacted with peculiar sensitivity to "the upward and downward trends within society" (45–46; cf. 39, 41). As examples of those in the middle class, however, he gives "fishermen," whom he had described earlier as destitute and penniless, and farmers, who, he explains at points, were heavily in debt. Almost certainly there was nothing in ancient Jewish society that corresponds to the modern "middle class." As Sherwin-White points out, the picture of Galilean society portrayed in the Synoptic Gospels is one of the very rich in contrast with the very poor peasantry (and fishermen).[1]

More generally, Theissen carries out analysis in terms of abstract and schematic categories with uncertain derivation from or relevance to the ancient social realities. Theissen's "sociology" is attractive partly because it is bold, sweeping, and concise. He zeroes in on a category of analysis, locates a few pieces of evidence, and draws a sharply stated conclusion. But this may have its cost in terms of the depth and comprehensiveness of sociological understanding ultimately attained. The interconnection of the categories or issues and the overall structure of the social situation may remain unilluminated. This appears at three levels in Theissen's "Analysis of Factors."

At the level of description of social behavior, for example, Theissen poses the issue of attitude toward possessions in order to probe the "intentions" of the movements treated. Especially with regard to the Jesus movement, however, he does this narrowly and with respect to individual disciples, not noticing the collective, relational, and "communal" way in which "riches and possessions" are understood in the movement as a whole (37–39). Focus on particular categories or issues should proceed relationally, especially in sociological analysis.

The second level is illustrated dramatically by his presentation of the four economic "causes" of uprootedness. He treats each of the causes *separately* (39–45). Besides lacking historical perspective, so that we cannot appreciate the change in circumstances he finds so important (e.g., how had population become so dense in Jewish Palestine? 40–41), this procedure "cause by cause" does not enable us to see their interconnection and cumulative effect. Because of this procedure we are not allowed to realize that "the concentration of possessions" was to some extent virtually the same thing as "the struggle for the distribution of goods." That is, the "resources" of the Herodian princes were precisely their claim to taxes or rents in the struggle with the producers and their own Roman competitors for "the distribution of goods." Of course, the same is true both for the Jewish high priests, in their claim to and use of tithes and other religiously legitimated offerings, and for the Roman overlords in their claim to tribute. "Concentration of possessions" in fact *occurred in the process* of "the struggle for distribution." Similarly, because of Theissen's procedure cause by cause we are not allowed to observe how overpopulation and serious drought and famine compounded the problems of Jewish peasants in their struggle to stay alive, given the heavy and increasing demands for tribute, tithes, and taxes. Hence, the problem of increasing peasant debt is related to all four of Theissen's "causes," and not only to the "competing tax system."

The third and most serious level at which the sociological analysis proceeds in terms of categories abstracted from actual social interconnections is the very isolation of the separate factors of socio-economic, socio-ecological, socio-political, and socio-cultural. Theissen justifies this because "we cannot achieve a direct understanding of the 'totality' of all social interconnections without confusing partial associations with the whole" (31). The problem, of course, is that in an undifferentiated traditional society, what modern sociologists assume as separable categories may not be even analytically separable. We have already noted how Theissen himself mixes his factors in what is supposedly a procedure that finds the appropriate "cause" to explain the "phenomenon" in that category of factors. For example, he offered an "economic" explanation for the "ecological" phenomenon.

At the very least a procedure "factor by factor" tends to obscure the interconnection between the various factors. For example, the social rootlessness to be explained under "socio-economic" factors resulted from the loss of land due to the heavy indebtedness of the peasantry. But in fact this was "caused" by the concentration of power and resources in the hands of the (Romans), Herodians and priestly aristocracy who held political power (socio-political aspect), the latter being legitimated in their political-economic position by religious traditions (socio-cultural aspect). Moreover, all of the "political" holders of "economic" power, Roman officials, Herodian princes, and high priests, lived in the cities and were supported ultimately by the products rendered up by the rural peasantry (socio-ecological aspect). But neither in ch V nor in Part Two as a whole do we get any sense of this interconnection, because of the procedure in terms of isolated and abstract categories. Moreover, ch VI is unnecessary. Not only did the "phenomenon" have only limited analogies, but the "ecological" factors were implicit in the political-economic factors: as in the ancient world generally, the city lived off the countryside through the mechanisms of tribute, taxation, tithes, and rents.

At the worst, Theissen's procedure separates the inseparable—that is, it becomes seriously reductionist. For example, in ch VII Theissen treats as a political matter what was irreducibly economic and cultural-religious as well. The "radical theocratic movements" were religious-cultural and economic as well as political. The occasion for the emergence of the "Fourth Philosophy" led by Judas of Galilee was the imposition of direct Roman rule and tribute, and its agenda was resistance to the tribute on the understanding that Jews were to serve God as their only Lord. The Essenes at Qumran formed a total, self-sufficient community. By the time of the Jesus movement there was a long cultural tradition of radical theocratic critique of and opposition to hierocracy that included both political and economic dimensions (see, e.g., the last section of the book of *1 Enoch* or the *Psalms of Solomon*).

The phenomena and their causes simply cannot be adequately discussed in a procedure that abstractly categorizes inseparable dimensions of historical reality. Although it may produce a few piecemeal flashes of insight into particular issues or connections, Theissen's procedure simply blocks any satisfactory understanding of the way in which the overall structure of ancient Jewish Palestine worked in the Roman imperial situation, and it only serves to obscure rather than elucidate "the reciprocal interaction" between Jewish society in Palestine and the Jesus movement.

Problems in Functionalist Sociology

There are, moreover, several weaknesses inherent in the structural-functional approach itself that Theissen is utilizing. The basic criticisms are of two kinds, methodological and substantive. Besides its typical problems with teleological and tautological explanations, functionalism deals in abstract "social systems" and not in concrete particular societies. It has attempted to build one grand scheme of analysis, which may be of questionable application to all societies. Structural-functionalism has been compared to utopia; one wonders whether the utopian elements of this social theory are ever encountered in real societies.[2] We have already noted the obfuscating effects of Theissen's application of abstract concepts and analytical schemes to Jewish Palestine and the Jesus movement.

The substantive criticisms of structural-functional sociology are principally that it so emphasizes whole social systems in equilibrium that it cannot deal adequately with history, social change, and the seriousness of conflict. Consequently, say its critics, it has a conservative bias in favor of the status quo and serves to support the established order through its emphasis on what is normative for the social system.[3] It goes without saying that these problems would be serious for attempts to apply functionalism to biblical history and literature, particularly to the "Jewish movement." Not surprisingly, we can see these problems illustrated in Theissen's analyses.

Inattentiveness to history. The functionalist antihistorical bent surely has something to do with its intellectual origins. It was developed in conscious reaction to the evolutionary assumptions of late-nineteenth-century anthropologists. It was also a healthy reaction to the common practice of resorting to conjectural constructions of "pseudo history" when few sources were available to the anthropologist-ethnographer. In both respects functionalism was thus an important step beyond the ethnocentric evolutionary and biological-psychological theories of the late nineteenth century. Thus history was not rejected in principle. Yet structural-functional social science retained its emphasis on social structure. To cite A. R. Radcliffe-Brown, one of the British social anthropologists influential in the transmission of functionalism to sociology: "In such an analysis we are dealing with a system as it exists at a certain time, abstracting as far as possible from any change that it may be undergoing."[4] Perhaps the most important critical result for the use of the structural-functional method itself is that it has an implicit bias against historical perspective on the conditions which affect or "cause" certain phenomena.[5]

The antihistorical bias of functionalism, of course, is illustrated most dramatically and obviously in its assumption that any given society is a bounded and self-contained entity. This is patently absurd especially for modern times, with our highly developed electronic media and extensive worldwide exchange of goods and ideas. But it is also impossible to treat historical "societies" in isolation. The use of functional sociology on ancient Jewish Palestine thus just tends to exacerbate the obfuscation entailed in attempting to treat a particular people or "society" in isolation from its broader historical context, in this case the Hellenistic world and the Roman Empire. The historical situation of ancient Jewish Palestine could be understood far more adequately in terms of changing patterns of interaction between village communities and the groups or cities that ruled them within the broader context of imperial influence and domination.[6]

Theissen's analysis of the causes of the Jesus movement has simply left historical developments out of consideration. Examination of the dramatic political-economic changes which had been taking place in Jewish Palestine since the second century B.C.E., and particularly since the Roman takeover of the eastern Mediterranean, might have helped elucidate the "socio-economic" factors. Theissen, in effect, with his abstract analytical scheme, juxtaposes historical materials that were not simultaneous. Despite the paucity of sources, much greater historical precision seems possible.

Underestimation of serious conflict. Because of its emphasis on social stability and integration, structural-functionalism tends to underestimate the degree and importance of conflict. With its focus on the integration of a whole social system, this method would seem to have great potential for comparative assessment of the tensions and conflicts that might threaten a system's equilibrium. In practice, however, functionalists have not devoted much attention to conflict and have virtually ignored serious conflicts which lead to genuine structural changes in favor of less dramatic and more "evolutionary" change within a social structure.[7] Functionalism maintains continuity with Durkheim, who treated conflict "as a form of social pathology." Functionalists such as Lewis Coser who have dealt with conflict emphasize the *integrative function* of conflict for society.[8]

Theissen's functional analysis, while acknowledging the many particular tensions or conflicts present in Jewish society, tends to ignore or discount serious, structure-challenging conflict. Social phenomena (such as radical theocratic movements) that he finds caused by tensions between ruling groups at the top of the social structure would more adequately be understood as rooted in the fundamental conflict within the political-economic structure itself (see ch 4 below). Theissen's overall framing of his presentation, in the methodological statement at the beginning and in the "functional" analysis at the conclusion, is in terms of the *integrative* function of religion or social phenomena. Accordingly, he deals with *conflict* as well ultimately in terms of how it contributes toward social integration.[9] Thus its integrative effects are the measure of success or failure of the Jesus movement; this is the sole issue in the concluding Part Three.

Conservative bias. Indeed, the whole enterprise of structural-functionalist sociology, by its very design, focus, and concerns, would appear to be inherently conservative.[10] Attention is devoted primarily to (narrowly conceived) *social* relations, with little concern for their material bodily and economic basis. Functionalism typically inquires into the needs of society or "social systems," but not necessarily into the needs of people. It focuses on the relations of the whole society and its component parts, but not necessarily on the relations between and among the people who comprise society.

That functionalists generally focus on social stability and integration in their actual analyses is perhaps the most obvious expression of the conservative bias in structural-functional theory. Moreover, because of its teleological orientation and its tautological tendencies, functionalist explanation becomes, in effect, justification. Thus, perhaps not surprisingly, anthropological functionalism was accused of being a new kind of "dismal science," whose own "function" was to provide social scientific rationalization especially in reference to the British policy of indirect (colonial) rule.[11] Malinowski even acknowledged this use of his anthropology:[12]

> The practical value of such a theory (functionalism) is that it teaches us the relative importance of various customs, how they dovetail into each other, how they have to be handled by missionaries, colonial authorities, and those who economically have to exploit savage trade and savage labor.

Now Theissen surely did not consciously select the functionalist approach because he was dealing with an analogous situation, that is, because a method developed in connection with British colonial rule might prove useful in analysis of ancient Jewish Palestine under Roman imperial rule. Yet it is at least interesting that sociological analysis coming from the North Atlantic "first world" emphasizes the *integrative* function of early Christianity through the control of aggression and concludes that the ethically more radical Jesus movement "failed." The conservative implications of the typical functional emphasis come out clearly in the long final paragraph of Theissen's book. Not understanding what was happening perhaps, the Romans may have persecuted the Christians from time to time. It was highly functional for the continuing integration and cohesion of the imperial society in late antiquity, however, that the Christians, emphasizing love-patriarchalism, organized communities which created "a social balance between the different classes within society" (117–18).

Certain studies of the political orientation of American sociologists, while acknowledging that functionalism is ideologically conservative, claimed that the large majority of sociologists did not understand functionalism in conservative terms and were themselves politically "liberal."[13] The critical concept of "ideology" as an unconscious or hidden aspect of culture, of course, is often used to analyze precisely such a situation in the "sociology of knowledge." Even a scientific theory can have an ideological dimension insofar as its holders unconsciously view reality in a way that is tilted toward their own interests.[14] Even those who see themselves as liberals, especially within the context of their own society, might develop or be attracted to an approach that implicitly favors and serves the maintenance of an overall societal and international situation in which they have a vested interest. It is possible that by adopting a functionalist sociological approach one would be giving a highly conservative interpretation of the "Jesus movement" even while entertaining a self-image as liberal, critical scholars, readers, and citizens.

Domestication of the Jesus Movement

One of the purposes of a "liberal education" was to assist people in liberating themselves from particular institutional and ideological forms of domination. Similarly, in its early phases the critical study of the Bible was used to gain leverage on the teachings and institutionalized power of the established churches. When sociological interpretation of Jesus and the Gospels first arose in the United States, it was influenced by and had links with the "social gospel" movement for justice in social relations. Even at the beginning of the current revival of sociological interpretation in the 1970s it seemed that it had implications for the pertinence of the Jesus movement and the Gospel materials for contemporary social struggles.

Adoption of the conservative functionalist sociological approach to the Jesus movement, however, threatens to subvert the liberating potential of the Jesus movement, the Gospels, and critical biblical studies. Theissen's presentation of the Jesus movement, its origins, and its function constitutes a modern domestication of the Gospel materials on which it is ostensibly based. This domestication would appear to be rooted in the conservative functionalist sociological approach he adopted (although perhaps not only there). What appears in the Gospel traditions to pose a sharp challenge to the ruling groups of the society is transformed, by means of functionalist sociology, into a movement supposedly striving to control conflict and maintain the social system. This can be seen in the principal arguments of the book, briefly sketched here, as well as in the other, subsidiary arguments to be examined in the next chapter.

In Part One Theissen claims that most of the sharply challenging sayings of Jesus that would be difficult if not impossible to follow in normal social relations were originally directed only to the wandering charismatics. Indeed, the only way that the itinerant radicalism intended by these sayings could be realized was for these special people, who were marginal in the first place, to deliberately abandon all normal social interaction. The hard sayings of Jesus thus were not originally intended for and did not pertain to regular social relations. They pertained only to the "roles" and "radical ethos" of a few dozen itinerants ("deviants"!) in first-century Palestine. The implications seem rather obvious for us modern sociologists and readers: the seriously challenging sayings of Jesus in the Gospel tradition are not relevant to ordinary social relations.

In Part Two Theissen locates the cause of the rise of radical theocratic movements in the tensions between the Jewish and Roman ruling groups. Attention is thus diverted from the more fundamental structural conflicts in ancient Palestine onto what were secondary or derivative conflicts. In the discussion of social-economic factors focused on how social rootlessness in the society affected the Jesus movement, Theissen finds that some among the "middle class(es)" threatened by upward and downward trends within society voluntarily abandoned their "possessions," etc., and became vagabonds. Thus attention is diverted from the evidence of concrete problems such as hunger and indebtedness, problems that the Jesus tradition ostensibly addresses, to the religious-ethical response of a handful of itinerant charismatics. The picture that emerges includes no serious structural conflict and no direct relation between concrete suffering and the Jesus movement.

In the concluding Part Three on the effects of the Jesus movement on society, Theissen emphasizes how that "renewal movement" attempted to overcome social tensions by controlling, even introjecting aggression. The focus is almost exclusively on how this movement served the needs of the society, controlling conflict through the intensification of norms, but no attention is given to how it may have responded to the needs of hungry and indebted people, let alone how that response may have been a threat to the established institutions, such as Temple and high priesthood (which, as suggested by Theissen's own evidence in Part Two, were a major cause of that hunger and indebtedness). The Jesus traditions that are critical of the governing authorities are not allowed to pose questions about any needed changes in the social system. In good functionalist fashion, emphasis falls rather on adjustment by people to the system by means of religious norms. Nor is Theissen led to question his own analysis when he is forced to recognize in the last chapter that the more radical Jesus movement of itinerant charismatics failed in its "function" of controlling conflict in Palestinian Jewish society. Rather, the conservative implications of his functionalist approach come out all the more clearly in the concluding section on early Christianity in the broader Hellenistic-Roman world. It was highly "functional" for the continuing integration and cohesion of the imperial society that the Christians, emphasizing love-patriarchalism, organized communities that created "social balance between the different classes within society" (117-18).

If the Jesus movement was merely a few dozen alienated middle-class people who had voluntarily chosen itinerant poverty, however, then why was Jesus executed by the Roman governor, why were his followers persecuted and killed by Jewish and Roman authorities, why were his brothers executed, and why were Paul and other apostles periodically arrested? One cannot resist the impression that the "function" of

Theissen's *Sociology* is a modern domestication of "early Palestinian Christianity."

Notes

1. Not surprisingly, the chapter on "The Middle Class" in J. Jeremias, *Jerusalem at the Time of Jesus* (Philadelphia: Fortress, 1969) 100–108, makes it sound both rather indeterminate and small; most of the chapter concerns the priests and the tithes they received.

2. Ralf Dahrendorf, "Out of Utopia: Toward a Reorientation of Sociological Analysis," *American Journal of Sociology* 64 (1958) 115–27; and *Class and Class-Conflict in Industrial Society* (Stanford, CA: Stanford University Press, 1959).

3. An attempt is now under way by some who stand directly in the Parsonsian tradition to revive functionalism, principally by arguing that it can indeed accommodate change and conflict and by simply denying its conservative ideological implications; see Jeffrey C. Alexander, ed., *Neofunctionalism* (Beverly Hills, CA: Sage, 1985). But this "neofunctionalism" inherits the same tendency toward an ahistorical orientation, which is rivaled only by the contributors' lack of historical self-understanding; see Charles Camic, "The Return of the Functionalists," *Contemporary Sociology* 15 (1986) 692–95.

4. "Introduction," in A. R. Radcliffe-Brown and C. D. Forde, eds., *African Systems of Kinship and Marriage* (London: Oxford, 1950) 3.

5. Marvin Harris, *The Rise of Anthropological Theory* (New York: Crowell, 1968) 516, 524–25; Jonathan Turner, *The Structure of Sociological Theory* (rev. ed.; Homewood, IL: Dorsey, 1978) 113. "Functional sociology, with its ahistorical character and its emphasis upon the *ongoing* consequences of existent social arrangements, reflects the loss of historical imagination that corresponds to the mature entrenchment of the middle class, which no longer fears the past and neither imagines nor desires a future radically different from the present" (Alvin Gouldner, *The Coming Crisis of Western Sociology* [New York: Basic Books, 1970] 107; cf. 157). John Schütz, in the "Introduction" to G. Theissen, *The Social Setting of Pauline Christianity* (Philadelphia: Fortress, 1982) 16, has an unusual assessment of functionalism.

6. See Eric Wolf, *Europe and the People Without History* (Berkeley: University of California Press, 1982); John Kautsky, *The Politics of Aristocratic Empires* (Chapel Hill: University of North Carolina Press, 1982); S. N. Eisenstadt, *The Political Systems of Empires* (New York: Free Press, 1963).

7. Harris, *The Rise of Anthropological Theory*, 558–59; Gouldner, *Coming Crisis*, 353; cf. Schütz, "Introduction," 18–19.

8. Lewis Coser, *The Functions of Social Conflict* (Glencoe: Free Press, 1956) 195; Harris, *History of Anthropological Theory*, 560–61; Peter Worsley, *The Third World* (London: Wiedenfeld & Nicolson, 1961) 28.

9. See also Theissen, "Theoretische Probleme religionssoziologischer Forschung und die Analyse des Urchristentums," in *Studien zur Soziologie des Urchristentums* (Tübingen: Mohr, 1979) 66.

10. Gouldner, among others, is sharply critical of the inherent conservatism of structural-functional sociology: "To make social order one's central concern, then, is indeed to be conservative" (*Coming Crisis*, 253; cf. 195–96, 281, 297, 331–33, 421, 430). Schütz's exposition of Theissen's functionalism ("Introduction," to *The Social Setting*, 17) reveals its inherent conservatism.

11. Gouldner, *Coming Crisis*, 126–32; Harris, *The Rise of Anthropological Theory*, 517, 534.

12. Malinowski, "The Life of Culture," in G. E. Smith et al., eds., *The Diffusion Controversy* (New York: Norton, 1927) 40–41.

13. E.g., S. M. Lipset and E. C. Ladd, "American Social Scientists and the Growth of Campus Political Activism in the 1960s," *Social Science Information* 10/2 (1971) 105–20.

14. George A. Huaco, "Ideology and General Theory: The Case of Sociological Functionalism," *Comparative Studies in Society and History* 28 (1986) 34–54.

3 ◊ Evidence and Arguments _____

Itinerant Radicalism

Theissen's reconstruction cannot stand up to critical analysis, primarily because of the lack of supporting evidence. The "Analysis of Roles" begins hypothetically enough: he claims merely to be testing against the sources his main argument that "Jesus did not primarily found local communities, but called into being a movement of wandering charismatics" (8). Very few of the sources he cites, however, support his presentation of the wandering charismatics themselves, let alone the contention that Jesus founded a movement of them. Most poorly attested of all is the ethos of "itinerant radicalism" that Theissen claimed to find particularly in the tradition of Jesus sayings.

The general problems with the way he reads or uses the sources are easily identifiable. A certain literalism prevents him from appreciating the subtlety or nuances of some sayings.[1] He applies only to his wandering charismatics a number of sayings that clearly applied or were addressed to a broader audience. Some texts are simply misconstrued. Sometimes, finally, the lack of any serious evidence at all is apparent. These problems can be readily observed in a point-for-point examination of various "conclusions." Because Theissen claims that the Jesus movement consisted primarily of the wandering charismatics and their "radicalism," it is important to discern from the outset that there is little or no evidence for this reconstruction. And because he adduces so little evidence, it is possible to examine critically virtually every text he does adduce.

The Wandering Charismatics

The "constructive conclusions" that the apostles and others were wandering charismatics (8–9) are largely arguments from silence (or rather "absence") or arguments by analogy with apostles such as Barnabas and Paul, who operated outside Palestine.[2] There is apparently no direct "information" to confirm his inferences by analogy.

The principal phrases that actually support his "analytical conclusions" regarding the "homelessness," "lack of family," and "lack of possessions" of the itinerants (10-14)[3] are taken from the same two passages in the synoptic tradition: (a) that on the calling of the first disciples (Mark 1:16, 20), which only by implication, but not in explicit terms, would evidence the abandonment of home and family—and that only temporarily; and (b) that on the sending out of the disciples (Luke 10:4=Q; par. Matt 10:9-10, a conflation of Q and Mark 6:8-9), which suggests that no possessions are to be carried during missionary journeys, although it does not mention abandoning home and family. The other principal passages that he draws on repeatedly, however, are problematic for his purposes. The sayings in Matt 8:18-22 (par. Luke 9:57-60) were surely addressed to a broader audience than a few dozen wandering charismatics, and it is highly questionable that sayings such as "leave the dead to bury the dead" are to be taken literally as addressed to a particular charismatic. Mark 10:28-29, if read in its context, 10:28-30 (or 10:17-31), places those addressed in a new "home" and the broader "family" of a renewed community (with lands!) rather than in an ethos of homeless wandering.[4]

Nearly all of the other texts he adduces as illustrations of one or another of the characteristics of the wandering charismatics are similarly problematic. On "homelessness" (10-11) his citations of *Didache* 11:8 and 11:5 appear to be twisted to fit his case, perhaps simply misread: far from suggesting that wandering is "the behavior of the Lord" to be imitated, *Didache* 11 appears to be a set of pronouncements aimed at curbing abuses by itinerant prophets. Surely fleeing to the next town to avoid persecution (Matt 10:23, taken from the synoptic apocalypse in Mark 13) does not indicate the supposedly intentional homelessness of the itinerant charismatics.

Many of the texts he adduces for the "lack of family" (11-12) are either pulled out of their immediate context in the Gospel tradition or taken literally without sensitivity to possible figurative or analogical meaning. For example, texts such as Mark 3:21 (". . . he is beside himself") and Matt 10:25 ("If they have called the master of the house Beelzebul . . .") had as their context a broader conflict than that between a "lost son" and his family who thought he was "mad"—indeed one of apocalyptic proportions. Theissen makes much of Luke 14:26 ("hating" father and mother, wife, children, etc.). Compared with its parallel in Matt 10:37, however, this saying has clearly been decisively reworked by Luke (for example, so that it pertains only to married males). Like the other sayings with which it is now linked in Luke, moreover, it would appear to be addressed to a more general audience than a few dozen itinerants. And far from being meant literally, the "hating" of one's family members as well as one's own life is a rather severe illustration of "counting the cost," parallel to the other illustrations such as "building a tower" in Luke 14:27, 28-30, 31-32.

Even as it stands in Luke, finally, it would appear to be understood properly not in the context of an individual family but in connection with the broader social conflict that comes with the advent of the kingdom and the decisions that requires, as in sayings such as Luke 12:52-53; Matt 10:20. Other texts adduced in support of the charismatics' "lack of family" are simply misconstrued. It is very difficult to find "praise of castration" in Matt 19:10-12 ("eunuchs for the kingdom of heaven"). Mark 6:4 does not imply that a family had been forsaken by a son but that an overly vocal local protester was rejected by his town of origin.[5]

In the section on "lack of possessions" (12-14) none of the texts except those from the "mission discourse" (Luke 10:4 par.) even suggests itinerancy. Sharing or selling possessions was expected of more than the wandering charismatics (Mark 10:17ff.; Acts 4:36-37; cf. 5:1; Mark 10:25; Matt 6:19ff.). Surely the beatitudes and woes (Luke 6:20-26) as well as sayings such as not serving both God and Mammon (Luke 16:13) have application far broader than the hypothetical itinerants. Moreover, typical apocalyptic imagery of judgment was not peculiar to wandering vagabonds who were "working off their aggression." Matt 10:42 (on giving "a cup of cold water to these little ones") may well have aimed at inducing "sympathizers" to support itinerant "beggars." But the lengthy passage which climaxes in "seek first the kingdom . . ." (Matt 6:25-33) is far broader in its address and application than merely expressing "the harshness of the free existence of the wandering charismatics, without homes and . . . with no possessions and no occupation" (13).

The final characteristic, "lack of protection" (14), appears to lack particular textual illustration or support from the Gospel sources. There is no question that guidance of the individual or community was understood to be by the Holy Spirit (Matt 10:17ff.; etc.). But turning the other cheek and going the second mile (Matt 5:38f., 41) must have had a reference broader than the wandering charismatics.

Besides this uncritical use of individual texts in support of contentions that most in fact do not attest, there is an apparent lack of critical assessment of the literary sources that might be relevant to the inquiry—a lack that is puzzling in an investigation that purports to practice the sociology of literature. As a fundamental procedural principle Theissen very appropriately excludes from consideration synoptic material that is of Hellenistic origin. But the only evidence he has, indirect at that, on the basis of which he deduced his "constructive conclusions" about the Palestinian Jewish situation are Hellenistic texts pertaining to Paul and Barnabas, who were operating in Hellenistic churches. Moreover, the literary sources from which we have access to earlier stages of the synoptic tradition are Hellenistic. Theissen draws heavily (and uncritically) from Luke as well as Acts, and some of the principal texts he emphasizes have clearly been shaped by Luke (e.g., 14:26, as mentioned above).

If we conduct the critical analysis of sources that Theissen omitted, however, the lack of evidence for his "wandering charismatics" is all the more striking. The renunciation of possessions by the disciples as an example for his readers from the pristine past is a prominent theme in Luke's Gospel. This makes Theissen's contention about the prominence of the wandering charismatics and their abandonment of home and possessions all the more questionable insofar as his case relies heavily on Lucan texts. Paul does not mention any activity of itinerant charismatics in Palestine. Theissen himself points out (8–9) that his argument here is one from "absence" (of the disciples from Jerusalem when Paul visited, Gal 1:18). One of the points at which Paul does mention traveling apostles, however, appears to contradict Theissen's contention that they were strictly without family: "Do we not have a right to be accompanied by a wife, as the other apostles and brothers of the Lord and Cephas?" (1 Cor 9:5). Acts 8:14–17 and 9:32–43 portray Peter (and John) as charismatics who travel from town to town in Palestine, but there is no hint of the "radical ethos" of intentional homelessness and poverty emphasized by Theissen.

A literary-sociological analysis of the synoptic tradition itself, finally, would appear to lead to a use of the sayings tradition virtually the opposite of Theissen's. The evidence is weakest for Theissen's claims about the "radical ethos" of the charismatics. Yet assume for a moment that we found credible that itinerant disciples were active in the Palestinian "Jesus movement."[6] It would then be inherently likely that they were instrumental in the transmission of Jesus sayings, since that would have been part of their "role." If such itinerant disciples shaped the sayings tradition in the process of transmission, they would likely have emphasized their own importance. In that case, however, we would have to discount that emphasis, not highlight it, in attempting to make historical and sociological generalizations regarding the Jesus movement. Historically the itinerant disciples would have been, if anything, less important than our literary sources portray (whether at the Q or the Lucan/Matthean stage).

The Cynic Analogy

Given the lack of evidence in the sayings tradition for the wandering charismatics and their "ethical radicalism," it is likely that Theissen's "Comparative Conclusion" is more determinative for his argument than he and we, at first, might realize. For the itinerant charismatics, he declares, "poverty was not only a fate, but a calling" (13). One wonders, however, whether this idea arises from the Gospel tradition or from portrayals of the wandering Cynic philosophers. Having excluded synoptic material of Hellenistic origin from consideration as a basic procedural principle, Theissen ironically appeals to vagabond Hellenistic philosophers as the comparative paradigm for his reconstruction of the itinerant charismatics of the Jesus movement. Theissen himself is aware of the procedural discrepancy when he states apologetically, "true, these analogies take us outside Palestine" (15). Apparently he is presupposing the more concrete analogy he had drawn in the earlier article, in which he found the similarity of ethos indicated in Jesus sayings and Epictetus's description of the Cynic's life-style to be evidence that the itinerant followers of Jesus "belonged to a comparable sociological group."[7]

On closer examination, however, there appear to be decisive differences between the Cynics and the traveling preachers and healers of the Jesus movement in Palestine.[8] First, as just explained, there is very little evidence in the sayings tradition or elsewhere for the "ethos" claimed by Theissen. Second, the principal texts upon which the very existence of the itinerant charismatics is projected, e.g., Luke 9:3; 10:4, make pointed distinctions between Jesus' disciples and the Cynics: the former are not to take purse and staff, some of the characteristic signs of the latter, as Theissen himself points out.[9] Third, assuming that the mission discourse refers to "wandering charismatics," they were sent primarily to village communities in Jewish Palestine, whereas the Cynics appeared primarily in cities, and throughout the Hellenistic-Roman world. Fourth, the Cynics apparently really were vagabond beggars, whereas those sent on mission by Jesus stayed in local houses, eating what was provided in those households. The Cynics and Jesus' disciples, finally, apparently had very different "callings." The Cynic virtuosi were called to be individual paradigms of virtue for other individuals who might emulate their example. Jesus' disciples were called as catalysts of a community-based movement (as Theissen himself assumes with the communities of "sympathizers"). Thus, whereas the Cynics lived without home and possessions and family as an intentional "ethos," those sent out in Mark 6:8–11 and Luke 10:4–11 (at least temporarily) left behind home, possessions, and family as an unavoidable but more incidental matter necessitated by the mission to which they were called.[10] Jesus' preachers and healers, while not a "sociological group" themselves (*contra* Theissen), worked in community bases. They were not simply supported by local communities, but were apparently engaged in attempts to revitalize community life (see further ch 7 below).

The Charismatics and Their Sympathizers

For Theissen's attempt to reconstruct "the role of sympathizers in the local communities" (17-23) the principal problem is again lack of information. "Unfortunately we know very little about them" (17). For "constructive conclusions" we have no more information than that certain (to Jesus) sympathetic families were *probably* the nucleus of *later* local communities" (my emphases). For "analytical conclusions," moreover, "there are very few synoptic traditions the unmistakable setting of which is the life of the local communities" (18). Much weight would therefore appear to rest on "a comparative conclusion": extrapolation by analogy from the Essenes, as portrayed primarily by Josephus (not the Dead Sea Scrolls). But not only were the traveling Essenes not wandering charismatics; the Essenes were withdrawn from the rest of society, whereas the early Palestinian-Christian communities attempted to remain within and open to the rest of the society (21-22).

Considering the shaky base of evidence, therefore, it is surprising that Theissen draws such sharp and firm conclusions about the local communities: i.e., that "they are to be understood exclusively in terms of their complementary relationship to the wandering charismatics" and that they lived in "compromise with the world" and according to "more moderate norms" than did the "radical" wandering charismatics (22-23, 18-19).

On the first point, Theissen's discussion of "analytical conclusions" demonstrates almost the opposite. That is, in two out of three categories discussed, "regulations for behavior" and "procedure for accepting and rejecting members," the communities' complementary relationship with the wandering charismatics has little or no effect. Theissen's conclusion thus rests primarily on his discussion of "the structure of authority" (19-21). But the only synoptic text he can cite that even suggests that "wandering charismatics were the authorities in the local communities" is that about Peter having been given power to bind and loose (Matt 16:19). Matt 23:34 (about sending "prophets, visionaries, and scribes") would not appear to be addressed to the local communities. Matt 23:8-11 suggests that the communities would recognize no "father" or "teacher" other than God and Jesus, and Matt 18:18, in context at least, gives the power to bind and loose to the community. There is simply no basis for Theissen's assertion that "the less the structures of authority in local communities had come under the control of an institution, the greater was the longing for the great charismatic authorities" (20).[11] Thus, a close scrutiny of the passages cited leads to a conclusion virtually the opposite of Theissen's: one can understand very little about the local communities from their relationship with the wandering charismatics.[12]

The Charismatics and the Son of Man

Lack of evidence, or perhaps rather unclarity about how to construe the evidence, again plagues Theissen's claims about the "homologue" he detects between the "Son of man" and the wandering charismatics. After whetting our appetite in the introduction to Part One, Theissen lets us down in ch IV. "The various christologies express the attitudes of expectation directed towards the bearer of revelation . . ." (7). The possibilities thus set up go largely unexplored when he concentrates on only "the Son of man." His presentation suffers from an apparent lack of acquaintance with the results of scholarly discussion of "the various christological titles," particularly investigations into the meaning and use of "son of man." With the rationalization that "sociological analysis cannot answer the question of who the Son of man is," he bypasses the hotly debated issues concerning Jesus and "the son of man." He simply assumes that the earliest followers of Jesus had identified "the earthly Son of man" (in sayings where Jesus refers to himself as "the son of man") and "the future Son of man" (in sayings where eventually many early Christians must have understood the exalted Jesus himself, although Jesus and his early followers may have understood a different, future figure or, as in the original vision of Daniel 7, an image of the judgment and/or of the restoration and renewal of the people).

His conclusion, with regard to "the role of the Son of man," that "his situation corresponded to their situation" is vague—the more so when "their situation" is not adequately explained sociologically. He tends to focus on the wandering charismatics (to the exclusion of the sympathizers). And by "corresponded to," he apparently means "to be the same as or similar to" through much of his discussion. Thus Theissen claims that the "vagabonds" were similar to the Son of man even in the judgment role (27).[13] As a proof text, of course, he cites Matt 19:28 *in translation*. But it has long been recognized as problematic to understand and translate the Hebrew *šāpaṭ/mišpāṭ* and the Greek *krinein* in terms of the English and German words for "judging." [14] The twelve in Matt 19:28 will not be so much "judging" as "saving/delivering/liberating" the twelve tribes of Israel. There is really no evidence that the wandering charismatics, let alone the members of the Jesus movement generally, "corresponded to" the Son of man's role as eschatological judge.

If "corresponded to" refers simply to the eschatological judge (the Son of man) as vindicator of the members of the Jesus movement, then the correspondence includes all members, not only the wandering charismatics. Thus it is puzzling, especially in a sociological analysis, to find the claim that "the conflict between 'man' and the 'Son of man' which appears in" the Son of man sayings such as Mark 8:38 has, as "a social foundation," "the conflict between vagabond outsiders and 'human' society" (27). Such sayings, however, clearly portray the Son of man as universal judge and vindicator of *all* Jesus' followers, not simply of the wandering charismatics (see, e.g., Mark 8:38; 14:62 and par.; 13:26-27; Matt 13:41; 24:27ff.; 25:31-46). One suspects that the social foundation (in the structural homologue) of "the Son of man" coming in judgment and other apocalyptic visions of vindication runs much deeper than the need of the "vagabond outsiders" for ultimate recognition.

In sum, the picture of the Jesus movement resulting from Theissen's analysis of "roles" bears little relation to the tradition of Jesus sayings that he claims as evidence. The very existence of "wandering charismatics" as he portrays them is postulated by Theissen primarily on the basis of Paul's comment that the disciples of the Lord were not in Jerusalem when he visited there, bolstered by an extrapolation from the existence of itinerant missionaries such as Paul and Barnabas outside Palestine. Moreover, the "ethical radicalism" of which they were the only conceivable practitioners—hence its being labeled "itinerant radicalism"—simply cannot be documented from the sayings tradition. Many of the sayings cited by Theissen clearly pertain to Jesus' followers generally. Indeed, the only sayings that clearly pertain to itinerant missionaries are from the "mission discourse." These sayings give regulations for the way in which traveling preachers and healers are to obtain support from local communities. They thus provide for a sort of elementary division of labor within the nascent Jesus movement. There is simply no justification in the sources for Theissen's writing at points later in the book as if the Jesus movement consisted primarily of wandering charismatics. Similarly, Theissen's contention that the wandering charismatics are the key to understanding the Jesus movement is simply not borne out by the evidence.

Analogies and Arguments

"The Resistance Movement" Never Existed; "The Essenes" Withdrew

Theissen's use of arguments from "analogies" also appears to founder on problems of evidence. The analogies that Theissen finds in the other Jewish renewal movements are crucial to both the procedure and the argument that the key "phenomena" of the Jesus movement were widespread in the society and therefore "influenced by that society." Indeed, "it is often the analogies which provide a first indication" of a social cause, "since the social conditioning of a phenomenon often emerges more clearly in contemporary parallels than in the Jesus movement itself" (32). In regard to the limitations of the evidence, it is therefore worth noting that Theissen relies on different analogies from "factor" to "factor," with "robbers," John the Baptist, "prophetic movements," and Pharisees figuring prominently in successive chapters. Then, far more significantly, of the two "analogies" that figure throughout under all the different factors, that is, "the resistance movement" and the Essenes, the one almost certainly never existed, at least in the form Theissen imagines, and the other may not be all that "analogous" sociologically.

Theissen relies perhaps most heavily on the analogy of the "resistance movement." His generalizations in this connection combine a less than critical analysis of the sources with an unquestioning acceptance of a standard modern scholarly reconstruction. At the time he wrote, the old construct of "the Zealots" as a movement organized to agitate for insurrection against Roman rule was still generally accepted. Although he appears to know better than to use the old nomenclature of the "Zealot" movement, he clearly has it in mind: "The *resistance movement* pursued its aim of a general rebellion against the Romans over a number of generations" (61). Following the standard older reconstruction, he views Judas of Galilee as "the founder of the movement" and suggests that he already had royal aspirations, based on the usual uncritical identification of the "teacher" Judas of Galilee, who was active in 6 C.E. in Judea (*Antiquities* 18.4–23), with the royal pretender Judas son of Hezekiah, who was active in Galilee in 4 B.C.E. (*Antiquities* 17.271–72).

Although there was some pointed criticism of this modern synthetic reconstruction available when Theissen wrote,[15] the diversity of groups behind the modern misunderstanding had not been generally discerned. Now, however, it can be seen that what he lumps together to illustrate the rural base of the resistance movement (e.g., on 49–50) were a number of quite different groups: (a) The "unrest after the death of Herod" took the form of movements led by popularly acclaimed "kings" (which he later realizes were "messianic pretenders," 75); (b) the "leaders of revolt," of course, did not all come from Galilee, and the ones he mentions did not lead revolts, but were either no more than "social bandits" (Eleazar son of Deinaeus or Tholomaeus) or a leader of a resistance to Roman taxation (Judas of Galilee); (c) those who "made the Jerusalem aristocracy the victims of their terror" were the scholarly-led Sicarii, who were based in the city, not the countryside; and (d) the "hordes" who entered Jerusalem during the great revolt were four quite different groups who were indeed from the country but who fought each other as much as or more than they did the Romans.[16]

Unfortunately, Theissen himself goes even beyond previous reconstructions in making claims about "the resistance movement" based on dubious use of the limited sources. For example, he adduces three texts from Josephus to document the assertion that the "resistance fighters" "drew their recruits from the farmers who were no longer able to pay taxes, from those in debt, and from the poor" (35–36). However, the first text (*Antiquities* 18.274) is Josephus's account of Jewish ruling groups concerned that an increase in social banditry might occur if the peasant protest (refusal to plant crops) against the imposition of Gaius's statue in the Temple continued and the tribute could not be met. The Sicarii, the principal referent Theissen seems to have in mind behind the vague phrase "resistance fighters," had not yet emerged as an active resistance group. The second text (*War* 2.424ff.) is Josephus's surmise that part of the motivation of the followers of Eleazar and others, including some Sicarii, active at the very outbreak of the revolt in Jerusalem in 66, was to provoke a broader uprising of the impoverished and indebted peasantry against the wealthy Jewish ruling class. But at the point they were hardly recruiting members for a movement. The third text (*War* 4.421) is part of a speech placed in the chief priest Jesus' mouth by Josephus denigrating as "scum and offscouring" the peasants-turned-brigands (i.e., the Zealots proper) who had fled to Jerusalem during the winter of 67–68 after the advancing Roman forces had devastated their villages and lands. All of these texts are relevant to the phenomenon of social uprootedness in first-century Palestine. But none of them provides any evidence for a renewal movement of resistance fighters analogous to the Jesus movement.[17]

It is ironic for Theissen's argument, which emphasizes both rural rootlessness and the basis of renewal movements in the countryside that the one group that could be seen as an organized resistance movement, albeit small and only short-lived (50s and 60s C.E.) was the *urban-based* group called the Sicarii, which was apparently at least led by intellectuals. But it becomes more serious historical distortion when a historically unattested "resistance movement" is used as a foil over against which to portray the Jesus movement as "the peace party among the renewal movements within Judaism" (64). The only peace party mentioned by Josephus consisted of the priestly aristocracy and their allies, who were eager to protect their property, power, and privilege in collaboration with Roman rule (*War* 2.338, 411–22).

The other principal renewal movement upon which Theissen relies may be a somewhat limited analogue. The Essenes (primarily at Qumran) were a literate, priestly-oriented community off in the wilderness of Judea almost totally withdrawn from interaction with the rest of the society. The Jesus movement, on the other hand, according to Theissen himself, consisted most importantly of the charismatics who were itinerant or of sympathizers based stably enough in local communities to provide support to the itinerants. The (initial) cause of the original "exodus" to Qumran was probably not economically induced rootlessness, and it is questionable whether we have any reliable evidence regarding subsequent generations' withdrawal to the wilderness community. Similarly, it may be doubted that the Essenes give us any analogy at all for the "ecological" factor of countryside versus city. Considering the priestly orientation and scholarly-scribal style of the community at Qumran, many of the members may have been Jerusalem expatriates for political and cultural reasons, not country-based peasants resentful of the political-economic exploitation by the city-based ruling groups. The analogy would remain limited in this case to the radical theocracy and the intensification of norms.

Problematic Arguments

Throughout ch V, "Socio-economic Factors" there would appear to be a fundamental unclarity or even confusion regarding the *phenomenon* to be explained and the *explanation* in terms of socio-economic factors itself. The phenomenon to be explained is "the social rootlessness of the wandering charismatics." But "by social rootlessness" Theissen means "that the followers of Jesus (now virtually identified with the wandering charismatics) left their ancestral homes" (33). Hence their social rootlessness is not their social-economic situation prior to being called to discipleship, but the result of their having joined the movement. Most of the rest of the chapter is devoted to supposedly analogous groups of socially rootless people and the social-economic causes of their rootlessness. Yet both in introducing the "causes" and in summarizing the explanation, Theissen argues basically that it was not those already socially rootless but those who may have felt threatened by economic insecurity who provided the social context and the participants of the renewal movements within Judaism, including the Jesus group. Not rootlessness but the threat of (or reaction to others') rootlessness turns out to be the explanation of why the wandering charismatics became rootless.

Theissen's attempt to be schematic may have caused part of the confusion. He treats together both those people who had actually been uprooted by economic and/or political circumstances (emigrants, robbers, beggars) and participants in renewal movements, some of whom retained their roots, some of whom became rootless, and some of whom established new social roots. He apparently assumes that socially rootless and dissatisfied people somehow had a choice about their behavior and pursuit in life (34–36). He even labels the "choices" of some as "evasive." For most of the "evidence of disintegration," however, this is absurd—unless the choice was between dying and becoming a beggar or a bandit or an emigrant. A historical sociologist must at least take into consideration the minimum basis for the support and "reproduction" of biological life.[18] Theissen has apparently accepted the usual sociological generalization that not the poorest, most desperate people, but those facing the threat of poverty are the likely participants in protest or renewal movements (39, 45–46). The principal confusion in his own argument thus seems to be rooted in the fact that the propertyless and homeless people in Galilee "shortly before the period of Jesus' ministry" are not very appropriate analogies for his "wandering charismatics," who chose to become homeless.

It is clear that the appropriate analogies to the wandering charismatics would be those who joined other renewal movements. But the particular renewal movements Theissen chooses to use as analogies are problematic if the phenomenon to be explained in terms of social-economic factors is voluntarily chosen social rootlessness. The Qumranites, far from becoming rootless, chose a utopian, new covenant community which, judging from its longevity, developed vigorous new roots. With regard to "the resistance movement," moreover, Theissen appears to have in mind primarily the Sicarii, who conducted their assassinations in a clandestine manner so they could continue their ordinary lives while engaged in resistance to the Jewish ruling class. Thus they were even less rootless than the Essenes. The only renewal movements that provide an appropriate analogy to the phenomenon of voluntarily chosen social rootlessness are thus the "eccentric undertakings" of the popular prophets who led their followers in anticipation of some new divine act of liberation (36). Even here, however, the analogy is good only for the wandering charismatics, and not for the Jesus movement generally; for the followers of the popular prophets all abandoned their homes, whereas the vast majority of those involved in the Jesus movement remained rooted in local communities.

Whereas the "wandering charismatics dominate ch V to the exclusion of the vast majority of people in the Jesus movement, these itinerants have totally disappeared from view in ch VI, "Social-ecological Factors." Indeed, aside from the one-paragraph section on the phenomenon to be explained—that the Jesus movement was based in the countryside—there is virtually no discussion of early Palestinian Christianity apart from the

Jerusalem community. In the concluding summary, Theissen states that "like the other renewal movements within Judaism, the Jesus movement had its roots in the hinterland of Judea" (57). The chapter, however, has not explained the phenomenon. The causes are either not relevant to the phenomenon or not socio-ecological. And the discussion of comparative material is highly problematic.

The comparative movements and the corresponding "intentions" are not good analogies for the supposed tension between city and country. If the latter conflict is so important, then the analogies should be critically analyzed with precisely this in focus. In fact, it is highly questionable whether "the other renewal movements within Judaism" were "rooted in the country and dominated by trends hostile to Jerusalem" (52). Theissen's statements are simply wrong or misleading on a number of counts.

The prophetic movements apparently did consist primarily of people from the countryside; but they also appear to have abandoned their roots there to head out into the wilderness. Theissen's other analogies were not even rooted in the country. Many of the Essenes at Qumran may well have originated from priestly families based in Jerusalem. The terrorist activity Theissen cites (49) was carried out by the Sicarii, a group rooted in the city, not the countryside. Moreover, the Essenes and some of the prophetic movements went out into the wilderness, not the settled countryside—for what in Theissen's analysis would have been cultural and political reasons. In imitation of past events of deliverance they were seeking purification and renewal in the wilderness and were getting away from alien or domestic ruling groups.

Furthermore, it is Theissen and not his source (Josephus) who finds in these renewal movements some hostility to the city itself. As we now know from the *Temple Scroll* found at Qumran, the "Essenes" were hoping to return eventually to a purified city as its faithful and proper priesthood. There is no reason whatever to believe that the Sicarii were anti-city. The one prophetic movement (led by the "Egyptian" Jew) that did not go out into the wilderness marched about Jerusalem; but this was not necessarily to see it destroyed; it may have been to experience its liberation by God and to gain access to it themselves (*Antiquities* 20.169–71; *War* 2.261–63). And the Zealots proper, a coalition of brigand bands who sought refuge in Jerusalem in the winter of 67–68, may have thought of themselves not as anti-city but as its liberators (of the city and people from the wealthy and powerful collaborating in Roman rule) as Theissen himself points out (51).[19] It would appear from at least the evidence on the Essenes, the Sicarii, the prophetic movement led by the "Egyptian" Jew, and the Zealots proper that these "renewal" groups were not simply hostile to the city as such but reacting against the ruling groups based in the city from whose control they wanted to see it liberated.

For "causes" of the key renewal groups being rooted in the country— which, as just pointed out, was not necessarily the case—Theissen reaches for "factors" which are not "ecological" but "economic." That is, the inhabitants of Jerusalem were conservative because nearly all of them were either indirectly or directly dependent economically on the Temple, while the economic pressure was greater in the country than in the city (a curious understatement, considering that in the ancient world the city lived off the countryside, on which see further ch 4 below). This generalization is questionable and hardly a sufficient explanation, considering the evidence that the Sicarii were urban based and some of the Essenes came originally from the city. Of his other "causes" for "the rebellious attitude of the country areas," that they "were harder to control" does not explain much and "begs the question," while that they "were border territory" is only partly true.

Two of the principal problems inherent in ch VII, "Socio-political Factors," are rooted in inadequate textual and historical analysis. Indeed, on the basis of the material and analysis Theissen presents in the sections on phenomena, analogies, and intentions, it is difficult to figure out what a "radical theocratic movement" was.

First, his statements about the Jesus movement and its contrast with "the resistance movement" or "the war party" or the Essenes are utterly unfounded. As noted already above, there is simply no historical evidence for the modern scholarly assumption of a longstanding ancient Jewish "resistance movement." There is similarly no evidence of any "war party" among "the renewal movements within Judaism." Furthermore, there is very limited textual evidence for Jewish "Messianology" before and during the life of Jesus (contra 63–64). Theissen does state forthrightly the political implications of the Jesus movement's "imminent eschatology": the rule of God meant the end of all other rule, including that of the Romans and the priestly aristocracy (59, 63). The other "radical theocratic movements," moreover, shared this imminent eschatology,[20] with its implication for Roman and Jewish high priestly rule. On what basis, then, is it so "unmistakable" that the Essenes were "aggressive" while the Jesus movement was "eirenic" in their respective "political ethics" (64–65)? Theissen has not carried out a sufficiently critical analysis of the "political ethics" of these "radical theocratic movements." His claim that the Jesus movement was "the peace party" is based on the usual collage of "proof texts" that Jesus was not "political"—texts about which there has been little recent exegetical consensus. Were the Essenes any more aggressive than the Jesus movement? Hatred of "the sons of Darkness/the pit" in fact does not mean an "aggressive" political stance at all (see 1QS 10). Nonretaliation can be rooted in Essene "hate" just as easily as in Pauline "love," and both were "intentionally rooted in the expectation that God's wrathful punishment of evildoers was imminent.[21]

Second, because of his lack of historical perspective, Theissen has linked the rise of the radical theocratic movements with a secondary or subsidiary factor, while overlooking a more primary cause. He claims that conflict between native Jewish and alien Roman structures of rule weakened and contributed to the illegitimacy of the Jewish priestly aristocracy and thus gave rise to dreams of theocracy in a radical form (65). Long before the first-century conflicts between Roman governors, Herodian client kings, and Jewish high priests, however, the Jewish hierocracy had been discredited and weakened in the eyes of the people, and radical theocratic movements had appeared. No sooner had the "Maccabean Revolt" resulted in the successful reassertion of Jewish independence from foreign rule than the upstart Hasmoneans were seen as illegitimate high priests by the Essenes and apparently also by the Pharisees. The Pharisees and others eventually fought a bloody civil war against Alexander Jannai, one of those illegitimate Hasmonean high priests. At the death of the hated tyrant Herod, the crowd in Jerusalem had called for the removal of the high priest appointed by Herod, the refusal of which became one of the provocations leading to the outbreak of massive insurrection against the whole ruling structure: Roman garrison, client king, and priestly aristocracy combined (*Antiquities* 17.204–85; *War* 2.4–13, 39–65). The Sicarii were certainly not the only Palestinian Jews who knew full well that the high priestly ruling clique were collaborating with the Roman imperial system, just as were the Herodians.

The socio-political "cause" of the rise of radical theocratic movements was thus not the tension between Roman and native rulers. The weakness and illegitimacy of the priestly aristocracy did not begin with or result from its own tensions with the Romans on whom their power and privilege were dependent. The socio-political cause of the rise of radical theocratic movements was illegitimate and oppressive rule, whether native or alien, or native collaborating with alien. The Essenes at Qumran, the only "analogy" for which Theissen has any evidence to speak of, had arisen nearly two centuries earlier, perhaps as an offshoot of an earlier "resistance movement" led by the Hasidim, who were fighting for the preservation of the people's traditions against a combination of apostate high priests and their imperial sponsors.

This recognition of the long history of "radical theocratic movements" prior to the rise of the Jesus movement suggests that they were the result of a "socio-cultural cause" as well. Theissen's presentation underplays the

role of religious and political ideological traditions. For several generations prior to Jesus, dreams of theocracy in radical form had been cultivated in the wilderness at Qumran—and therefore probably elsewhere in
Jewish society—and before that in the Danielic and Enochic apocalyptic
literature. The "cause" of the rise of radical theocratic movements would
therefore appear to be the intolerable discrepancy between the ideal of
God's rule of justice and the oppressive rule of native high priests in collaboration with imperial regimes.

By ch VIII, "Socio-cultural Factors," Theissen's interest has reached
beyond the Jesus movement to what developed outside of and/or after
early Palestinian Christianity. He has clearly moved to Hellenistic
(including Hellenistic Jewish) society, the role of Paul, and the universalization of Judaism in the rise of Christianity. The shift of focus is evident
already in his discussion of "the phenomenon" (77). Ostensibly the
phenomenon is the stricter interpretation of the Torah in Jewish renewal
movements. Theissen's attention, however, focuses more on "the crisis of
identity" in "Judaism," more particularly on the question of assimilation
or detachment from Hellenistic culture. Thus, it is not surprising that the
"summary" (93) on the results of the crisis of cultural identity drives
quickly toward "the universalization of Judaism," a breakthrough the
final consequences of which were drawn "only with Paul." As noted in
the previous paragraph, an examination of cultural factors such as Palestinian Jewish religious-political ideologies of radical theocracy would be
absolutely essential for an understanding of the rise of "radical theocratic
movements" such as that catalyzed by Jesus. But by ch VIII interest has
simply shifted to issues of cultural assimilation and individualistic ethics.

Introjection of Aggression

The first and perhaps most fundamental difficulty for Theissen in Part
Three as in Part One is the lack of evidence for his assertions. In ch X,
in fact, he makes no effort even to cite any textual evidence apart from
Acts 12:20ff. to support his claim that the Jesus movement was a failure
in Palestine. He does cite many a text in his arguments concerning aggression, but virtually none of them illustrates or attests his arguments.
Regarding the two texts provided in illustration of "compensation for
aggression" (99–100), it is an unwarranted assumption that Matt 5:43–44
("love your enemies") involves "intensified aggression"—which supposedly then turns into its opposite—rather than, say, alleviated aggression;
and Matt 18:21–22, used in reference to aggression by outsiders, actually
pertains to forgiveness within the community. On the substitution of the
subject of aggression, the pronouncement of judgment against the town

that rejects Jesus' envoys, Matt 10:15, does illustrate the point. The other citations (Matt 12:31f.; Mark 8:38; Luke 12:4–7) appear to be misconstrued and do not even indirectly pertain to "the transference of aggression." Mark 5:1ff., concerning the Gadarene demons, does indeed illustrate the transference of aggression, but the whole phenomenon of belief in demons would appear to be most obviously an illustration of the substitution of the subject of aggression (demons substituted for Romans, etc.) rather than its object. But, of course, Theissen has posed the whole discussion in terms of the oppressed, poverty-stricken *Jesus movement's* aggression and its containment, rather than the general problem of aggression and relative power relations in the Roman imperial situation.[22] Moreover, in the only, cursory reference to what "was endured by the Jesus movement" (102), the illustrative text, Matt 25:40, is misconstrued. The point of the whole passage, Matt 25:31–46, would appear to be precisely *against* "transference of aggression" or mercy, a sort of sanction directing people to focus on other humans rather than on some substitute, such as God or the Son of man.

In his focal analysis of "the reversal of aggression" it is unclear that any of the texts cited could be construed even indirectly to involve "introjection" of aggressiveness. As noted, Theissen sees introjection of aggression in the call to repentance and in the intensification of norms. But Luke 13:1–5, at least through the argument that the slain Galileans were *not* worse sinners than others, is an argument explicitly against introjection, i.e., that one's suffering is due to one's own sin. Most of the other texts cited are simply irrelevant to the issue, while the text on John the Baptist, Mark 1:3, is simply misread to mean "withdrawal" in the sense of geographical separation, like the Qumranites. On "the intensification of norms" Theissen has misread a number of texts, such as Matt 5:22 and 29 (prohibiting even anger or lust), in a "Lutheran" sense of the "impossibility of fulfilling the intensified norms" pointing or leading to "the grace of God" rather than the reverse, as in the Sermon on the Mount, where the proclamation of the kingdom in the beatitudes (grace) leads to the intensification of norms. Most puzzling is where Theissen gets the idea that the Jesus movement in Palestine "accepted defeat" by introjecting their own guilt in the sense that "Jesus had to die for our sins." In Part One he claimed clearly that the wandering charismatics symbolized their own eventual vindication in the exaltation and judgment role of the Son of man. The "sayings source," on which he based most of his sketch of the "itinerant radicalism" of the Jesus movement does not appear to focus on the sacrificial or expiatory death of Jesus at all. Indeed, when Theissen comes to the section on "the symbolization of aggression," the only good texts he cites for his Freudian interpretation of the "scapegoat" are Mark

10:45 and 1 Cor 15:3. The latter is surely an early, pre-Pauline "creedal formula" about Christ's dying for sins, but not necessarily evidence for Palestinian communities, and Mark 10:45 stands out as one of the *only* two or three synoptic texts that make any reference to an expiatory interpretation of Jesus' death ("a ransom for many"). Theissen's "Analysis of Function" has virtually no basis in textual or other evidence pertaining to the Palestinian Jesus movement.

Theissen's presentation in Part Three also has problems of argument and analysis. The whole procedure whereby he attributes psychological properties to a movement is, of course, invalid.[23] Only individuals in a group, not a group itself, can project or introject or transfer in various analytically conceived psychological processes. Besides the fundamental procedural fallacy, however, Theissen's analysis is problematic, even simply wrong in some ways. This may be partly due to an uncritical acceptance of certain traditional interpretations. Far more serious are a number of fundamental discrepancies or inconsistencies both within the "analysis of function" and between the latter and his analyses earlier in the book.

At points Theissen appears simply to be projecting a typical traditional interpretation back onto the Gospel texts. He suggests, for example, that by "not resisting one who is evil" and by "turning the other cheek" the "hope is that part of his (the aggressor's) aggression will be directed inwards, so that aggressive actions will call forth shame and awareness of guilt" (107-8). This sounds similar to a traditional (Jewish and) Christian (but not necessarily Jesus movement) interpretation of a related exhortation by Paul in Romans 12. Stendahl, however, has argued conclusively that by "heaping burning coals" upon the evildoer's head Paul was not thinking of an appeal to the aggressor's conscience. There is simply little or nothing in Matt 5:38-42 to suggest the intention of provoking shame and guilt in the aggressor. In parallel fashion, Theissen's analysis of how a rich man could possibly enter the kingdom of God (Mark 10:27) and of "some of the intensified demands in the antitheses in the Sermon on the Mount" (105-6) would appear to project a particular Christian interpretation onto the Jesus sayings. Statements such as "the impossibility of fulfilling the intensified norms here becomes a pointer towards the grace of God" sound very much like the introspectively Western (Augustinian-Lutheran) interpretation of Paul's reflections on the law (in Galatians 3-4 or Romans 7). Correspondingly, we might well be cautious about such a statement in analysis of how "ethical radicalism" turned into "a radical proclamation of the grace of God" in the Jesus movement.[24]

Besides these projections, however, there are a number of serious discrepancies in the argument. Within Part Three, Theissen shifts back and forth on the character of the Jesus movement between "an eirenic movement" and "the ethical radicalism" of the wandering charismatics. This shift is connected with the particular point he is making. In relation to the containment of aggression in Jewish society so charged with tension, he concludes that the eirenic Jesus movement "experimented with a vision of love and reconciliation . . . in order to renew this society from within" (110). But then in the final chapter on functional effects he reverts to his earlier (Part One) emphasis on "the extreme ethical pattern" of "dispensing with family, homeland, possessions and protection," when the argument is the movement's failure in Jewish Palestine and the success of the "more moderate patriarchalism of love" in the Pauline communities (111, 115).

Even in the discussion of "the reversal of aggression" through introjection, which he sees as the key to the Jesus movement's containment of society's tensions, there is an apparent discrepancy. He declares at one point that "what was needed was a new relationship to all norms: putting trust and freedom from anxiety before demands of any kind" (107). This statement, however, stands in contrast with several other formulations that appear to reverse the structure or sequence of "grace" and "the intensification of norms" that one finds in the sayings of Jesus. To cite only the most extreme of these formulations (mostly on p. 105): "the impossibility of fulfilling the intensified norms here becomes a pointer towards the grace of God." Throughout this whole central section of his analysis of "functional outline," Theissen does not explain but merely asserts that (somehow) the intensification or impossibility of the problem becomes the solution, for example, that the intensification of introjected aggressiveness "turned into" self-acceptance.

Discrepancies between principal points in Part Three and the analysis in Part Two further compound the discrepancies within Part Three. The eirenic Jesus movement's "way of dealing with aggression," primarily through introjection and "the intensification of norms," "made room for the new vision of love and reconciliation" (110) supposedly in order to renew the society from within. Yet it was this same "intensification of norms" in the drive to realize the rule of God that led to inter-cultural and intra-cultural demarcations and tensions according to the analysis of "socio-cultural factors" in ch VIII (86).

Such discrepancies suggest that Theissen's approach is inappropriate to the material requiring analysis. He is focusing on "the function of religion" understood as contributing toward "the basic aims of a society, namely in achieving the integration of its members and overcoming conflicts through change" (2). "When a society is involved in crisis, its chief concern is to overcome and reduce the tensions within itself" (98). From what Theissen himself has described in Part Two and the chapter on functional effects (ch X), Palestinian Jewish "society" was so divided into conflicting groups and so fragmented into rival renewal movements that the tensions were insurmountable and reintegration impossible. Since the eirenic Jesus movement was, in effect, doomed to failure in this regard from the start, it makes little sense to emphasize how it could overcome society's tensions through the introjection of aggression. Indeed, one must question whether, if it is so clear that the Jesus movement had no effect on (i.e., no function in) Palestinian Jewish society (ch X), there is anything to be gained from such an analysis of the "functional outline" of this "eirenic" renewal movement (ch IX).

One must also question, on a more theoretical level, whether anything is to be gained in this case from analysis focused on the "integration" of "society." Given the inherent social-structural conflicts in Palestinian Jewish society, it is difficult to imagine any realistic way in which "society" as a whole could have "considered" or "approved" anything. Indeed, the very concept "society" in this case would appear to be a sociological abstraction of doubtful utility for understanding either social conflicts or functional effects. Theissen claims, of course (114), that his analysis of the Jesus movement in Palestine was based on "a sociological theory of conflict," in contrast with his analysis of the effects of the movement in Hellenistic society in terms of "a sociological theory of integration." From his own description (114) and his actual procedure, however, it is evident that there is little difference in practice between the two, and his own orientation is consistently toward "the resolution" of social tensions. In any case, one has the impression that the serious discrepancies as well as the misreading of evidence evident in Theissen's analysis of the effects of the Jesus movement on "society" are rooted in his approach. And that approach, sociological functionalism, is heavily invested in societal integration and social control.

Notes

1. "There should be no doubt that Jesus' sayings are meant seriously and literally" ("Itinerant Radicalism," 85).

2. This makes it all the more puzzling to find Theissen making such a sharp distinction between the itinerant charismatics and the "community organizers" Paul and Barnabas in an earlier article, "Legitimation and Lebensunterhalt: Ein Beitrag zur Soziologie urchristlicher Missionare," *New Testament Studies* 21 (1974-75) 192-221, translated in Theissen, *The Social Setting of Pauline Christianity* (Philadelphia: Fortress, 1982) 27-67.

3. See also "Itinerant Radicalism," 85–87.

4. W. Stegemann ("Vagabond Radicalism in Early Christianity," in *The God of the Lowly* [Maryknoll, NY: Orbis, 1986] 135) discerns, *contra* Theissen, the *community situation* inherent in Mark 10:28–30. His observation, however, that the community members have "changed their religion" and passed "to a different religious communion" projects a modern situation and concept back into first-century Palestine. Sociologically Theissen is on the mark with the opening sentence of the book (except for the abstractions in his formulation): "Earliest Christianity began as a renewal movement within Judaism" (1).

5. Martin Hengel's comment that such texts call for the abandonment of or break with "all human ties" is clearly an overinterpretation (*The Charismatic Leader and His Followers* [New York: Crossroad, 1981] 15, 71, etc.).

6. Stegemann is so convinced ("Vagabond Radicalism," 136).

7. "Itinerant Radicalism," 87.

8. W. Michaelis ("*pera*," in *Theological Dictionary of the New Testament*, ed. G. Kittel and G. Friedrich [Grand Rapids: Eerdmans, 1964–76] 6:119–21) and Hengel (*Charismatic Leader*, 128, 133) point out some of the differences between the Cynics and the key Gospel texts. A. J. Malherbe points out the necessity of taking into account the "rich diversity" of Cynicism which emerges from a wider selection of sources than has been used in the past by New Testament scholars (*Cynic Epistles* [Missoula, MT: Scholars Press, 1977] 3); see also his article "Cynics," in *Interpreter's Dictionary of the Bible: Supplementary Volume*, ed. K. Crim [Nashville: Abingdon, 1976] 201–3). The parallels between certain Pauline expressions, especially in the Corinthian correspondence, and the standard texts on the Cynics are far more striking than any parallels suggested between Cynic and Gospel texts; see W. Schmithals, *The Office of the Apostle in the Early Church* (Nashville: Abingdon, 1969) 111–13. R. MacMullen (*Enemies of the Roman Order* [Cambridge, MA: Harvard University Press, 1966] 59–66) and Wayne Meeks (*The Moral World of the First Christians* [Philadelphia: Westminster, 1986] 52–56) paint a picture of the wandering Cynics that seems very different from Theissen's wandering charismatics. But see further ch 6 below for more recent and precise studies of similarities between parts of the mission discourse in Q, Luke 10:3–11, and portrayals of the Cynics.

9. "Itinerant Radicalism," 88.

10. Theissen could just as appropriately have said of the itinerant charismatics' abandonment of home, etc., what he said of the community organizers' renunciation of financial support in another article: "Behind it there is to be found a deliberate missionary design. . . . The renunciation arose from concrete conditions in order to make the pioneering mission as effective as possible" (*The Social Setting of Pauline Christianity*, 40).

11. Otherwise Theissen's evidence for "the structure of authority" comes partly from Paul's letters and primarily from the *Didache*. However, were the passages from the *Didache* to be subjected to a redactional analysis they would provide weak evidence indeed for Theissen's claim.

12. "More generally, the earliest Christian documents are remarkable for their neglect of questions concerning leadership within individual communities" (John Gager, *Kingdom and Community: The Social World of Early Christianity* (Englewood Cliffs, NJ: Prentice-Hall, 1975) 33.

13. To claim that Matt 12:32 is "a saying in which the earliest Christian preachers set themselves above the Son of man" (28) betrays a literalistic lack of subtlety and an avoidance of critical issues.

14. V. Herntrich, "*krino*," in *Theological Dictionary of the New Testament*, 3:923–32.

15. S. Zeitlin, "Zealots and Sicarii," *Journal of Biblical Literature* 82 (1962) 395–99; M. Smith, "Zealots and Sicarii, Their Origins and Relation," *Harvard Theological Review* 64 (1971) 1–19.

16. See the attempts at more precise reconstruction in R. A. Horsley, "Josephus and the Bandits," *Journal for the Study of Judaism* 10 (1979) 37–63; "The Sicarii: Ancient Jewish Terrorists," *Journal of Religion* 59 (1979) 435–58; "The Zealots: Their Origin, Relationships and Importance in the Jewish Revolt," *Novum Testamentum* 28 (1986) 159–92; and Horsley and J. S. Hanson, *Bandits, Prophets and Messiahs: Popular Movements in the Time of Jesus* (Minneapolis: Winston-Seabury, 1985).

17. Theissen also occasionally engages in simple unsubstantiated statements, such as that "the zealots murdered large numbers of the temple aristocracy. . . ." It is clear from the relevant passages in Josephus, however, that although the Zealots did attack Herodians, and although the priestly aristocracy attempted to mobilize the Jerusalemites to attack the Zealots, the latter apparently did not go after the chief priests. See Horsley, "The Zealots."

18. Anthropologists address the issue. On peasants in a traditional agrarian situation, see Eric Wolf, *Peasants* (Englewood Cliffs, NJ: Prentice-Hall, 1966) 4–6.

19. But Theissen again misconstrues a source: it is clearly Josephus who uses the Hellenistic imperial language of "benefactors and saviors of the city" in his biting description of the Zealots' actions, not the Zealots describing themselves, in *War* 4.146.

20. We may want to question the applicability of the concept "eschatology." Apparently most of these groups focused not on the end of history but on the imminent action by God to resolve the historical crisis in which they stood.

21. See K. Stendahl, "Hate, Non-Retaliation and Love: 1QS X.17–20 and Romans 12:19–21," *Harvard Theological Review* 55 (1962) 343–55.

22. On the latter, see, e.g., Klaus Wengst, *Pax Romana and the Peace of Jesus Christ* (Philadelphia: Fortress, 1987) Part I; and R. A. Horsley, *The Liberation of Christmas* (New York: Crossroad, 1988) ch 2.

23. See John H. Elliott, "Social Scientific Criticism of the New Testament and its Social World: More on Methods and Models," *Semeia* 35 (1986) 24; and Matilda White Riley, *Sociological Research I: A Case Approach* (New York: Harcourt, Brace & World, 1962) 704–6.

24. K. Stendahl, "Paul and the Introspective Conscience of the West," *Harvard Theological Review* 56 (1964) 199–215.

Part II
Social Conditions in Jewish Palestine

4 ◊ Issues and Structures _____

On Asking Appropriate Questions

Life in ancient Jewish Palestine was very different from life in modern urban industrialized America or Europe. Thus, rather than impose an abstract analytical scheme on biblical history and literature, we should begin by asking what needs explaining sociologically and what the concrete patterns of social life may have been in ancient Palestine. Some of the issues that require explanation are suggested by the minimal sources we have from the Jesus movement itself. But those issues must be understood in the context of the general historical situation of social life in first-century Palestine.

As noted above, it was not so much social rootlessness as the threat of rootlessness that lay behind the Jesus movement and similar social phenomena. Moreover, once we broaden our concerns from a few dozen "wandering charismatics" to the whole Jesus movement and attend more concretely to more of the Synoptic Gospel tradition, it becomes abundantly evident that underlying the seemingly abstract "threat of rootlessness" lay fundamental social-religious problems many of which were explicitly addressed by the Jesus movement.

It is precisely these social problems that need explanation. Behind a movement that offers hopes of enough to eat and other blessings to "the poor" must lie serious problems of hunger and poverty. Underlying a movement concerned to alleviate the poverty and debts of its people must be some serious problems of indebtedness. Similarly, we may want to inquire what particular social malaise gives rise to the conception of renewed local community relations in nonpatriarchal familial terms. If the distinctive activities of the charismatic disciples focus on healing and exorcism, then surely sickness and demon-possession must be a serious problem in the society. Indeed, the very occurrence of belief in demons must be explained sociologically-historically, especially considering that such belief was unprecedented in traditional (biblical) Israelite-Jewish culture. We may similarly want to understand why it is that the movement emphasizes forgiveness of sin, apparently in a situation in which sin serves as an explanation for suffering and illness. Also clearly manifested in the Synoptic Gospel traditions stemming from the Jesus movement and requiring sociological explanation are sharp conflicts between the movement and both the Pharisees and the high priests. Other contemporaneous or near contemporaneous movements may provide some helpful comparisons and contrasts with the Jesus movement on some of these issues that require explanation.

As an alternative to Theissen's "Analysis of Factors" in an attempt to understand "the reciprocal interaction between Jewish society in Palestine and the Jesus movement," we can explore the social conditions of and for the Jesus movement. The concept "social conditions" has the double implication (a) that certain conditions may have been necessary and/or were present in order for a historical movement, figure, or series of events to emerge (conditions for), and (b) that those conditions also affected or even determined the possibilities and course of development of that movement or figure or series of events (conditions of). In order even to begin consideration of such matters, of course, we need to know the fundamental social structure in Jewish Palestine and the different social strata's respective interests in that situation. In addition we need to take into consideration the subjection of Jewish Palestine to Roman rule. Then once we have in mind the structure of the overall situation (ch 4), we can consider some of the dynamics of the situation that constituted the "social conditions" of the Jesus movement (ch 5).

To understand the actual social structure of ancient Palestine in its historical situation may require some serious adjustment of the usual sociological conceptual and theoretical apparatus, which has been developed to deal with highly differentiated industrialized "societies." Until we understand better the fundamental structures of traditional social life, in fact, it may be necessary to give first priority to what has been called "social description" and then to adjust our analytical concepts and theories accordingly. Since sociological analysis of the Jesus movement and its Palestinian Jewish socio-historical context is in its infancy, generalizations and explanations will be necessarily provisional at this point, in some cases little more than a set of hypotheses or questions to be further investigated.

As an obvious first step, we can make some elementary extrapolations from historical sociological studies that have made generalizations on the basis of analysis of societies comparable to ancient Jewish Palestine.[1] In contrast to modern, highly urbanized and industrialized societies, ancient agrarian societies had a relatively simple social structure divided fundamentally between the rulers and the ruled. A tiny (under 5 percent) ruling group with a virtual monopoly on political-military power lived from the produce they took from the vast majority (90 percent) of the population. The rulers organized the society so that the peasants were forced to produce more than they would have needed for their own subsistence. The rulers could then take this "surplus" in the form of tax, rent, or tribute to support themselves as well as the artisans and others who served their needs and the military, sacerdotal, and scribal "retainers" who helped them control and exploit the producers. The rulers, their servants, and retainers lived principally in (fortified) cities, with the peasant producers living and working in the surrounding countryside villages. Thus the interests and outlooks of rulers and ruled would have been very different.

Assuming that ancient Jewish Palestine had a social structure somewhat like this, then it may be necessary to work consciously against some of our standard assumptions about social life. Perhaps the first step for those involved in theological or religious studies is to recognize that traditional societies knew no differentiation between the various aspects of life that we automatically think of in terms of religion, politics, economics, etc. Since at least the nineteenth century, theologically influenced biblical studies have presumed to treat biblical and related literature primarily as religious phenomena, often without much attention to concrete historical context. Concepts such as "Judaism" and "Christianity" have determined exegetical and historical discourse, as if such abstractions corresponded to some historical realities. But there was no separable "religious" dimension of life in ancient Jewish Palestine, just as there was no term or concept of "religion." Religion was rather embedded with the political and economic aspects in the concrete social forms of family, local community, and forms of domination by which one group ruled others (such as the Temple in Jerusalem). It is important, indeed essential, to recognize that literature such as the Synoptic Gospels traditions, as products of such traditional social life, are concerned with the whole of life, not simply some separable religious dimension.

The second step, especially insofar as sociological thinking has tended to reify "society," is to recognize that a historical social entity the scope of Palestine in the first century C.E. was hardly a bounded, self-contained "society" such as sociologists write about. As the transmitters of the Gospel traditions were acutely aware, with Jesus having been executed by order of a Roman imperial official, Palestine was part of the Roman Empire. Historical sociological analysis of traditional empires indicates that they are not like modern societies, "not only because they are not modern, but because they are not societies."[2] Such empires are agglomerations of agrarian societies ruled and exploited economically by yet another society, the aristocracy. In an extensive and highly complex empire such as that ruled by Rome, the same pattern prevailed even within subordinate regions such as Palestine, where, for example, the Roman client king Herod ruled several distinctive districts. Hence, the concept of a "social system" is not applicable to Palestine. Even with the phrase "Palestinian Jewish society" we may be projecting something unhistorical, hence not susceptible of sociological analysis. At the very least, we would have to take into account that Jewish Palestine was an imperial situation, the Jewish rulers as well as the people being subjected in direct and indirect ways to foreign domination and influence.

Third, and closely related to the previous point, there was a virtually unbridgeable gap between the ruling groups and the common people in ancient empires. The gulf between the aristocracy and the peasantry was "far wider than that between modern classes," there was no "middle class" between the rulers and ruled, and no mobility to speak of between them.[3] Furthermore, the ruling class virtually monopolized political-economic-religious power, leaving little or no possibility of any significant participation by those they ruled in any supposed "national" or society-wide "political" or "religious" life. Thus, even if we were to continue to abstract some religious entity called "Judaism" from the social context in which it was embedded, it would still be necessary to designate *which* or *whose* Judaism in order to account for essential class and regional differences.

Fourth, because Palestinian peoples had only recently come under Roman domination, because Roman rule involved frequent changes in its divisions and patterns, and because traditional societies are strongly informed by "tradition," it is essential to maintain historical perspective on any significant development or conflict. Because the concrete situation in Jewish Palestine was changing from generation to generation, even decade to decade, synchronic analysis would be pointless as well as misleading.[4]

Fifth, as implied by the last two observations, in agrarian societies in which there was some common cultural heritage shared by rulers and ruled, there were likely some significant differences between what anthropologists have called the "little" or popular tradition and the "great" or "official" tradition, reflecting the respective interests of rulers (and/or their clerical-scribal retainers) and peasants.

Finally, as suggested by the previous point, we have been and remain heavily dependent on literary sources in our attempts to reconstruct social history. This means that modern scholars who themselves occupy a privileged social position tend to be influenced by the ancient social elite whose interests are reflected in the literature that, ordinarily, only they left. Once aware of the extent to which established biblical and theological studies have reflected the views and interests of a social elite, it seems appropriate to make a special effort to appreciate the circumstances and interests of ordinary people, who were usually in a position of subordination to those who left the literary sources on which we are so heavily dependent. This may be especially important, as well as complicated, for biblical studies since much of the traditional material that found its way into such documents as "the law and the prophets" and the Synoptic Gospels reflects the circumstances and interests of ordinary people. Thus we are in the unusual position of having literary sources for popular life and culture which it may be inappropriate to interpret in the same way as the more usual literary sources that reflect concerns of the cultural elite.

Fundamental Social Structures

The Imperial Situation

The people of Palestine were subjected to one empire after another following the Assyrian conquest of Israel in 722 B.C.E. and the Babylonian conquest of Judah in 587. In succession, the Persian, Hellenistic, and Roman empires conquered Palestine along with other areas by force of arms, subjected the local rulers, and took tribute, usually through the local aristocracies or their own imperial officers. Persian imperial policy permitted Judea to be reestablished as a tribute-paying temple community. The high priesthood thus functioned as part of the imperial regime. Following a brief period of relative independence for the Hasmonean high priests, the Romans conquered Palestine, controlled the area initially through the last Hasmonean rulers, then through their own clients, the Herods, and finally imposed direct rule in the first century C.E. By installing the Herodian kings in Palestine while leaving the high priestly Temple apparatus intact, the Romans added another layer to the ruling strata that had to be supported by the people. The Romans themselves, of course, took tribute—Caesar having decreed, as it were, that "all the world" should be taxed. That the Romans viewed failure to render up the tribute as tantamount to rebellion well illustrates that the political and economic aspects of ancient imperialism were inseparable.

After the Roman takeover of the eastern Mediterranean, Palestine was a diverse conglomerate of districts under the control of one or several client rulers. Herod had ruled over the five districts of Judea, Idumea, Samaria, Perea, and Galilee, along with other areas such as the royal estates just south of Galilee and the newly subjected Trachonitis to the northeast. His administration and mercenary army were Hellenistic and alien to the largely "Jewish" population of Judea, Perea, and Galilee.

Briefly under Agrippa I in 41–44 and then under Roman governors for the decades preceding the great revolt of 66–70, all of these districts and cities were again under the same "administration." During the lifetime of Jesus, Galilee and Perea were ruled by Herod's son Antipas, while Judea, under the oversight of the Roman governor in Caesarea, was governed by the high priesthood based in the Jerusalem Temple.

It is thus utterly inappropriate to speak in facile fashion of "Palestinian Jewish society," let alone of the religious abstraction "Judaism." We must rather attend to the particular (and shifting) ways or forms through which the people of Palestine were exploited by the overlapping ruling strata. It makes sense to start with the Temple/high priesthood in Jerusalem because we have more evidence for it and because it ruled (or shared in ruling) at least Judea continuously from its institution by the Persians until disrupted and destroyed during the great revolt of 66–70 c.e. We can then picture how the Herodian regimes complicated the ruling class and compounded the burden on the peasantry, and finally we can speculate about the situation in Galilee on the basis of the fragmentary evidence available.

The Temple-State

At the head of Judea, with certain powers over Jewish inhabitants of other areas in Jewish Palestine, stood the Temple and high priesthood. These were not merely religious institutions, but economic and political as well. Indeed, the religious dimension served to legitimate the political-economic aspects of the Temple and high priesthood. The Torah provided both the divinely given "constitution" of the political-economic-religious rule of the Temple and high priesthood along with the fundamental traditions through which the people were governed. The ultimate head of the society was understood to be God. As articulated in the Torah, since the sixth century, the people owed tithes and offerings to God. That provided the legitimating form in which the peasant producers supported the Temple apparatus and priestly aristocracy. As laid out elaborately in Nehemiah (10:35–39; etc.), the people "were obligated to bring the first-fruits of every tree, year by year, to the house of the Lord . . . and to bring the Levites the tithes from our ground . . . in all our rural towns, . . . and (to bring to) the priest, the son of Aaron, the contributions of grain, wine, and oil." The basic structure at the time of Jesus would have remained the same as it was at the time of Nehemiah, even though the obvious adaptations must have been made to deal with the much greater territory and population that had come under the jurisdiction of the Temple in the wake of the Hasmonean conquests.

It was this religiously sanctioned economic support from the people's tithes and offerings that enabled the high priests to exert political power over the peasant producers, although ultimately their position of power and privilege depended on their backing by and cooperation with the imperial regime. High priestly rule was perhaps mediated somewhat through the courses of ordinary priests, but the latter resided primarily in villages, as did the peasant producers. The priestly aristocracy that governed the society was hereditary. The office of high priest itself had been hereditary in one (Zadokite) family until, building on their leadership of the "Maccabean" revolt, the Hasmoneans usurped control of the high priesthood and Temple apparatus. Although no longer in the control of one family, the office of high priest, and apparently the other key offices such as Temple captain and treasurers, were controlled by four families during the decades between the death of Herod the Great and the revolt of 66–70. Some of those powerful priestly families had been brought by Herod from Babylon or Egypt; hence, they were not even native Palestinian Jewish priestly aristocracy.

The governing class or ruling group of any such traditional agrarian society lived apart from the peasant producers from whom they drew their living in a (fortress) city. From that capital, in this case the Temple in Jerusalem, they ruled and taxed the people through their own agents and "retainers," and provided for their own life-style with a supporting cast of artisans, traders, and various types of servants.

Instrumental in the process of government would have been some "bureaucrats" or "retainers" supported by the Temple establishment and functioning as scholars, teachers, judges, lawyers, and government counselors.[5] Most scribes or sages in Jewish Palestine would have been "retainers" working for the rulers or ruling institutions. Sirach portrays the scribes as performing just such functions in government service before "great men" and "rulers"–and in sharp contrast to mere farmers and artisans (38:24–39:11). The scribes in the Gospels appear as mid- to high-level officials subordinate to the high priestly rulers.[6]

The Pharisees at the time of Jesus (as portrayed both in the Gospels and by Josephus) were most likely some sort of association or "political-interest group" among such retainers (with the Sadducees perhaps having been a parallel political-interest group among the priestly aristocracy itself). However personally pious and rigorous they may have been individually or collectively, most Pharisees must have functioned as "subordinate officials, bureaucrats, judges, and educators."[7] Some Pharisees, along with certain scribes, of course, played highly influential roles as members of the Sanhedrin, the high council which was the principal instrument of high priestly government.

The importance of the Pharisees in Jewish Palestine has been blown out of proportion because of their portrayal as principal opponents of Jesus in the Gospels and because they were supposedly the precursors of the rabbis. Furthermore, the understanding of "Judaism" at the time of Jesus in terms of the four "sects" (Pharisees, Sadducees, Essenes, and Zealots) that has prevailed until recently in New Testament studies is a vivid illustration of how pseudo knowledge can become built into the structure of a field. It would appear to be a projection of the modern European Christian phenomenon of a split between "church" and "sects" studied and developed as a typology by E. Troeltsch and M. Weber. But the church–sect typology presupposes a differentiation of religious from other social institutions that had simply not occurred in ancient Judea, where the Temple and high priesthood were the ruling political-economic as well as religious institution. Moreover, in the modern European experience, sects either withdrew from or were put out of the established church. But the Pharisees and Sadducees were apparently groups among either retainers or the aristocracy who, far from withdrawing, were actively engaged in struggles for influence in the ruling institutions of Temple, high priesthood, and Sanhedrin.

From the fragmentary evidence in Josephus and the New Testament, it is clear that the Pharisees as a political-interest group were involved in the government of the temple-state for nearly two hundred years, from John Hyrcanus to the great revolt of 66-70. They were apparently involved in the significant opposition to the expansionist and tyrannical practices of Alexander Jannai, after which they dominated the government themselves under his widow Alexandra Salome early in the first century B.C.E. (*Antiquities* 13.379-83, 401-15). When Herodian kingship was superimposed on the Temple and priestly apparatus (see just below), they and other retainers would likely have suffered serious diminution of status and influence in the expanded political hierarchy. Thus, it is not surprising that they resisted Herod to a degree, refusing to sign his loyalty oaths (*Antiquities* 17.41-43). The very fact that they engaged in political intrigue at the court (*Antiquities* 17.44-45), however, indicates that they still actively sought influence in political affairs. They may well have formed special associations or fellowships and may well have been committed to rigorous personal observance of purity regulations.[8] But they apparently did not withdraw from political involvement during the first century C.E. As Josephus indicates quite clearly, "the leading Pharisees" were important and influential figures in the high priestly governing circles at the outbreak of the revolt in 66.

Although most of the Pharisees were apparently based in Jerusalem, the Gospels portray them as active in Galilee as well, that is, thus extending the influence or jurisdiction of the high priestly government beyond the political "borders" of Judea; and Saul (the Pharisee who became Paul the apostle) is portrayed as acting under high priestly authority further north into Syria (Acts 9:1–3; cf. Gal 1:13–14). As we might expect of retainers responsible for cultivation and application of the "great tradition" (the Torah) and the administration of the rulers' policies in this political-economic-religious structure, the Pharisees appear in the Gospels as rigorous in application of the tithing laws—and as suspect to and resented by the ordinary people.[9]

Besides many of the "scribes" and "Pharisees," a goodly number of artisans and workers would have been resident in Jerusalem, directly or indirectly dependent economically and politically on the Temple establishment.[10] There was, to be sure, a goodly amount of trade centered in Jerusalem, which was a pilgrimage city and the center of world Jewry; hence, merchants and tradespeople were active in the city. But most of such activities were directly or indirectly related to the Temple apparatus and perhaps even were supervised by and subordinate to the priestly rulers as well. The urban-based artisans and tradespeople certainly did not constitute any sort of "middle class" in the modern North Atlantic sense. Whether "retainers," artisans, or workers, these urban dwellers were dependent on and served the needs and pleasures of the rulers.

The high priestly families were apparently prepared to take whatever steps might be necessary to maintain their own position of power and privilege. At mid-first century C.E., perhaps in response to serious slippage in their actual power and "religious-cultural" legitimacy, these families were engaged in virtually predatory actions against their own people. Josephus, who was himself close to these very families in the years preceding the Jewish revolt, reports that they maintained gangs of ruffians, which they used, for example, to seize by force from the threshing floors the tithes intended for support of the ordinary priests (*Antiquities* 20.181, 213). An oft-quoted passage from the Talmud provides evidence of how the people felt about their use and abuse of power, whether through the pen, the courts, or simple brutality: "Woe is me because of the house of Boethus, . . . Hanan, etc. For they are high priests, and their sons are treasurers, and their sons-in-law are temple overseers, and their servants beat the people with clubs" (*b. Pesaḥim* 57a).

Herodian Kingship

The Roman imposition of client Herodian kings in Palestine complicated the structure of imperial control and compounded the pressures on the Jewish peasantry. Herod's kingship over all of Palestine and then his son

Antipas's rule of Galilee and Perea added another layer of rulers to be supported by the demands on the peasant producers, for the priestly aristocracy and Temple apparatus remained in place and continued to draw support from and to govern Judea in many respects and perhaps Galilee and Perea as well in some regards. With his massive building projects in Palestine, his exorbitant "gifts" to members of the imperial family, and his sponsorship of Hellenistic cultural projects abroad, Herod exhausted his subjects economically. Under Herod there was thus not simply a double but a triple demand for taxes from the peasantry, at least in Judea and perhaps in the other districts as well: tribute to the Romans, tithes and offerings for the Temple establishment and priests, and taxes to support Herod's vast expenditures and thereafter the many-branched Herodian family that continued to play a prominent role in Palestine.

The people in the predominantly Jewish districts of Herod's realm were clearly feeling the pressures, even though we may not have sufficient evidence to estimate the percentage or exact form of the multilayered taxation. Having conquered his kingdom with the help of Roman troops in the first place, Herod then maintained in unusually tight control of the people through excessively repressive means. The surface tranquillity of "peace and prosperity" merely masked the underlying repression and exploitation that exploded in popular rebellion in each of the three major Jewish districts—Judea, Galilee, and Perea—when Herod died in 4 B.C.E.

Galilee

Palestinian Jews would thus appear to have had a certain unity, even if it was one imposed from above by the Temple, high priesthood, and Herodian kingship—or even if it was perhaps over against those ruling institutions. But there were additional, complicating factors of historical and contemporaneous shifts of rulers' jurisdiction and the foundation of Hellenistic cities impinging on the Jewish population, particularly for the district of Galilee. The fragmentary character of our evidence means that it is especially difficult to attain a very precise sense of the situation among the Galilean people. Hence, some of our hypothetical reconstruction depends on our knowledge of the general structure of such imperial situations.

The Galilean area was taken over by the Assyrian Empire in 722 B.C.E. and remained thereafter subject to some form of imperial administration until the Hasmonean expansion in the late second century B.C.E. There would be some reason to believe that ancient Israelite traditions might have been continuously cultivated by the formerly "Israelite" inhabitants of the area. But only very infrequently was there any serious possibility of official "oversight" of these traditions by the Judean rulers, such as under King Josiah in the late seventh century. It is sometimes simply assumed that the Galileans eagerly and without incident fell under Hasmonean rule, whether at the time of the Maccabean revolt or later.[11] It is clear, however, that the ambitious expansionist wars of the Hasmoneans, particularly of Alexander Jannai, brought the people he ruled under severe economic pressure and that there was popular discontent as well as virtual "civil war" between the ruling class and the retainers, including the Pharisees (*Antiquities* 13.372-76, 379-83). Although there is no evidence that the Galileans were simply conquered and forcibly Judaized, as were the Idumeans (1 Maccabees 5), we should be fully aware that they had become subject to the political-religious control and economic exploitation of the high priesthood in Jerusalem only about a hundred years before the time of Jesus.

Under Herod, Galilee continued to be subject to the central regime in Jerusalem. One would assume that this meant continuing subordination to the Temple authorities as well as to Herodian officials. Under Herod's son Antipas, who ruled Galilee from 4 B.C.E. to 39 C.E., however, the Galileans came under separate—or perhaps overlapping—jurisdiction. We have no way of knowing whether it was any less unacceptable to Galilean Jews that they were not under direct Roman rule, as were the Judeans. But clearly for all of the life and career of Jesus and for most of the time prior to the great revolt of 66-70, Galilee was not "politically" united with Judea under the same rule. Moreover, in the decades after Antipas was deposed, there were frequent shifts in the administration of Galilee, from Agrippa I, 40-44 C.E., through Roman governors from 44, to the division of administration in the assignment of the toparchies of Tarichaeae and Tiberias to Agrippa II from ca. 54 on (*War* 2.218-20, 247, 252). Thus, there was a certain political power vacuum in Galilee during the very time when the Jesus movement was developing—the significance of which we can better appreciate once we recognize the importance of local communities in ancient Palestine (see next section below).

We should also note another complicating factor for Galilee that intensified under Antipas. Like royal or temple cities, Hellenistic urban foundations depended on the surrounding villages as their economic base. The foundation of Hellenistic cities of the Decapolis (southeast of Galilee) following the conquest by Alexander the Great would have had an indirect impact on Galileans. The urban foundations in lower Galilee under Antipas would have made a direct and far more serious impact, however. Following its devastation by the Romans in 4 B.C.E. in retaliation against the popular revolt centered there, Sepphoris was rebuilt as a Greek-speaking Hellenistic city. Significantly, in contrast to the surrounding rural area, it remained loyal to Roman rule at the outbreak of the great revolt in 66. Then around 20 C.E. Antipas founded Tiberias as his new capital along the shore of the Lake of Galilee. Both of these cities must have been dependent on lower Galilee for an economic base, whatever the specific arrangement may have been. And these Hellenistic centers of administration and culture must have made a serious impact, however negative and/or positive, on the Galilean peasantry.[12]

The situation in Galilee was thus more complex than that in Judea, with shifting centers and multiple layers of administration and the immediate proximity of centers of Hellenistic culture. It might be only what we should expect when the Gospel of Mark has both "Pharisees," as representatives of the high priestly government in Jerusalem,[13] and "Herodians," officials of Antipas, appear in Galilean villages, concerned about Jesus' activities. This complex situation in Galilee should make us cautious about simply assuming a consistency across some hypothetical pan-Palestinian "Jewish society" or "Judaism." Even if we assume that Israelite (biblical?) traditions were remembered among Galileans, this would not be the same as—indeed, might even be opposed to—the current traditions espoused by "retainers" of the rulers, such as the Pharisees.[14] Certainly such traditional memories and loyalties would not necessarily translate into eager service to Temple and high priesthood.

Indeed, if we examine the fragments of evidence available we find just such a picture of popular sensitivity regarding fundamental symbols such as circumcision or the Torah, but resistance to the demands of the Temple and priestly establishment in Jerusalem. Thus, many Galileans joined in a peasant strike against the attempt by the emperor Gaius to place a bust of himself in the Jerusalem Temple (*Antiquities* 18.261-74), and at the beginning of the revolt in 66 C.E. Galilean Jews insisted on the circumcision of foreign nobles joining their cause and appealed to the Torah as the embodiment of their independence and traditional way of life (*Life* 112-14, 149-54, 126-35). The Jerusalem authorities believed that they had jurisdiction over Galilee, as indicated by their move immediately to assert control over Galilee at the outset of the great revolt in 66. And as their aristocratic priestly "general" discovered, many Galileans felt obliged to render up tithes to priests at least when they appeared on the scene (*Life* 63). But, generally speaking, the Pharisaic and other representatives of central authority had little influence in Galilee,[15] and Galileans apparently were slow and reluctant to pay their dues to Temple and priests.[16] A combination of historical and structural factors makes it likely that there were significant differences in political-economic interests and cultural traditions between official Jerusalem, including the scribes and Pharisees, on the one hand, and ordinary people in Galilee, on the other.

Villages and Towns

The Herodian court, governmental apparatus, and building projects (in Jerusalem or Tiberias), the high priestly and Temple apparatus and the supporting services in Jerusalem, and the Roman tribute all depended on the produce they took from the peasantry. In the already classic definition by Eric Wolf, the Jewish (and other) peasants in Palestine were "rural cultivators whose surpluses [were] transferred to a dominant group of rulers that used the surpluses both to underwrite its own standard of living and to distribute the remainder to groups . . . for their specific goods and services."[17] We have no statistical evidence from ancient Palestine, of course, but it is clear that—the urban foundations on the coast, in the Decapolis, and in Galilee notwithstanding—it was a traditional agrarian situation, the bulk of the population consisting largely of peasants in villages and towns. It was certainly more exclusively an agricultural society than was apparently the norm in the Hellenistic world, judging from Josephus's apologetic explanation: "Ours is not a maritime country; neither commerce nor the intercourse which it promotes with the outside world has any attraction for us. Our cities are built inland, remote from the sea; and we devote ourselves to the cultivation of the productive country with which we are blessed" (*Apion* 1.60; cf. *War* 2.42–44, 48–50).

In order adequately to understand social relations in a traditional agrarian situation such as ancient Palestine, we must recognize that the ancient state, local as well as imperial, did not govern or directly administrate a bounded (boundaried) and coherent society in the same way as a modern nation-state does. The relationship between the local community (village, town) and the state focused primarily, sometimes almost exclusively, on the taking of taxes or tribute. "To rule in aristocratic empires is, above all, to tax."[18] This tributary relationship was often established originally by military conquest, and the state's threat of punitive military force was usually sufficient sanction to guarantee the flow of resources from local communities to the state apparatus. In a temple state or community such as Judea, of course, the tributary relationship was grounded and legitimated by the whole established religious apparatus and tradition. Beyond the primarily tributary relationship, as sanctioned by military force and religious rites and traditions, however, the state did not directly "govern" the people, and certainly had nothing of the modern state's apparatus of "surveillance" of its populace.[19]

Thus, although individual families and local communities were economically burdened (see further in ch 5 below), village communities were self-governing. Social relations in the local communities proceeded according to custom and tradition, with the patriarchal family and village elders providing guidance in cases of conflict, disruption, or crisis. This is also precisely the context in which we must understand the Gospel references to "the synagogues" in which Jesus was teaching and healing (whether in Capernaum, Mark 1:21, 23, 29, or "throughout all Galilee," Mark 2:39), in which the Pharisees like "the best seats" (Mark 12:38-39; Luke 11:43), and in which Jesus' followers would "be beaten" (Mark 13:9-11). There has been an understandable tendency to project something like "a place of worship" onto these references, probably from modern presuppositions regarding Jewish and Christian religious gatherings in buildings, that is, "churches" and "synagogues." But there is no evidence of synagogues as *buildings* in Galilee before the second century c.e. The unique references to a building in Luke 7:5 (a Lucan addition to Q) and Acts 18:4 stand out by contrast with other occurrences of "synagogue(s)," which refer apparently to an assembly of people. Various studies that have attempted to solve the puzzling question of the origins of "the synagogue" as a Jewish institution would seem to point in precisely this direction. In each town or village of any size, there was an assembly in which various matters of community life were dealt with from the teaching to religious rites to local community deliberations.[20]

The people of Judea proper, with a centuries-long tradition of political-economic-religious affairs focused in the Temple and administered by the high priesthood according to the Torah, would likely have had far greater coherence among the village communities. That coherence, reinforced by the successful experience of rebellion against alien influence and domination in the Maccabean Revolt, however, may also have served to undergird resistance to client rulers of an alien empire more than to cement loyalties to the rulers. In outlying areas such as Galilee that had only recently come under the domination or influence of Jerusalem, the traditions that might support wider social solidarity were probably weaker. The network of ordinary priests, many of whom lived in Judean villages most of the year while serving in the Temple during their designated "courses" and at the great festivals such as Passover, surely helped knit together the local communities that constituted Judea. Again, the outlying areas such as Galilee that had only recently come under Jerusalem's jurisdiction or influence would have been far less affected. Thus, the further the "distance" from Jerusalem, the more would local custom and tradition have informed and guided social relations. And while local communities were indeed dominated and burdened by the various layers of rulers, they also had a degree of identity, coherence, and independence that must be recognized in our attempts to understand the social conditions of the Jesus movement and related social phenomena.

Notes

1. See esp. Gerhard Lenski, *Human Societies* (New York: McGraw-Hill, 1970); idem, *Power and Privilege: A Theory of Social Stratification* (New York: McGraw, 1966); John H. Kautsky, *The Politics of Aristocratic Empires* (Chapel Hill: University of North Carolina Press, 1982).
2. Kautsky, *Aristocratic Empires*, 72; similarly, Lenski, *Power and Privilege*.
3. Kautsky, *Aristocratic Empires*, 74–75.
4. Anthony Giddens argues generally against the distinction between diachronic and synchronic analyses (*Central Problems in Social Theory* [Berkeley and Los Angeles: University of California Press, 1979]).
5. On the role of "retainers" in traditional agrarian societies, see Lenski, *Power and Privilege*, 243–48. Anthony J. Saldarini, relying on basically the same comparative sociological literature as does this study, has cautiously analyzed the fragmentary evidence available and sketched out a picture of the scribal and Pharisaic "retainers" in the Palestinian Jewish temple-state that should replace previous sociological treatments (*Pharisees, Scribes, and Sadducees in Palestinian Society* [Wilmington: Glazier, 1988]).
6. Saldarini, *Pharisees*, 250, 255, 266.
7. Ibid., esp. ch 12.
8. Ibid., 214–20.
9. Josephus's laudatory sketch of the Pharisees, to which "philosophy" he himself belonged, as influential among the townspeople (*Antiquities* 18.15; cf. 13.298), is hardly a good indication of the people's own attitudes.
10. Most of the evidence in J. Jeremias's *Jerusalem at the Time of Jesus* (Philadelphia: Fortress, 1969) pertains to such people.
11. Sean Freyne, *Galilee from Alexander the Great to Hadrian* (Wilmington: Glazier, 1980) 41–50.
12. On Sepphoris, see esp. Eric M. Meyers, Ehud Netzer, and Carol L. Meyers, "Sepphoris, 'Ornament of All Gailiee,'" *Biblical Archaeologist* 49 (1986) 4–18; on Tiberias, see R. Horsley, "Bandits, Messiahs, and Longshoremen: Popular Unrest in Galilee Around the Time of Jesus," *Society of Biblical Literature 1988 Seminar Papers* (Atlanta: Scholars Press, 1988) esp. 194–99.
13. It is conceivable that such Pharisees were somehow retainers in the employ of Herod Antipas; but Saldarini concludes that Pharisees active in Galilee were probably representatives of the Jerusalem priestly rulers (*Pharisees*, 291–93).
14. See further the section on "Popular Memories" in ch 5 below.
15. So Saldarini, *Pharisees*, 294–95.
16. Freyne has laid out the available evidence (*Galilee*, 277, 280, 282, 285, 293–94, etc.); ironically, he draws the curious conclusion that Galileans were deeply attached to Jerusalem and the Temple. He repeats his conclusion in "Galilee-Jerusalem Relations According to Josephus' *Life*," *New Testament Studies* 33 (1987) 600–609.
17. E. Wolf, *Peasants* (Englewood Cliffs, NJ: Prentice-Hall, 1966) 3–4.
18. Kautsky, *Aristocratic Empires*, 73, 150.
19. Anthony Giddens, *The Nation State and Violence* (Berkeley: University of California Press, 1986).
20. Recent analyses of the origins or some particular aspect of the synagogue include Joseph Gutman, "The Origins of the Synagogue: The Current State of Research," in *The Synagogue: Studies in Origins, Archaeology, and Structure*, ed. J. Gutman (New York: Ktav, 1975) 72–76; Martin Hengel, "Proseuche und Synagogue: Jüdische Gemeinde, Gotteshaus und Gottesdienst in der Diaspora und in Palaestina," in *The Synagogue*, ed. J. Gutman, 157–84; Sidney B. Hoenig, "The Ancient City Square: The Forerunner of the Synagogue,"

in *Aufstieg und Niedergang der römischen Welt*, II.19.1, ed. W. Haase (Berlin: Walter de Gruyter, 1979) 448–76; Eric M. Meyers and James F. Strange, *Archaeology, the Rabbis and Early Christianity* (Nashville: Abingdon, 1981) ch 7; S. Safrai, "The Synagogue," and "Jewish Self-Government," in *The Jewish People in the First Century* (2 vols.; Assen: Van Gorcum, 1974, 1976) 1:377–449; 2:908–44; H. C. Kee, "The Transformation of the Synagogue after 70 C.E.: Its Import for Early Christianity" (paper read at the 1987 Annual Meeting of the Society of Biblical Literature).

5 ◊ Social Conflicts _____

The fundamental social structure of and divisions within Jewish Palestine under Roman rule can be seen most clearly in the actual conflicts which erupted into sufficiently visible form that our historical sources have described them. Much of the previous discussion, by using vague general concepts such as "renewal movement" and "sect," has obscured both the fundamental divisions and the dynamics in ancient Jewish Palestine. By noting more precisely what social strata were involved in various conflicts it may be possible to distinguish the fundamental structural conflict in Palestine from the more superficial and less structural tensions that emerged from time to time. Some of the reasons for the fundamental conflict can be discerned in the effects of the economic pressures to which the peasantry was subjected. But the more distinctively Jewish movements that challenged the established order must be explained out of particular Israelite-Jewish cultural (biblical) traditions among popular circles.

Tensions and Conflicts

In most ancient "aristocratic empires" political conflict, like political activity generally, took place either between the imperial regime and the collaborating aristocracies or between the retainers and the ruling monarchies or aristocracies. The ordinary people, largely the peasantry, were generally excluded from participation in the political process by the very structure of things.

There were surely tensions, periodically acute, between the Jewish high priests and/or client kings and the imperial regime on which they were dependent. The feud between the Herodian Agrippa II (and the Roman governor Festus) and the high priests (ca. 61 C.E.) regarding the tower added to the royal palace that allowed the king a view over the Temple proceedings provides an illustration (*Antiquities* 20.189–96). But even when Roman governors or emperors purposely or inadvertently stumbled into a serious provocation, there is no evidence that the high priestly or Herodian rulers became involved until the popular demonstrations threatened to get out of hand and undermine their own privileged positions as client rulers. The case of apparent conflict between Roman governor and Jewish aristocracy at the time of Cumanus at mid-century illustrates rather precisely the functioning of that imperial chain of domination. The governor Cumanus dispatched some representative Jewish aristocrats to Rome to render accounts because they had failed to keep "law and order," and then Cumanus himself was called to account for his own failure to maintain strict control (*Antiquities* 20.118–36; *War* 2.232–46).

Far from the Jewish priestly aristocracy and the Herodian families having resisted Roman rule, their position of power and privilege was dependent on it. Far from leading protests against provocations by the Romans, they attempted to pacify the people's outrage. In a highly symbolic as well as concrete manifestation of the structure of the situation, when the tribute to Rome was seriously in arrears on the eve of the popular revolt in 66, the high priestly officers (as those institutionally responsible for it) set about collecting the tribute from the Judean countryside (*War* 2.405).[1]

There were more serious tensions and some significant conflicts between the Jewish "retainer" class, on the one hand, and the Jewish priestly rulers and/or the imperial rule, on the other. These are understandable in terms of the special mediating position that the retainers such as scholars, scribes, or Pharisees occupied in the imperial situation and their mediating role with regard to the sacred traditions according to which Jewish political-economic-religious life was supposedly regulated. The professional role of such scholars-teachers-lawyers was as guardians and interpreters of the sacred traditions embodied in the Torah and other rulings based upon it. But if the priestly rulers for whom these retainers were working to help govern the people according to the sacred traditions appeared to have wandered too far from those traditions in collaboration with the dominant imperial rule and ethos, then the retainers were involved in a conflict of loyalties, between the sacred traditions and their rulers.

Thus, in certain circumstances of acute conflict some alienated retainers who were dependent on the established institutions actively opposed rulers who they thought were subverting those institutions. By the first century C.E., in fact, there was a fairly substantial tradition of protests or resistance by literate retainers. Most notably, to faithful scribes and Torah-scholars, the usurping high priestly group who headed the hellenizing "reform" in the 170s B.C.E. seemed simply to have abandoned their heritage. The *maskîlîm* who produced the book of Daniel (11:33–35), and perhaps the Hasideans and others who resisted first the reform and then the violent repression by the emperor Antiochus Epiphanes, would appear to be such retainers, who stood by the sacred traditions in opposition to their apostate rulers.[2]

Around the time of Jesus the tensions between the native Jewish rulers and those who were apparently retainers erupted into protest or serious conflict at three notable points. As Herod lay on his deathbed in 4 B.C.E., two revered sages had their students cut down the Roman golden eagle from over the Temple gate—for which they paid with their lives (*Antiquities* 17.146–67; *War* 1.648–55). Then in 6 C.E., the high priestly submission to direct Roman rule appeared to the "teacher" Judas of Galilee and Saddok the Pharisee as an abandonment of the sole rule of God (the first commandment). Hence, in what Josephus labels as the "Fourth Philosophy," they attempted to organize resistance to the Roman tribute. The continuing collaboration of the ruling high priestly families in mid-first century, following the disastrous drought and famine, must have left the scholar-teachers who formed the Sicarii feeling desperate enough to strike out in selective assassination of their own officials.[3]

With the possible exception of the resistance to the tribute in 6 C.E., however, such resistance by these groups of retainers involved no serious challenge to the fundamental structure of political-economic-religious life. Rather, such protests by the scholarly-scribal retainers served, in effect, to mitigate and moderate the most intrusive cultural effects of the imperial situation, just as the very role of the retainers served to mediate the domination of the imperial as well as Jewish rulers. It has been surmised that the Pharisees in particular were attempting to reform or change Jewish society. That is highly unlikely. If their position in the social structure was that of retainers, then the limited evidence we have for their activities can most easily be interpreted as indicating an attempt to influence political affairs and to control social relations. In the context of the imperial situation, midst alien economic and cultural pressures, they were apparently attempting to maintain discipline and coherence in the Palestinian Jewish temple-state and some of the outlying areas under its influence.[4]

There were also tensions, even an occasional face-off, between the Jerusalem crowd and the Jewish rulers. For example, immediately after the death of Herod when Archelaus appeared as the presumed successor to his father, the Jerusalem crowd clamored for relief from taxes and more just appointees to the high priestly office. But these tensions did not pose a challenge to the fundamental political-economic structure.

The fundamental conflict in Jewish Palestine was not between the different layers of political-economic (religious) rulers, but between the ruling groups on the one hand and the bulk of the people on the other. Perhaps in most traditional agrarian empires there is no "class conflict" because there is such an extreme difference between the powerful rulers, on the one hand, and the hapless peasants that they exploit, on the other, and because they are, basically, even different "societies."[5] Ancient Palestinian Jews, however, were in this regard a distinctive people even if not a unified and bounded "society." Both ruling priests and ruled peasants and artisans shared, to a degree, the same sacred traditions. And they, or at least the rulers and/or literate strata who left literary remains, considered themselves an ethnic unity, centered in a hereditary priesthood and headed by hereditary high priestly families. Ironic as it may seem, this common history and tradition formed a basis for disagreements and conflicts. "Peasant revolts" may have been infrequent among other precommercial agrarian empires, but they were strikingly frequent in Jewish Palestine.

Many discussions of Jewish resistance and rebellion in the first century C.E. have labored under one or both of two misconceptions, for neither of which there is much evidence. First, the notion that "the Zealots" were a long-standing, organized movement that advocated armed rebellion against Roman rule for several decades until it finally provoked the revolt in 66 has blocked recognition of the diversity and extent of popular resistance. As noted above, however, the Zealots proper did not originate until the middle of the revolt against Rome in 66–70, and there is no evidence for any sustained, organized "revolutionary" movement earlier in the first century.

The second misconception has been that the entire Jewish nation was united against Roman rule, particularly in the great revolt of 66–70. The Temple and the high priesthood stood symbolically at the head of the Jewish "nation," and it is surely the case that these institutions did serve to mediate the impact of Roman domination and alien Hellenistic cultural influences on Palestinian Jews. But, as noted just above, the high priestly families as well as the Herodian rulers were part of the imperial as well as domestic pattern of domination and exploitation. At the outbreak of the revolt in 66, the people attacked their own rulers as well as the Roman garrisons. Once the popular insurrectionaries had driven out the Roman forces, the high priests and leading Pharisees who did not simply flee then played a mediating role, pretending to prepare for war while attempting to negotiate an arrangement with the Romans (as Josephus explains explicitly in *Life* 20–23 and elsewhere). The subsequent course of the war, with the Zealots proper and other groups from various country districts attacking the high priestly junta once they entered Jerusalem (*War*, books 3–4), further illustrates that the primary division and conflict lay between the ruled and the domestic as well as foreign rulers.

It is striking how much evidence we have for a wide variety of popular protest against the dominant situation and particularly for active resistance to or rebellion against the ruling groups. Indeed, the period of Jesus' ministry and the nascent Jesus movement is neatly framed by two massive popular revolts. The frustration and resentment that had been building up under Herodian oppression and repression erupted in the form of movements led by popularly acclaimed "kings" in every major Jewish district at Herod's death in 4 B.C.E. It is abundantly clear from Josephus's reports that these were rebellions of the peasantry against the Herodian regime and high priesthood as well as against the Romans (*Antiquities* 17.271–85; *War* 2.55–65).

Seventy years later the opposition was basically the same, the popular forces engaging in a sustained rebellion against the high priestly government, prominent Herodians, and the Roman troops. Indeed, we can see from Josephus's reports how the Jewish people were pushed toward open rebellion in 65–66 by the arrogant provocations of the Roman governor and by the predatory behavior of their own high priestly families. The latter then joined with the Herodian client king Agrippa II and other prominent Herodians in a desperate effort to head off and finally to suppress the nascent popular insurgency (*War* 2.336–44, 402–7, 417–22). The same fundamental division appears to have prevailed in Galilee as well as in Judea, judging from Josephus's reports (*Life* and *War* 2–3). The city of Sepphoris remained loyal to the Romans, and the wealthy "principal men" of the formerly royal city of Tiberias attempted repeatedly to hand the city over to the control of Agrippa II. The country people, on the other hand, displayed a hostility both to the administrative cities, including the royal palace in Tiberias, and to the Romans that was clearly deeply rooted in their life situation (*Life* 33–34, 38–39, 66–67, 97–100, 102–4, 124, 155, etc.).

Overt conflicts during the intervening decades display the same structure. The priestly aristocracy even felt threatened by the prophetic laments of the "crude peasant" Jesus son of Hananiah, and asked the Roman governor to dispatch him. Although the Roman governor Albinus (62–64) was not particularly troubled by this individual "maniac" (*War* 6.300–309), his predecessors Fadus (44–45) and Felix (52–60) were surely quick to send out the troops against the popular prophetic movements led by Theudas and "the Egyptian" (*Antiquities* 20.97–98, 169–71). Even the largely nonviolent protests against Roman provocations were primarily popular in character, with the priestly aristocracy and prominent Herodian figures becoming involved only when the protests threatened to "get out of hand"—and then in councils with the Roman officials on how to terminate the popular demonstrations, such as the peasant strike against the imposition of Gaius's statue in the Temple.[6]

The principal conflict in Palestinian Jewish society was thus clearly between the rulers, domestic and foreign, on the one hand, and the ruled on the other. From the discussion in the previous chapter it should be evident that this conflict is rooted in the very structure of the situation in Jewish Palestine. The Romans, the Herodian rulers, and the priestly aristocracy all extracted produce from the peasantry through mechanisms of tribute, taxes or rents, and tithes and offerings. They were able to do this because they had political power and/or religious-cultural legitimation. Their rule was based in the cities, where they resided, their needs served by artisans and traders, and their position secured by military retainers. Jerusalem in particular enjoyed explicit religious legitimation, with the religious-economic-political domination of the priestly aristocracy based in the Temple as the form through which the theocracy was mediated.[7]

The Dynamics of Indebtedness

Although it may be clear how the principal conflict in Jewish Palestine was rooted in the fundamental political-economic-religious structure of life, further analysis is necessary to help explain the frequency and extent of popular resistance and rebellion. As comparative sociological analyses have emphasized, peasant revolts and movements are infrequent and require special explanation. Although peasants have found many a way to resist the exactions of their rulers,[8] historically they have not generally produced movements of restoration or renewal, much less mounted widespread revolts.[9] We need a greater appreciation of the dynamics of peasant life to understand the circumstances in which they may take such unusual action. And we need some sense of the particular historical-cultural circumstances among Palestinian Jews to appreciate the occurrence and social forms that their actions and movements assumed in the first century. More particularly, this may help us to discern the conditions of the Jesus movement, including the circumstances of hunger, poverty, and sickness (and the threat to the traditional way of life and viability of the traditional social forms) to which that movement was responding.

The vast majority of the Palestinian Jewish people would have been peasants living in villages and working the land to support the Temple, priests, Herodian regime(s), and Roman tribute as well as their own families. In virtually any traditional agrarian society the peasants managed a marginal economic existence at best. The peasantry in ancient Jewish Palestine would have been no exception.[10] Although we have very little evidence on the basis of which to estimate the quantity or even the percentage of the peasants' produce that was taken in tribute, taxation, and tithes, it is clear that the double or triple layer of demands brought unusually heavy economic pressures on the Jewish people under Roman rule.[11] For example, with his lavish court and extensive building projects, Herod had exhausted the country. By the time of Tiberias the Romans found it advisable to mitigate the burden of taxation in Judea somewhat (Tacitus, *Annals* 2.42), but the basic structure and the multiple layers of taxation remained the same.[12]

When peasant producers under pressure for taxes did not have enough grain and oil to feed their families until the next harvest after rendering both to Caesar's agents and to God's, their only alternative would have been to borrow. But the limited resources of fellow villagers and of neighboring villages would have been quickly exhausted. Hence, hungry peasants would have been forced to seek loans from those who controlled larger stores of grain, oil, or money. This is indeed the picture one receives of the typical life situation from the parables of Jesus. Families or householders were indebted in smaller or greater amounts to those who controlled large estates or stores of grain, oil, or money, either the rulers-owners themselves or their servants-stewards (Matt 18:23-33; Luke 16:1-7). That much of this wealth and loaning to the poor was centered in Jerusalem, either substantively or "legally," is indicated by Josephus's report that at the outbreak of the great revolt in the summer of 66 the insurgents set the archives on fire in order to destroy the moneylenders' bonds (*War* 2.427).[13] That is, those who provided and controlled credit were the very rulers of the system that placed the difficult economic demands in the first place. Moreover, whatever the traditional prohibitions of "increase" (interest) as stated in the Torah, the loans were made at such rates as 25 percent (grain) or 100 percent (oil; see Luke 16:5-7).

Structurally, the heavy demands placed on the peasant producers were causing economic hardship, particularly the threat of poverty and hunger. But the mechanism by which these economic pressures gradually effected the disintegration of the socio-economic infrastructure of peasant life was clearly indebtedness. Peasant families could seek relief from short-term hunger by borrowing. But the continuing pressures of the system drove them increasingly into debt. Some might seek a partial solution by surrendering a son or daughter into debt-slavery. Some suffered the loss of the family inheritance to the creditor, or were allowed to remain on the land but utterly at the mercy of the creditor.

Indebtedness is thus the mechanism by which Theissen's various "factors" resulted in the "rootlessness" and the threat of rootlessness he wants to explain. More comprehensively, it is the means by which the dynamics of the Roman imperial situation in Palestine resulted in other forms of social malaise. Despair as well as poverty and hunger plagued the pressured peasantry generally, but particularly those who had lost their traditional lands or whose situation was deteriorating. As some families lost their land to, or came under the power of, the wealthy and powerful creditors, village communities disintegrated. As fathers were unable to maintain their hold on the traditional family inheritance, confidence in patriarchal authority deteriorated along with their own self-respect.

Insofar as the high priestly officials and Herodians were also the creditors taking advantage of the plight of the villagers, the higher levels of authority must have been questioned, if not indeed condemned outright (as in the prophetic lament of Jesus son of Hananiah). And insofar as those operating the official courts enforced the established order to the detriment of the indebted (cf. Matt 5:25–26) or insofar as the "Pharisees" or "lawyers" insisted that the people render up the tithes despite their circumstances (Luke 11:42, 46), the traditional patriarchal authority of scribes and scholar-teachers would have come into question as well. From the latter two examples of the decline of the authority structure in traditional Jewish society, moreover, we can also begin to understand the social conditions of the conflict between popular movements and both rulers and retainers.

Popular Memories and Movements

At the beginning of the current revival of sociological approaches to the New Testament, the model of "millenarian movements" was fruitfully applied to early Christianity.[14] Earliest Christianity was similar to millenarian movements, sharing some of their most fundamental characteristics, such as the imminent realization of "heaven on earth," the reversal of the present social order, a remarkable release of emotional energy, and the brief life of the movement itself.[15]

Despite the many parallels, however, Palestinian Jewish movements display a major and highly distinctive difference from the "cargo cults" of Melanesia on which much of the "millenarian movements" model was based. The peoples of Melanesia had only recently come under the control of Western imperial powers; hence, they had no historical basis for dealing with their sudden domination by others with overwhelmingly superior military, technological, and economic power. Ancient Palestinian Jews, however, had been subjected to foreign empires for centuries and had a long *tradition* of resistance against such alien domination to draw on. Indeed, the very core of their sacred traditions consisted of stories of how their God had decisively and repeatedly delivered his people from alien domination. Passover, one of the three principal

festivals of the people, celebrated the foundational events of God's liberation of the people from bondage in Egypt. The Jewish cultural (biblical)
traditions are striking and distinctive for the degree to which they feature
resistance to oppressive alien domination.

Palestinian Jews, moreover, differed from the Melanesian peoples on
whose experiences the "millenarian movements" model was based also
in that they had lived for centuries in a class society in which their own
Jewish rulers formed part of the imperial governing structure. Insofar as
the rulers and their retainers could control interpretation of the sacred
traditions, the potential disruptive effects of the long-standing Jewish
tradition of resistance may well have been blunted. But we must also take
fully into account a reality that anthropologists have long seen even if
biblical scholars have been somewhat oblivious to it. Biblical scholars
understandably concentrate on the reconstruction, analysis, and interpretation of the sacred *scripture*, the *written* biblical text. Insofar as the
biblical traditions have been *written*, of course, they have been the
products of people who could write, which in any traditional agrarian
society means probably those in the employ of the rulers. Alongside, or
rather underneath, this officially sponsored "great tradition," however,
many peoples actively cultivate a popular or "little tradition." Far from
being completely separate, the "great" and the "little" traditions can stem
from a common historical heritage and exert mutual influence in their
periodic interaction.[16] In the case of the Hebrew Bible, the scribes who
produced the official text incorporated many narratives originally from
popular tradition. Yet many of those stories, while also included in the
sacred text, continued to be told in oral form in popular circles that,
however illiterate, were not "uneducated" in, or "uninformed" from,
their own heritage.

While the "great" and the "little" traditions would thus share a
common heritage, there would be distinctive differences in emphases,
interpretations, and implications. For example, we can observe in the
Torah how the "great tradition" legitimated the centrality of the Temple
in Judea and the support of the Temple and priests by tithes and offerings. The "little tradition" on the other hand, while cultivating many of
the same historical memories as the "great tradition," would likely have
emphasized stories that expressed or supported the people's own interests. And a great deal of such material had been included even in the
officially recognized scripture, largely because these stories formed parts
of the constitutive history of the Israelite-Jewish people. Thus, besides
the foundational exodus story and the stories of the "judges-liberators,"
there were narratives of popular revolts against oppressive Israelite kings
as well as extensive collections of prophetic oracles directed primarily

against abuse and oppression of the people by their own ruling priests and kings. If even Judean scribes such as Ben Sira, who served before "rulers," remembered that Elijah had "brought kings down to destruction," how much more would (Galilean) peasants have remembered his mighty deeds on behalf of the people (Sirach 48:1–11). Moreover, the ideals of social justice to which these historical rebellions or protests had appealed were legitimated and sanctioned as the will of God revealed in the establishment of the covenant on Sinai.

Thus, along with the legitimation of the Temple and high priesthood, the Torah also included the ideal of and historical prototype for a free and egalitarian peasant society under the direct kingship of God, unmediated by such institutions. The Jewish notion of a radical theocracy turns out to have very deep historical-cultural roots.[17] If even the ancient Jewish "great tradition" contained such a heritage of resistance to both alien and domestic oppression, how much more would the "little tradition" have cultivated historical memories of divinely inspired resistance and liberation. Almost certainly the principal conflict in Jewish Palestine, that between rulers (both Roman and Jewish) and ruled, should be correlated with these parallel "great" and "little" traditions.

Indeed, it is out of the background of this determinative Jewish cultural heritage, particularly the "little tradition," that we must understand the distinctive social forms that popular Jewish movements (or individual figures) assumed in the Roman period. Early Christians' interpretation of Jesus as "the messiah" or "the eschatological prophet" has previously been dealt with primarily in terms of the history of ideas, particularly in terms of synthetically constructed "expectations" and the equally synthetically constructed "fulfillment" of those expectations. That whole synthetic idealistic approach is now being questioned under the impact of the recognition that there is precious little evidence for any "expectation," let alone a standard and pervasive Jewish expectation, either of a "messiah" (or "son of David") or of an "eschatological prophet."[18] However, historical-cultural traditions can operate in far more concrete form than free-floating "ideas" and "expectations." In the case of ancient Jewish Palestine, moreover, we have far better evidence for these traditions in the concrete form of popular movements than we do for the "expectations" supposedly prevailing in "Judaism." These concrete popular figures and movements thus provide a far more secure basis for understanding Jesus and his movement than the abstract synthetic construct of "expectations." It may be particularly important in utilizing sociology, which focuses on general patterns of social relations, to recognize that not simply the self-expressions but even the concrete social forms taken by many of the Palestinian Jewish movements under Roman domination were distinctive to ancient Jewish society. Thus, to understand that and how they were informed by biblical traditions of resistance to domination may be more important than classifying them in some taxonomy of social movements.[19]

How distinctive the popular prophetic and messianic movements were can be better appreciated by comparison with the banditry that was endemic in Jewish Palestine in Roman times; for banditry is a typical feature of most traditional agrarian societies and is usually only incidentally a serious or very political form of resistance. The degree of banditry may be a key barometer of peasant distress in a given society, one that helps us appreciate the level of popular unrest that could result in other movements of protest or resistance. The escalation of banditry in the late 50s and early 60s was perhaps an indication that the peasantry could simply no longer carry the burden imposed upon them by the overlapping layers of Roman and Jewish rulers and that the "system" was about to break down. But, like banditry generally, ancient Jewish banditry did not have any broader perspective or distinctive cultural memory that could inform a concrete social formation that could take root in the local communities of a given area or that could inspire a socially transformative challenge to the established order.

The appearance of popular prophets delivering oracles of judgment or deliverance in mid-first-century Palestine is, by comparison, highly distinctive. Jesus son of Hananiah's dirge announcing the imminent judgment of Jerusalem (*War* 6.300–301) is clearly reminiscent of the "classical" prophets of Israel, particularly of Jeremiah and his pronouncements of the imminent destruction of the Temple. The occurrence of this clearly traditional form of prophecy suggests that, although according to the "great tradition" officially recognized prophecy may have ceased with Malachi (who proclaimed the renewal of the Temple!), popular prophecy against the ruling institutions was very much alive.

It is worth noting also that the distinctively Jewish popular protests that occurred during the first century were provoked by challenges either to the Passover, the celebration of the exodus liberation from oppressive alien rule, or to the central covenantal prohibitions protecting the exclusive sovereignty of God—all key items of popular as well as official tradition. That is, however we may assess the importance of the economic pressures, the people were apparently actively attuned to and acutely sensitive to their traditions that symbolized their historical liberation and their independence of life under the direct rule of God.[20]

Most striking historically and sociologically are the distinctive forms taken by the widespread popular movements. The significance of these movements for more precise understanding of both Jewish Palestine generally and the Jesus movement in particular have been obscured by the utilization of the synthetic construct "messianic" into which evidence of all sorts of expectations and movements was funneled partly because of christological concerns. Closer analysis reveals three particular types of movements.

First, the revolts in the three principal Jewish districts of Palestine at the death of Herod as well as that led by Simon bar Giora in 68–70 all took the form of movements led by a popularly acclaimed "king." Second, the large popular movements in the mid-first century in Judea (and one in Samaria) were headed by "prophets" (Theudas and the "Egyptian"), who led their followers, respectively, to experience deliverance with the dividing of the waters of the Jordan River or to see the collapse of the walls around Jerusalem, giving them access to the city. It would seem fairly clear that both of these types of movements assumed their particular forms because they were modeled on particular biblical traditions. The movements led by popularly acclaimed kings (which might more properly be termed "messianic movements") were a revival of or patterned after the historical movements led by the popularly acclaimed ("anointed"=messiah) kings such as Saul, particularly David, or Jehu. Theudas and "the Egyptian" patterned their actions in anticipation of divine deliverance after the exodus led by Moses and the conquest (battle of Jericho?) led by Joshua respectively. In both cases the biblical traditions of popular rebellion or liberation had remained alive or been remembered and had come to inform the concrete social form taken by these movements.

Third, the action of the Zealots proper in restoring a legitimate and *popular* hierocracy in 68 C.E. should also be understood in this connection. It would appear to be yet another manifestation of how the proper structure and conduct of social relations should be constituted according to the "little tradition," at least among people from northwestern Judean villages. Jesus son of Hananiah had pronounced God's judgment against the Temple and high priestly rulers in Jerusalem. The Zealots proper took the further step of electing by lot new priestly leaders from among legitimate Zadokite families now resident in Judean villages. They understood that the theocracy should function through biblically required hereditary "high priestly" leaders. But that did not mean hereditary power and privilege! Indeed, it required an alternative to, and clearly a rejection of, the then hereditary and privileged ruling and priestly families and their imperial Roman sponsors.[21]

It should be clear by now that some of the popular movements posed a genuine revolutionary threat to the established order in Palestine. This threat can be highlighted by contrast with movements among the Jewish retainers (scholars, scribes, etc.) and priests aimed at purification or restoration of the traditional temple-state and/or apocalyptically oriented movements, particularly the scribal-priestly community at Qumran. The "Fourth Philosophy" was unable to mobilize serious widespread resistance to direct Roman rule. The terrorist group of Sicarii, while serving to point up the vulnerability as well as illegitimacy of the collaborationist high priestly families, displayed the impotence of any group of supersensitive teachers or retainers by their having to resort to terrorist tactics against their own Jewish rulers. The popular movements led by the prophets Theudas and the "Egyptian," having been caught up in intense anticipation, seemed oblivious to the concrete "realities" of political power.

The Qumranites (probably to be identified with the Essenes) had simply withdrawn to await their time. Having fought desperately to preserve the traditional ways, and perhaps having come to believe, in terms such as those dreamed of in Daniel 7, that the sovereignty was about to be given to the people, this priestly oriented group decided that the way to pursue the restoration of Israel was "to prepare the way of the Lord in the wilderness" of Judea. Over against the Hasmonean high priesthood that they viewed as utterly illegitimate and "wicked," they acted in imitation of the exodus and Mosaic covenantal traditions, setting up a new covenant community. The Qumranites come the closest to fitting the concept of "sect."[22] They might more appropriately be described as an apocalyptically oriented utopian community. What neither of those categories comprehend, however, is the Qumranites' expectation (and intention) that they are the only righteous and proper leaders, as priests and scribes, etc., of the whole people. Membership was "voluntary." But this literarily highly productive group's orientation, and probably membership as well, was clearly elitist. The most remarkable aspect of the group was the length of its survival—two hundred years. This must be attributed partly to its intense apocalyptic orientation, and largely to its having constituted no real threat to the actual ruling groups in Jerusalem, whether the Hasmoneans or, later, the Herodians.

By contrast, the movements led by the popularly acclaimed kings in 4 B.C.E. and then that led by Simon bar Giora, the Zealots proper, and other groups that originated in the countryside during the great revolt of 66–70 provide a dramatic manifestation of well-organized and widespread popular revolt capable both of pushing out the high priestly rulers and the garrison of troops ostensibly protecting their position and of governing the people independently of Jewish or Roman overlords. Resonance to the ideal of "radical theocracy" was at least dormant among the peasantry in Jewish Palestine. At crucial points of crisis it erupted in organized action that formed a distinctive alternative to the established imperial order in a particular area of Jewish Palestine.

A Note on Apocalypticism

Jewish "apocalypticism" (and/or the closely related term "eschatology") has figured prominently in much of the twentieth-century discussion of the origins of Christianity and other Jewish movements. Because "apocalypticism" and related concepts have been so synthetically constructed by a theologically oriented scholarship, however, it is necessary critically to reexamine all asumptions and generalizations regarding Jewish "apocalypticism" or "eschatology" around the time of Jesus. Insofar as the term eschatology/eschatological is used in the sense of "endtime" or the "last days" of historical reality, the term should simply be dropped as inappropriate and misleading. Unless apocalyptic literature is read literalistically or as theological doctrine instead of as a special symbolic language, there is very little in the documents prior to the time of the Jesus movement that refers to any sort of "end of history," let alone to some "cosmic catastrophe." Beyond the abandonment of inappropriate concepts, the pertinence of apocalyptic literature to the Jesus movement must be extensively reconsidered before any definitive hypotheses can be ventured. In this context we can only probe a few pertinent factors.

A critical review of the often assumed apocalyptic perspective in Jewish Palestine is particularly important in analysis of Jewish movements' basis in tradition because "apocalypticism" is often viewed as an unprecedented departure from biblical traditions and orientation. In particular, the apparent dualism between God and Satan or the demonic forces (and that between "this age/world" and the "next"–Theissen's "crude dualism of the ages") is often seen as alien to previous Jewish tradition. In biblical studies in particular, Jewish apocalyptic literature has been (mis)understood somewhat literalistically and treated in terms of doctrine, with little sensitivity to distinctive use of language and little attention to the concrete historical situation.[23] Recent analyses of apocalyptic literature have laid the basis for a far more adequate understanding of the concrete situations of alienation, oppression, and even persecution in which the otherwise seemingly fantastic apocalyptic writings were likely rooted.[24]

Apocalyptic literature, far from containing an unprecedented theological doctrine or alien worldview, can be seen as visionary literature seeking understanding of and consolation in difficult historical circumstances. Literature such as Daniel and the various sections of 1 Enoch, while likely written by sages/scribes, can be seen to stand in continuity with late prophetic literature. Their fundamental concerns are for the renewal or restoration of the people of Israel, for the eventual divine judgment against their oppressors, and for the vindication of the righteous Jews who endure abuse and even death in their faithful adherence to the traditional covenantal way of life.

Apocalypticism is often described as the product of "exclusive conventicles" standing over against "the dominant society."[25] From the historical social structural analysis above, it is clear that there was no dominant "society," although there were surely dominant ruling institutions and families. Judging from the amount of apocalyptic literature that survived despite efforts to suppress it, moreover, the corresponding mood or orientation was probably not confined to a few "exclusive conventicles." On the other hand, the actual apocalyptic literature on which synthetic generalizations have previously been based stems from literate groups, and not from popular circles. Moreover, the principal apocalyptic documents other than the Qumran literature date from either the second century B.C.E. (e.g., Daniel, the Enoch literature) or from a few decades after the Roman destruction of Jerusalem in 70 C.E. (e.g., 2 Baruch, 4 Ezra), while the limited literature from closer to the time of Jesus (e.g., Psalms of Solomon) displays little apocalyptic language or orientation. Thus, on the basis of the utter lack of evidence for it, as well as judging from comparative materials, it seems unlikely that any sort of general apocalyptic mentality was pervasive among the people over a continuous period of time. That is, once we discern the actual structure of social relations in ancient Jewish Palestine, "apocalypticism" as a general explanation of popular Jewish movements at the time of Jesus no longer appears well based, let alone convincing.[26]

The question then becomes whether the apocalyptic literature produced by scribes or sages can be used as evidence for the orientation and mood of circles among the common people, who left no literary remains as direct evidence for their own frame of mind. This can be done—but only with extreme caution—because the scribes and other "retainers" had come to share a situation similar to the common people under foreign domination during the late Hellenistic and Roman periods.[27] Since there is simply no justification for believing that all or most Jewish movements were apocalyptically oriented and motivated, it appears necessary to assume that given movements were not so motivated unless there is some compelling evidence to suggest otherwise. For some, such as the popular messianic movements, there is no evidence one way or the other. For a few movements such as those led by the popular prophets Theudas and "the Egyptian" (see below), the judgment that they were caught up in a keen anticipation of divine deliverance can be based on comparison with certain carefully analyzed apocalyptic literature. If and when a widespread apocalyptic mood emerged it would likely have been a temporary, localized phenomenon in connection with some crisis, such as the suppression of the traditional Jewish way of life by Antiochus Epiphanes in 168 B.C.E. (reflected in Daniel 7–12) or the Roman siege of Jerusalem in 69–70 (reflected in Josephus's reports of collective visions, etc., *War* 6.285–99).

Although there is no evidence of a pervasive apocalypticism in ancient Jewish Palestine, it is evident from apocalyptic literature such as the Dead Sea Scrolls and from Synoptic Gospel materials that at least some Palestinian Jewish circles lived in the understanding that their lives and situation were under the control of demonic forces. Sociologically, the key to a more adequate understanding of particular apocalyptic visions and/or the more general sense that life was caught up in a struggle between divine and demonic forces is surely their relation to the fundamental conflict in the historical situation. That is, "mythical fantasies" of a more humane future were almost certainly rooted in the experience of a concrete dualism, between the people's traditional way of life lived according to their sacred traditions, on the one hand, and political, economic, and/or cultural oppression that was breaking down or making impossible that traditional way of life, on the other. The dualism of God's agents versus Satan reflected the political-economic situation in which the people's lives were out of their own control and under hostile and/or alien control.

Belief in demons or, more broadly, Jewish apocalyptic symbolization is thus yet another important aspect of the social conditions of and for certain (but not all) Jewish renewal or resistance movements. Besides simply reflecting the concrete situation, however, this belief in demon possession and a struggle between God's agents and demonic powers provided (at least some involved in) the Jesus movement and certain others (such as the Qumranites and apparently the popular prophetic movements) both with a way of understanding their oppressive situation and with a way of dealing with it. It would have been intolerable to believe that their God either had abandoned them to the dominant imperial forces or was too weak to defend them. And it would have been impossible, simply suicidal, to have attempted a direct political solution, given the overwhelming military might of the Romans. Hence, in order to persist in their own traditional way of life and/or actively to resist their rulers' domination, it was necessary for Palestinian Jews to have a broader historical and spiritual perspective. In the confidence that God was indeed still in control and would restore them, judge their oppressors, and vindicate their efforts, they could (variously) simply "wait out" the imperial forces or pursue particular renewal programs or actively protest their circumstances. Precisely because Jewish demonology reflected the concrete political-economic conditions, precisely because more generally the apocalyptic perspective was rooted in the concrete historical circumstances, the belief in demons and confidence in God's ultimate deliverance provided an important social condition of and for the emergence and effectiveness of (at least some involved in) the Jesus movement.

Notes

1. See further R. A. Horsley, "High Priests and the Politics of Roman Palestine," *Journal for the Study of Judaism* 17 (1986) 23–55; A. N. Sherwin White, *Roman Society and Roman Law in the New Testament* (Oxford: Oxford University Press, 1963).

2. Our first glimpse of a group of scribes (and others?) alienated from the high priestly rulers is provided by the authors of sections of *1 Enoch*. They view themselves as faithful to biblical traditions, whereas the rulers are wicked and oppressive. The *maskîlîm* who produced the apocalyptic visions in the book of Daniel actively resisted the hellenizing "reform" led by their own high priestly rulers—and were sure of divine vindication for their martyrdom in defense of the traditional ways. See further J. J. Collins, *The Apocalyptic Imagination* (New York: Crossroad, 1984) ch 2 on *1 Enoch*, and ch 3 on Daniel and the *maskîlîm*; on the "Hasidim," see P. Davies, "Hasidim in the Maccabean Period," *Journal of Jewish Studies* 28 (1977) 127–40; on subsequent protests by scholarly retainers, see further R. Horsley, *Jesus and the Spiral of Violence* (San Francisco: Harper & Row, 1987) ch 3.

3. On the "Fourth Philosophy" and the Sicarii, see further Horsley, *Jesus and the Spiral of Violence*, 77–89; "The Sicarii: Ancient Jewish Terrorists," *Journal of Religion* 59 (1979) 435–58; and Horsley and Hanson, *Bandits, Prophets, and Messiahs*, 190–216.

4. See the interpretation in *Jesus and the Spiral of Violence*, ch 1.

5. See further John H. Kautsky, *The Politics of Aristocratic Empires* (Chapel Hill: University of North Carolina Press, 1982) esp. 72–75.

6. See further *Jesus and the Spiral of Violence*, ch 4.

7. Theissen also discerned "deep-rooted tensions" in every type of factor: "between productive groups and those who enjoy the profit, between city and country, between alien and native structures of government, between Hellenistic and Jewish culture" (94, etc.). Besides mistaking secondary for primary conflict within Palestinian Jewish society in the last two cases, however, Theissen more seriously blocks any understanding of the structural conflict underlying the tensions he discerns because he has divided the analysis into abstract categories. By focusing directly on the actual social structure of Jewish Palestine under Roman rule, fully aware that the "economic," "political," and "cultural-religious" were in fact inseparable dimensions of the particular historical situation, we are able to discern that the people actually involved on either side of the fundamental conflict are the same across every one of the categories. What Theissen presents as different sets of tensions were all simply aspects of the same fundamental social-structural conflict, that between the rulers on the one side and the ruled on the other.

8. See James C. Scott, *Weapons of the Weak: Everyday Forms of Peasant Resistance* (New Haven: Yale University Press, 1985).

9. Kautsky, *Aristocratic Empires*, esp. chs 12 and 13.

10. Partly because of the scarcity of solid evidence, we have a very rudimentary understanding of the basic economics of peasant life in Palestine. An important beginning

toward a more precise understanding has been made by Douglas Oakman, *Jesus and the Economic Questions of his Day* (Lewiston, NY: Edwin Mellen, 1987) esp. ch 2.

11. Gerhard Lenski has some illustrative figures from various traditional agrarian societies (*Power and Privilege* [New York: McGraw, 1966] 267–69).

12. On the economic situation in Palestine, see S. Applebaum, "Economic Life in Palestine," in *The Jewish People in the First Century*, ed. S. Safrai and M. Stern (Assen: Van Gorcum, 1974) 1:631–700; and "Judea as a Roman Province: The Countryside as a Political and Economic Factor, in *Aufstieg und Niedergang der römischen Welt*, II.8, ed. H. Temporini and W. Haase (Berlin: Walter de Gruyter, 1977) 355–96.

13. On the crucial role of the Jerusalem ruling groups in peasant indebtedness, see M. Goodman, "The First Jewish Revolt: Social Conflict and the Problem of Debt," *Journal of Jewish Studies* 33 (1982) 418–27.

14. See particularly John Gager, *Kingdom and Community* (Englewood Cliffs, NJ: Prentice-Hall, 1975).

15. I. C. Jarvie, *The Revolution in Anthropology* (Chicago: Regnery, 1967) 51; and Gager, *Kingdom*, 20–37.

16. See R. Redfield, *Peasant Society and Culture* (Chicago: University of Chicago, 1969) 70–72.

17. That is, it can hardly be explained merely by Theissen's "political factors" of tensions between rival structures of government (*Sociology*, 65–76).

18. See M. de Jonge, "The Use of the Word 'anointed' in the Time of Jesus," *Novum Testamentum* 8 (1966) 132–48; *Judaisms and Their Messiahs at the Turn of the Christian Era*, ed. J. Neusner, W. S. Green, and E. S. Frerichs (Cambridge: Cambridge University Press, 1987); and Horsley, "'Like one of the Prophets of Old': Two Types of Popular Prophets at the Time of Jesus," *Catholic Biblical Quarterly* 47 (1985) esp. 437–43.

19. These popular movements have been more extensively examined in *Bandits, Prophets, and Messiahs*, and the evidence is more carefully examined and analysis more critically argued in a series of articles, esp. "Popular Messianic Movements around the Time of Jesus," *Catholic Biblical Quarterly* 46 (1984) 471–95; "'Like One of the Prophets of Old': Two Types of Popular Prophets at the Time of Jesus," *Catholic Biblical Quarterly* 47 (1985) 435–63. Important here is to appreciate the determinative influence of certain Jewish biblical traditions on the concrete social forms taken by these figures and movements.

20. See further *Jesus and the Spiral of Violence*, ch 4.

21. See further R. A. Horsley, "The Zealots: Their Origins, and Relationships, and Importance in the Jewish Revolt," *Novum Testamentum* 27 (1986) 159–92.

22. They are the only group that fits most of the characteristics laid out as typical of a "sect" by R. Scroggs, "The Earliest Christian Communities as Sectarian Movement," in *Christianity, Judaism and Other Greco-Roman Cults: Studies for Morton Smith at Sixty*, ed. J. Neusner (2 vols.; Leiden: Brill, 1975) 2:1–23, and discussed at greater length in W. Stark, *The Sociology of Religion: Vol. 2, Sectarian Religion* (London: Routledge and Kegan Paul, 1967). B. R. Wilson has broken this otherwise impossibly vague term down into a sevenfold typology (*Magic and the Millennium* [New York: Harper & Row, 1973] chs 1 and 2). But in order to comprehend the various characteristics of particular cases we would have to use two or more of Wilson's subcategories. In the case of the Qumranites, the "conversionist," "revolutionist," "introversionist," and "utopian" types all seem necessary to comprehend the group as known through the Dead Sea Scrolls.

23. See critiques in K. Koch, *The Rediscovery of Apocalyptic* (Naperville, IL: Allenson, 1972); Amos Wilder, "Eschatological Imagery and Earthly Circumstance," and "Apocalyptic Rhetorics," reprinted as chs 6 and 7 in *Jesus' Parables and the War of Myths* (Philadelphia: Fortress, 1982).

24. See especially Collins, *Apocalyptic Imagination* and numerous important articles; and George W. E. Nickelsburg, *Jewish Literature Between the Bible and the Mishnah* (Philadelphia: Fortress, 1981).

25. E.g., P. Hanson, "Apocalypticism," in *Interpreter's Dictionary of the Bible: Supplementary Volume*, 28-34.

26. It is thus also clear that the "millenarian movement" analogy is based on cross-cultural material that could only have appeared comparable to the old, inadequate understanding of Jewish apocalypticism.

27. See the explanation in *Jesus and the Spiral of Violence*, 129-31.

Part III

Toward a Social Reconstruction
of the Jesus Movement

6 ◊ The Jesus Movement in Jewish Palestine: A Provisional Sketch _____

According to the standard older picture, early Christianity started with the outpouring of the Spirit in Jerusalem, then expanded quickly beyond Palestine into the eastern Mediterranean under the leadership of Paul's mission to the Gentiles, finally reaching the imperial capital of Rome. Because Christian New Testament scholarship emphasizes "Gentile Christianity," and because Jerusalem was destroyed by the Romans in 70 C.E., the assumption is that once the Jerusalem community supposedly fled across the Jordan to Pella, Jewish Christianity is largely lost to historical view.

That simplified and schematic older picture is now being seriously questioned. We are now more aware that there must have been some continuity of communities of Jesus' followers in Galilee, for example, from the time of Jesus to the second or third century, from which we have archaeological or Jewish textual evidence for churches in Sepphoris or Capernaum. What is even more significant, intensive recent study of synoptic traditions and the Gospels is suggesting that much of this material was developed in Galilee, even to the point of "Q" or "Mark" having been written in Galilee or southern Syria. These developments help explain the recent interest in the "Jesus movement(s)" in Palestine.

The principal problem for investigation of the Jesus movement, of course, is the paucity of evidence. Thus, any attempt to sketch a full or detailed picture would quickly become mere speculation. What follows can rather be presented more as explorations of relatively uncharted territory, attempts to discern the contours of the land, and some suggestions for some of the principal agenda that require further critical "sociological" attention. While occasionally critical of other recent reconstructions, this project is clearly heavily indebted to them.[1]

Sources and Communities

The most striking thing sociologically about the Jesus movement was that it seems to have taken the form of local communities. We virtually take this for granted for "the early church" in Hellenistic cities such as Ephesus, Thessalonica, or Corinth, although the matter becomes more problematic when we ponder why, what particular community form(s) were involved, and where they came from. In comparison with this admittedly vague picture of tight-knit communities as the "churches" in the Hellenistic cities, we have an even vaguer sense of how the Jesus movement in Palestine took form. To be sure we have the idealized projection by Luke in Acts 2:44-45 and 4:32-35 of a joyous group of Jesus' followers gathered in Jerusalem who held everything in common and sold what individual possessions they might have had in order to care for the needy. We have little or no sense, however, of how the Jesus movement in the rest of Palestine was taking shape or of its possible continuity with Jesus' ministry.[2]

Part of our problem is the paucity of texts that would provide any direct evidence concerning the concrete social form of the Jesus movement in Palestine. But unless we are prepared to imagine that there was no continuity between Jesus' ministry and the Christian churches that produced and read the Gospels—since supposedly that body of Jesus' teachings that "was later to take independent form as Christianity" was handed on by a handful of itinerants anyhow[3]—then we must imagine a social context at the outset of the movement to which those sayings pertained. As noted in the previous chapter, in a traditional agrarian society such as that in ancient Jewish Palestine, the basic social form in which life was lived was a peasant village. The vast majority of people (90 percent or more) would have lived in villages and towns. Significantly, the rural setting of much of the Gospel tradition corresponds to what would have been the living situation of most people in Palestine. We can thus surmise simply on the basis of the social-historical context that during the first forty years in Palestine the Jesus movement must have been based initially in villages and towns and then in certain cities, and it must have been oriented toward the renewal of local community (villages and towns) or the foundation of communities (cities). Since the life of the people had village communities as its basic social form, it is no contradiction of this at all that the Jesus movement thought of itself as a renewal of Israel generally.

Since our sources for the Jesus movement(s) in Palestine are limited (basically to the Synoptic Gospel traditions) and often provide incidental or indirect information at best, we must examine them critically for whatever indications they may provide of social relations and social locations.

Acts and Paul[4]

It is important to cut through some of our standard impressions of the early group of Jesus' followers in Jerusalem, impressions which are rooted partly in the book of Acts' highly schematic account, partly in the special viewpoint of the apostle Paul, and partly in Christian theological viewpoints. Luke's portrayal of the earliest community in Jerusalem dramatizes elements such as the outpouring of the Spirit and the selling of possessions, and he presents a highly schematic picture of the expansion of the movement from a base in Jerusalem to Palestinian villages and towns, as well as around the eastern Mediterranean and finally to the imperial capital of Rome. It is because of Paul's special concerns and Pauline influence on scholarly interpretation that we might think that the significant things about the early followers of Jesus in Jerusalem were that they practiced circumcision and observed the Jewish dietary laws, or that the leaders such as Peter and James held "hasidic" values or pursued practices that might look somewhat "Pharisaic." There would be nothing noteworthy, of course, for Jews in Jerusalem to have been circumcised and to observe customary dietary practices. Of course, the standard assumption that the earliest followers of Jesus in Jerusalem participated in the Temple cult projects modern assumptions about religion and religious institutions back onto passages such as Acts 2:46, which says only that Peter and company were spending time in the Temple complex, the principal place available for public meeting, not that they were "attending Temple" (religious services or sacrifices).

Even if we allow for considerable exaggeration in Luke's nostalgic and romanticizing summaries (e.g., 2:41–47; 4:32–37; 5:42), we can still imagine a group excitedly celebrating table fellowship, sharing resources, and energetically preaching and healing in the Temple area. Behind Luke's account of the reconstitution of the Twelve in Acts 1 may well be the group's sense of being the reconstitution of "Israel," which appears elsewhere in early traditions. The repeated accounts of sharp conflict between the leaders of the group and the priestly governing authorities (Acts 4; 5:17–18; 8:1–3; 9:1–2; 12:1–5) surely reflects, even if it overplays, the historical significance of the mutual hostility that must have existed from the beginning and escalated into sharp repression and persecution by the high priests.

Paul confirms the impression from Acts that Peter and eventually Jesus' brother James were the principal leaders of the Jerusalem group (Gal 1:18–2:12). Of course, his reports also lead us to question just how egalitarian the Jerusalem group was, at least in its authority structure, however they may have shared their resources. Paul's account of his own conflict with these "pillars" illustrates clearly how various communities or movements, both ostensibly loyal to Jesus as Lord, could develop from different "gospels" and in different ways virtually from the outset, even though there was some "communication" between them. Moreover, Paul's reference to his own earliest ministry in Arabia and Cilicia in Galatians 1-2 helps us realize just how quickly "Jesus movements" or "churches" sprang up even outside of Palestine. This makes all the more credible the picture in Acts of the rapid spread of Jesus movements into the villages and towns of Judea, Samaria, and Galilee, as well as into the immediately surrounding areas of the Decapolis or Tyre and Sidon, although it seems questionable that the expansion radiated out primarily from a center in Jerusalem (Acts 8–10; cf., e.g., Mark 3:7; 7:24, 31).

What neither Acts nor Paul (nor any other source) provides is any indication that "the pillars" or "the Twelve" in Jerusalem have any connection with the Gospel traditions. The critical portrayal of the disciples in the Gospel of Mark might even suggest that at some point in the development of the synoptic tradition, the latter stood over against those who had assumed authority positions in Jerusalem. In any case, we must assume diversity and independent development of whatever movement(s) lay behind Synoptic Gospel materials, rather than a somewhat unified, Jerusalem-led movement. We cannot assume that Jesus people elsewhere in Palestine looked to Jerusalem even as a symbolic center or for leadership from the "disciples" centered there.

The Sayings Source, Q

Sophisticated analysis of the sayings source used by both Matthew and Luke claims that there was an earlier and formative "sapiential" layer followed by a redactional "apocalyptic" layer.[5] Such a distinction of earlier and later stages in the development of Q would make possible the tracing of a "social history" of the movement or community behind the cultivation and development of Q materials.[6]

However, the recent hypotheses regarding an earlier "sapiential" layer and a later "apocalyptic" layer within Q appear to be questionable. John Kloppenborg assigns five complexes of Q sayings—3:7-9, 16-17; 7:1-10, 18-35; 11:14-26, 29-32, 39-52; 12:39-59; and 17:23-35—to the same secondary redactional stratum on the basis of "several common features": *a projected audience* with the "target group" as "all of Israel," the *form* of chriae which encapsulate the prophetic judgment and apocalyptic words typical of this stratum, and *motifs* related to the theme of judgment such as imminence and the parousia.[7]

When one examines the actual complexes of Q sayings assigned to this redactional stratum, it is difficult to find these "common features." Little of the material in those five complexes appears to be "directed at the 'outgroup'" of the impenitent and the opponents. Most of the material in these five complexes consists of rationalizations, exhortations, and particularly sanctions directed at the "in-group" of Jesus' followers themselves (7:18–23, 24–28; 12:39–46, 51–53, 57–59; 17:23–35) or is not particularly threatening in the first place (11:14–26). There is no reason internal to the key texts of 11:29–32 and 49–51 to think that "this generation" refers to "Israel" as opposed to "Gentiles." The only occurrence of "Israel" is in 7:1–10. Here in this one text, indeed, a Gentile responds to Jesus with faith. But the point of the story is not to exemplify a mission to Gentiles,[8] but to challenge (or embarrass) Jews/Israel into fuller response. And beyond 7:1–10, there is no indication in Q of "actual Gentile belief." There is thus simply no basis in Q for "Gentile faith" as a significant theme, let alone its interpretation as a sign of condemnation for Israel.

As for the "common feature" of form, only one of the chriae listed (11:29+31–32) actually criticizes the response of "this generation" to the preaching of the kingdom. Moreover, of the sayings that these chriae "encapsulate," none of them appear to be "apocalyptic words," but are "prophetic sayings," and of the other sayings that supposedly articulate a threat, only three of the nine listed could intelligibly be interpreted that way. Moreover, with regard to the supposedly common "motifs," the assumption that Q speaks of "the parousia" is probably rooted in a Pauline understanding of Christ's return. But "(the day of) the son of man" in Luke 12:40; 17:24, 26, 30 is merely a symbol for the judgment, and not a reference to an individual figure of redemption. And judgment is not particularly "imminent" in Q, except perhaps in the Baptist's preaching. The sayings in 12:51–53 and 12:54–56 refer rather to the present crisis.

Strictly speaking, only two texts (11:29–32 and 11:49–51) actually attest the three common features used as criteria for the secondary "apocalyptic" or judgmental layer, and then not quite in the distinctive ways Kloppenborg has characterized them: that is, they are prophetic sayings (but not apocalyptic sayings) in form; they contain the motif of rejection of Jesus' preaching as a basis for condemnation (but no apocalyptic traits); and they also focus on "this generation" (but not "Israel") as the projected audience. It hardly seems justified to assign five whole complexes of sayings to a particular "redactional stratum" on the basis of only two sayings that actually manifest the "common features" used as criteria.

The stated criteria of assignment of Q material into redactional strata thus appear to have come not from the texts but rather from the interpretive concepts of modern New Testament scholarship. But scholarly concepts derived from an earlier, more synthetic scholarly understanding of "early Christianity" and heavily influenced by Christian theology and Christology, such as "apocalyptic" or "eschatological" motifs and concepts, "the parousia," and what are often taken as "christological titles," such as "Son of man," may not be expressed in or applicable to Q materials.[9] The general scholarly distinction between "sapiential" and "apocalyptic" traditions makes little sense sociologically, for the same literate social stratum of scribes or sages would be responsible for both. Indeed, a mixture of the two supposedly different types of material can be seen clearly in literature such as 1 Enoch. Thus, care must be taken not to let literary distinctions such as those of genre dictate (or become) differences of social situation. It seems that there is no basis within Q for distinguishing two clear redactional strata and correspondingly different social situations for the two strata. Meanwhile, however, until a more convincing hypothesis of different layers in Q emerges, it is possible to use Q as a source for a movement or community located apparently in Galilee and apparently prior to the great revolt of 66–70.

Rather than look for the "life-style" or (religious) ideals expressed in Q, which results in vague characterizations abstracted from the concrete historical situation, we should examine what social relations are indicated in Q materials. As a first step, we can narrow the possibilities for the social location of Q material by noting what is missing or negatively treated. It is obvious that Q was not produced by Pharisees, lawyers, scribes, or other Jewish retainers, who are the subject of criticism and condemnation in Luke 11:39–52. Jerusalem, including the Temple, seems remote, and indeed the "house" of the rulers is doomed for its rejection of the prophets and other envoys of God (Luke 13:34–35a). There is no attention to priestly (ritual or purification) activities.

Similarly, the Torah does not appear to function at all as sacred writ or law. Rather, aspects of its teachings can be discerned more as if it were the popular tradition underlying sayings such as those in 6:27–35. There are few if any signs of exegetical activity. The only quotation is from Mal 3:1 in the attempt to clarify the prophetic role of John in Luke 7:27; the closest things to quotations otherwise are the allusions to Isa 35:5 and 61:1 in Luke 7:22. But those, along with all of the references to the persons of or events associated with Abraham, Isaac, Jacob, the prophets, Solomon, Noah, Jonah and the Ninevites, Lot, or the queen of the south, appear to come out of common popular tradition and not learned interpretation of scripture.

However, as indicated by the abundant allusions to figures and events in Israelite historical tradition, particularly as groundings for (judgment about) response or rejection of Jesus, the Q people identify with and see themselves as the continuation, indeed the fulfillment of the hopes, of Israel. "Many prophets and kings desired to see what you see . . ." (10:24). "Israel" is being restored according to its "twelve tribes," with the disciples in the role of "liberating/establishing justice for" the people (Matt 19:28/Luke 22:28-30).[10] The "Israel" that is being renewed under the coming or presence of "the kingdom of God" is not concerned about maintaining boundaries over against the Gentiles, but is open to them, on the one hand. On the other hand, the "Israel" of the Q people is defined over against Jerusalem and the representatives of the government and official traditions, and participation is based not on one's proper lineage as children of Abraham but on repentance and action according to the teachings of Jesus (3:7-9; 6:46-49; etc.). In particular, the Q people understand John and Jesus as the climactic figures in the line of the prophets who, almost by definition, stood over against and were rejected by the ruling institutions and their representatives (7:18-35; 11:47-51; 13:34-35).

Judging from certain Q material addressed to the ingroup, the social location or setting in which the renewal of the people/Israel was taking place appears to have been local communities, probably villages and towns. Agricultural imagery is prominent in Q. It is assumed that the hearers of the sayings are involved in families and villages, with neighbors, children, and marriages on which there are pressures (11:9-13; 14:26; 16:18). They are also acquainted with very large households, with several servants and run by a steward (Luke 12:35-38, 42-46). The most direct instructions in Q, however, concern local social-economic relationships among individuals or ordinary households, such as periodic mutual borrowing and assistance, the conflicts that could emerge from one person being indebted to another, the importance of mutual aid despite reluctance and tensions, and the mitigation and resolution of tensions and conflicts (6:27-31, 37-38, 41-42; 17:1-2, 3-4). The Jesus movement behind Q is clearly not primarily one of "itinerant charismatics" who have abandoned home, family, and possessions.[11] The only indication of itinerancy of any sort is in Luke 10:3-4, while in the same "mission" context 10:7 appears to counter any appearance of vagrancy. The only place-names, apart from the doomed Jerusalem, are of towns at the northern end of the Sea of Galilee, Capernaum, Chorazin, and Bethsaida. The occurrence of only these particular place-names does not mean that the Q people were located only or primarily in central Galilee, but these passages do indicate that Jesus and/or his movement had been active in such towns. There is no particular indication in Q that the movement was located also in a city such as Sepphoris or Tiberias.

Mark and Pre-Marcan Material

Recent work on the Gospel of Mark has given us a heightened sense both of Mark as an original narrative in its own right and of the character of already shaped pre-Marcan materials utilized in Mark. In fact, whole sets of miracle stories and distinctive types of pronouncement stories can be seen to have taken definitive form prior to their use in Mark.[12] Such collections of types of materials, however, would appear to be too limited as a basis on which to project a separate "community" or "movement."[13] Moreover, as we shall see below, the social relations and location indicated in the sets of miracle stories and in the pronouncement stories are similar, and are similar to those indicated elsewhere in Mark. Hence, it seems best not to attempt greater precision than the sources allow, and to view the various types of material in Mark, some of which clearly predate Mark, as expressions of the same general movement. Choice of such a strategy would appear to be confirmed by the appearance of many of the same characteristics and social indicators in both distinctive sets of pre-Marcan material.

Distinctive chains of miracle stories have been discerned in Mark and in John. Taking into account an obvious editorial transposition in one case by Mark, two chains of such stories can be seen behind Mark 4–8, each beginning with a miracle on the sea and ending with a miraculous feeding, which thus frame three stories of healing or exorcism (respectively, Mark 4:35–41; 5:1–20; 5:21–24, 35–43; 5:25–34; 6:34–44; and Mark 6:45–51; 7:24b–30; 7:32–37; 8:22–26; 8:1–10). Both chains of stories combine allusions to Moses and the exodus with reminiscences of the Elijah-Elisha cycle of miracles. The implications are obvious: Israel is being liberated and restored or reconstituted. These events are taking place far away from the Temple, and the Torah as a "redemptive medium" is nowhere in sight. To think that these stories represent "marginal" or "unclean" candidates being collected for a new congregation mistakes the special concerns of a tiny stratum of Jewish scribes and sages for some sort of standard conventions or normative view that the Jesus movement was "challenging" or some generally recognized "social boundaries" that were being transgressed/crossed. The chain of miracle stories rather represents a renewal of people's lives and life-possibilities on the basis of a paradigm derived from *popular* traditions of Moses and Elijah-Elisha (who were active in "Israel," not in Judea!). Moreover, "Jesus" and the people being restored are simply not concerned with priestly and scribal-Pharisaic issues such as "clean- unclean" or purity-(normalcy-)marginality, which served to maintain distinctions of social order and privilege. These sets of miracle stories that suggest a new exodus and portray a revitalization of the people both presuppose and expose the worthlessness, or perhaps even the oppressiveness of the authorities. The social location is popular culture, apparently Galilean, remote from Temple and official tradition.

The elaborated pronouncement stories behind Mark, usually dated in the 50s and 60s C.E., present speech-in-character, often in controversy, and culminate in a clever and/or pithy saying. On the assumptions that there were "synagogues" as religious institutions and that (although they do not necessarily go together with synagogues) "the Pharisees" represent a sort of normative understanding in Jewish life, it would be credible to imagine these pronouncement stories as the products of a "synagogue reform movement." On the other hand, if what is usually called a "synagogue" in Mark or these pre-Marcan stories was a local assembly and the scribes and Pharisees represented official, probably Jerusalem-based views and concerns, then we must read the pronouncement stories in different terms in order to discern the social relations they presuppose and express.

In many of these controversies Jesus can be understood better defending not "unconventional behavior" (it being doubtful that Pharisaic views had become "conventional" among the people) but popular conventions and interests (and fundamental human values and common sense) over against the official codes. The sabbath was made for people! Thus, how ridiculous if it were not "lawful" to do good or heal on the sabbath! (Mark 2:23–28; 3:1–5). The Jesus group or movement reflected in the pronouncement stories does not appear to be so much a mixture of peoples (the Syrophoenician woman in 7:26–28 appears to be the only non-Galilean/ Jew) as ordinary people in a frontier area where social identity was more flexible and oriented toward local interaction as opposed to the Pharisaic or (high) priestly concern for rigorous protection of group boundaries and purity (e.g., Mark 2:15–17).

Certain pronouncement stories not only assert what must be conventional popular values but make clear as well that those conventions are rooted in the popular tradition, in contrast or even in conflict with the official tradition and its interpreters.[14] In Mark 10:2–9, for example, Jesus defends the conventional popular commitment to and expectation of marriage. In Mark 7:5–8 and 9–13 he insists on loyalty to the basic "commandment of God," which is apparently also local popular tradition, as opposed to "the traditions of the elders" pressed upon the people by the Pharisees and scribes. (Note the implied contrast between regional customs in the [Marcan?] explanation of 7:3–4, particularly if "all the Jews" should rather be translated "all the *Judeans*.") The Pharisees' concerns about issues of purity are rejected. These pronouncement stories,

in fact, do not deal simply with "religious" matters. At issue are fundamental social (familial-economic) obligations sanctioned by God's command that are being undermined by the official codes and scholarly
rulings (7:9-13; cf. 12:38, 40-44). These pronouncement stories cite the
Torah (key creation or covenantal passages probably known in popular,
oral tradition). But, if anything, Jesus is not represented as a scribe, but
as an *anti*-scribe who has a "down-to-earth" practical (and conventional)
wisdom "that frustrates the official scribal principles of interpretation."[15]
The pronouncement stories also reflect people who identify with the
history of Israel (note the sort of story recalled in 2:25-26!) and even see
events in their own time as fulfillment of the implications of that history
(9:9-13, which may be Marcan). The picture that emerges is of local or
popular interests over against official. The people whose interests the
stories represent are the insiders of local communities, while the Pharisees or scribes are the ones who come from outside the local community,
representing the ruling institutions.

Insofar as some of the pronouncement stories may reflect typical social
situations of those involved in a movement, we discern local community
life. Family or friends are determined to find help for the paralytic;
maintenance of marriage and family is absolutely essential (2:3-5;
10:2-9). Table fellowship is important regardless of the reputation of those
gathered together (2:15-27). Especially leaders of the movement should
maintain a humble, childlike bearing in the community (9:33-37). The
people whose situation such stories reflect must be of modest circumstances, with sharp resentment of the wealthy and powerful (10:17-22,
23-27; 12:41-44). It is difficult to tell whether the location is urban or rural
(2:23), but the social situations are clearly local communities of ordinary
poor people.

It is also possible to project back somewhat from the Gospel of Mark
itself, insofar as it reflects the circumstances and experiences in which the
Jesus traditions have been shaped. Surely the conflict between Jesus and
the scribes and Pharisees that escalates throughout the Gospel and the
direct "face-off" between Jesus and rulers in the Jerusalem Temple are not
merely literary artifice. The arena of Jesus' activity is primarily Galilee,
although he also devotes attention to the area east of the Sea of Galilee
and even ventures up into the villages of Caesarea Philippi and the
regions of Tyre and Sidon. The ending of the Gospel (16:7), moreover,
points back to Galilee as the scene of the continuation of the story. More
particularly, the activity is devoted exclusively to villages and towns. He
and his followers never enter the cities proper, either Tiberias or
Sepphoris in Galilee or Tyre, Caesarea Philippi, or the Decapolis beyond.
Although the first half of the story is one of an itinerant ministry of Jesus

and his disciples (1:35–38; 3:14–15; 6:7–13), that is not an indication that the movement reflected in Mark is primarily one of "itinerant charismatics." The sharp criticism and negative portrayal of the disciples suggests that the story of Jesus' ministry is not a paradigm of/for that of the disciples. If Mark is to be placed in Galilee or southern Syria, then the fact that it was written in Greek may indicate that it was written for urban readers. (Does the allegorical interpretation of the parables in Mark 4 also indicate an urban author who no longer understands the immediate analogical application of the agrarian images and stories?) But Mark reflects a social situation of village and town communities as the setting of the traditions it utilizes.

Although the movement reflected in Mark is remote from and has sharply condemned the Temple and sacerdotal government in Jerusalem (12:1–12), it nevertheless understands John's and Jesus' ministries, and apparently the experience of its own community, as the fulfillment of the traditions of Israel. What were reminiscences of and allusions to Moses and Elijah in the chains of miracle stories have become explicit statements of historical typology (1:2–3; 9:2–8; 9:9–13). The sense of fulfillment and the renewal or restoration of Israel, however, is explicitly anti-scribal and anti-establishment (12:35–37).

This examination of Mark and the sets of both miracle stories and pronouncement stories utilized in the Gospel indicates much the same social relations as are indicated in Q. All of these potential sources for the Jesus movement(s) explicitly or implicitly reject Jerusalem, the Temple, and the hierocracy. Clearly none of these strata of Gospel materials is the product of learned Jewish scribal circles; indeed, Mark and the pronouncement stories as well as Q sharply reject and/or condemn the scribes, lawyers, and Pharisees. These strata, moreover, show no interest in priestly matters, or they explicitly reject concerns with purity and ethnic boundary definitions.

Yet all of these strata of Gospel materials indicate a movement that identifies itself with the traditions of Israel to the point of understanding its experience as the fulfillment of Israel's hopes and the renewal of the people. The prophetic prototypes of Moses and Elijah and the liberation and restoration they accomplished are more or less prominent in every one of these sets of materials. There is little or no evidence in either Q or Mark for the Jesus movement as primarily a bunch of "itinerant charismatics." Rather, the renewal of "Israel" appears to be taking place in local community situations. The locations, by all indicators, are primarily in Galilee, with Mark suggesting that the movement(s) had also taken root in the villages and towns elsewhere in southern Syria.

The principal sources we can utilize for the Jesus movement(s) in

Galilee thus appear to be Q and the sets of materials used by Mark. Other materials in the Synoptic Gospel tradition (e.g., special Matthean or Lucan materials) and elsewhere can be utilized, but only after critical determination that they reflect conditions in or traditions from the Galilean or Palestinian situation. Materials of other provenance can be used only for critical projection or comparison. Throughout the provisional sketches that follow, finally, the attempt will be made to read textual and other evidence in concrete historical social context, as outlined in the previous two chapters.

An Alternative Reconstruction

The principal alternative to this view of the sources for the Jesus movement and their implications for its reconstruction builds on Theissen's and others' hypothesis of an itinerant ethos, but sees it as less charismatic and more Cynic-like. The alternative reconstruction focuses primarily on Q, discounts the features from Israelite-Jewish tradition, and emphasizes rather the sayings that have parallels with Cynic philosophy. Indeed, according to recent analyses of Q, the latter are so striking that those who shaped and transmitted Q material must have been much more Cynic-like than Theissen allowed in their "countercultural" life-style.

As in Theissen's presentation of the wandering charismatics, so in the Q-based reconstruction of the Jesus movement as fundamentally Cynic-like, the key text is the "mission discourse" in Luke 10:3–11.[16] Not only does Luke 10:3–11 supposedly hold the key to the identity of the Q people, but 10:4 by itself represents "a way of life," in particular one of "self-sufficiency and independence," as indicated by the extensive parallels discerned between the characteristics of Jesus' disciples and itinerant Cynic philosophers.[17] Luke 10:3–11 and particularly 10:4 would appear to be the paradigmatic "test case" for the Cynic-like reconstruction of the Jesus movement.

The numerous Hellenistic-Roman texts offered in illustration of various parallel motifs, however, seem mixed in their implications. The parallels offered for healing the sick in Luke 10:9 are not close or convincing, and it is not evident that 10:5–6 is about begging, for which the parallels are offered. With regard to the key parts of Luke 10 paralleled by the mission charge in Mark 6:8–11, no Cynic comparative materials are offered for Luke 10:7–8 (which is not surprising, since other materials indicate that Cynics went "house to house," i.e., counter to 10:7c) and, strictly speaking, 10:10–11 is not paralleled in Greco-Roman Cynic sources. What is perhaps most significant, for the key passage, supposedly attesting a "way of life" (10:4; cf. Mark 6:8–9), the "parallels" represent a contrast, often explicit, as much as or more than a similarity. Reconstruction of Q (Luke) 10:4 indicates five prohibitions: of money, wallet (bag), footwear, staff, and of greeting or talking (Mark mentions all but the last). The Cynic materials cited clearly offer parallels to the prohibition of money and to going barefoot. But the prohibition of a wallet does not conform to the typical description of the Cynic, who proverbially wore a *pera*, which supposedly indicated his "self-sufficiency." In contrast to the (reconstructed) prohibition of a staff in Q, it was a typical piece of equipment for the Cynic. And whereas Luke 10:4 prohibits greeting on the road, Cynics were famous for their so-called "boldness of speech."[18] Thus, in three of its five prohibitions, Q 10:4 could thus be understood almost as *anti*-Cynic.

One might want to argue that the items in Luke 10:4 represent by themselves a certain "way of life" that is sufficiently Cynic-like that it must distinguish itself by two or three distinctive differences. But Luke 10:4, (5-)7a(8), 10-11 and Mark 6:8-9, 10, 11 must derive from a common tradition. And there seems no justification for tearing Q 10:4 and Mark 6:8-9 out of their pre-Q or pre-Marcan context(s) for which Cynic comparative materials offer no parallels. The other parts of the common tradition of the "mission discourse," Mark 6:10-11 and Q 10:(5-)7a, (7c), (8), 10-11, instruct the envoys to offer a severe gesture of judgment against those who reject them and to maintain a certain stability in the way they obtain support from local households. Far from suggesting homeless beggary as a way of life, these other parts of the common tradition indicate that there was a distinctive purpose to their activities (the kingdom of God?) and a nascent network of people responding to their activities and providing hospitality and support. The "mission" would thus appear to have more to do with the revitalization of local community life than with a new, itinerant "way of life" as an object in itself. The key seems to be the purpose and pattern of the itinerancy as focused on social renewal, not an individual life-style of self-sufficiency and independence.

Indeed, as noted in ch 3 above, there appear to be several decisive differences between the Cynics and the envoys of the Jesus movement in Palestine. Particularly when we attempt to place them in concrete social contexts, the Cynics and Jesus' envoys appear to have had very different "callings." The former were individual paradigms of virtue, whether only in themselves or also for others who might emulate their example. In Luke 10:3-11 Jesus' envoys are charged as catalysts of a broader movement based in local communities. Accordingly, whereas the Cynics lived without home and possessions as an intentional "way of life," the delegates of Jesus left home, possessions, and family behind temporarily as an unavoidable but more incidental matter necessitated by their mission.

Cynics are indeed portrayed as vagabond beggars going from house to house. By contrast, Jesus' envoys are instructed to stay in local houses, eating what was provided in those households. Thus, even for the key text of Luke 10:4, the portrayal of Cynic philosophers in late Hellenistic and Roman literature is not particularly compelling and hardly suggests that the Q people were Cynic-like.

The Cynic hypothesis for the Jesus movement would provide a possibility for a reading of Q if we were to reconstruct the historical context differently from chs 4 and 5 above. That is, if we concentrated on the degree to which Hellenistic culture had already become prominent in the newly "Hellenized" city of Sepphoris or the newly built administrative city of Tiberias or on the older Hellenistic ethos of the Decapolis (and discounted the apparent implications of the rural ethos reflected in the Gospel traditions generally), then we could easily imagine a Cynic-like critique of the pretensions of established Hellenistic life appealing to some of the residents of those cities.

But there are more appropriate ways of explaining the Cynic "parallels" to Q materials. The similarities between Jesus traditions in Q and Cynic sayings or descriptions can be accounted for from the Cynic side (instead of from the Q side). That is, Cynic philosophers who took a radically critical stance toward established Hellenistic urban life and culture, would likely long since have found affinities with popular rural criticisms of the elite culture (that the peasants' productivity had always made possible but which was alien and oppressive to them). Pithy critical sayings borrowed or adapted by Cynics—and become "typical" Cynic—would thus not surprisingly bear many similarities to the sayings of a popular prophet or wise man such as Jesus, especially once those sayings were translated into Greek. Alternatively, Q could be understood as a collection (and development) of Jesus sayings in a Hellenistic urban milieu such as the Decapolis or Sepphoris that had some Cynic influence. This would account for both continuity and change in the development of Jesus traditions. That is, core Jesus traditions can have originated in a Jesus movement based originally in Galilean towns and villages, then have been translated and adapted in a Hellenistic urban milieu still in close proximity to and even in touch with those towns. But in this case, there is no reason to posit any actual itinerant vagabonds, for the Cynic-like layer would be basically adaptation or interpretation influenced by the Cynic lore known in such a Hellenistic urban context.

In any case, any hypothesis that, because of the similarities between certain Jesus sayings and Cynic philosophy, there were Cynic-like itinerant followers of Jesus in Palestine does not help us account for the (earlier or later) formation of communities by the Jesus movement. It is difficult to imagine how a number of individual paradigms of self-sufficiency could have called forth the existence of communities or have bothered with the sort of local social interaction with which significant parts of the Q material are concerned.

Comparisons and Implications

That the Jesus movement was initially based in and oriented toward the renewal of local communities (in Palestinian villages and towns) may be more concretely conceivable through comparison with two other types of movements, the wilderness community at Qumran and the popular prophetic movements. The Qumranites, like the Jesus movement, thought of themselves as a renewal of Israel. But the Qumranites had left their hometown or city in order to join a "utopian" community of other priests and intellectuals, completely away from the patterns and problems of ordinary life. By contrast, the members of the Jesus movement not only remained in their residential communities, but attempted to revitalize local community life, facing directly all the problems of poverty, anxiety, and local tensions as well as conflicts with the authorities, as we shall see further below.

The people who followed the popular prophet Theudas out to the Jordan River in anticipation of God's new act of exodus and/or conquest and those who followed the "Egyptian" up to the Mount of Olives to experience the new "battle of Jericho" in God's liberation of Jerusalem were clearly ordinary folk, like those in the Jesus movement. There may have been a further essential similarity insofar as some of the Jesus people were also caught up in unrealistic fantasies, such as "sitting at table with Abraham, Isaac, and Jacob in the kingdom of God" (Matt 8:11; Luke 13:28–29) or "sitting on twelve thrones liberating the twelve tribes of Israel" (Matt 19:28; Luke 22:29–30). But those who joined the popular prophetic movements had apparently simply abandoned their homes in anticipation of their fantastic new liberation, while the more "realistic" members of the Jesus movement remained in their towns (or were on mission to other towns) working out renewed community life.

If the Jesus movement originated in and was initially based on some villages and towns of Jewish Palestine, then it is more readily understandable how it could then fairly quickly spread into the villages of Samaria and Judea (Acts 8 and 9:31) and gain a foothold not only in a Judean district town such as Lydda (Acts 9:32) but also in places such as the coastal town of Joppa (Acts 9:36) and the Syrian city of Damascus. The author of Acts portrays the movement as spreading from its base in Jerusalem to the Samaritan and Judean villages as a result of the authorities' attempts to suppress the movement in the holy city. But that is almost certainly determined by Luke's schematic presentation of church history as having begun in and radiated outward from Jerusalem. Sociologically it is far more credible that the Jesus movement was based initially in (probably Galilean) villages and towns and spread into district towns and cities further along trade routes, as well as into other villages. Some of those who would have been attracted by the movement in towns or cities may well have been people recently displaced from their ancestral villages because of debts, that is, people for whom the traditional forms of community had completely broken down. In any case, it seems clear from fragmentary reports and allusions that the Jesus movement expanded rapidly within and beyond Palestine, into towns and cities such as Lydda, Joppa, Caesarea, but also into villages beyond Galilee and Judea (e.g., in Idumea, Perea, and in the "regions" around Tyre and Sidon or those around the cities of the Decapolis, as suggested by Mark 3:7; 7:24, 31).

The rural origins of the Jesus movement in Palestine would also provide a sociological component of an explanation of why a movement that was Jewish in origins and orientation (its purpose being the renewal of Israel) would so easily and quickly accept non-Jews into its communities. As is well known from New Testament literature such as Acts 10, Galatians 1–2, Romans 9–11, the issues of when and under what conditions the Gentiles would be brought into the churches was the focus of serious soul searching and struggle, particularly for some of the leaders (e.g., James, Peter). For such leaders, the necessity of deliberation and decision about inclusion was almost certainly provoked by actual practice in the communities of the early Jesus movement. An issue such as the inclusion of Gentiles would have been much less problematic for the ordinary people than for retainers of the Temple government, the hereditary regular priests, and especially the hereditary high priestly rulers. These groups, in escalating degree, were both the embodiment (and beneficiaries!) and the guardians of the purity system; hence, they were at pains to maintain the boundaries and degrees of purity scrupulously. Thus, for Paul the former Pharisee, the inclusion of the Gentiles was part of a dramatic "about-face" for a fanatic persecutor of the churches that happened in a paranormal experience (an *apokalypsis*, Gal 1:16; 2 Cor 12:1–5), and not the result of reasoned reflection.

But ordinary Jews in a district such as Galilee had no real stake in the purity system and boundary regulations. In fact, they may well have identified with non-Jewish peasants who were in a similar situation in the social structure over against their (ostensibly) Jewish rulers (e.g., Antipas, Agrippa I, as well as the high priestly government in Jerusalem) and

Roman domination. One would simply expect ordinary Jews to be more open to Gentiles than the priests and "scribes and Pharisees" would have been. Thus, this sociological reason can take its place alongside the practice of Jesus (the Syrophoenician woman), a few "revelations" (Acts 10; Gal 1:16), and the sense that the promise to Abraham (all nations would receive blessings) was now being fulfilled, as partial explanation for the inclusion of the Gentiles at an early point in the movement.

Characteristics of the Communities

Composition

As already indicated from the information gleaned regarding social relations in the previous section, most of the people who comprised the Jesus movement in Galilean and other villages would have been peasants, including fishermen and craftspeople. The composition would have been more diverse as communities became established in larger towns. Although people of modest means would not have been excluded, most of the participants would have been poor. In such a traditional agrarian society, there was simply no "middle class"; the vast majority of villagers and townspeople would have been marginal economically and therefore threatened with indebtedness if not actually heavily in debt. It would not be surprising if some who joined the movement in towns or cities had moved there because they had been dispossessed of their land. This composition of the movement is reflected in the numerous binary oppositions between rich and poor, the well-fed and the hungry, or the first and the last (e.g., Luke 6:20–26). Such contrasts clearly represent the social-economic circumstances as well as the self-image of Jesus' followers. There would have been a greater variety of people in the Jesus communities in the larger towns and cities. But people of considerable means, such as Susanna and Joanna, the wife of Chuza, Herod's steward (note that these names are in special Lucan material, 8:3), would still have been the exception in urban communities comprising largely ordinary people resident in the larger district towns and cities.

In such contexts the Jesus movement may well have attracted some socially disreputable or despised people such as "toll collectors," although the evidence is weak and problematic. It has been suggested that many (even the majority) of Jesus' followers were from some particular groups in Palestinian Jewish society, such as "tax collectors" and "prostitutes." Aside from such people not being identifiable social *groups*, there is little or no evidence that Jesus himself ministered to or associated with such people as tax collectors or prostitutes.[19] In the earliest tradition, Matthew

11:18-19/Luke 7:33-34, Jesus is *accused* of eating with "toll collectors and sinners," but the accusation, like the charge that John the Baptist had a demon, is assumed to be false. This makes it all the more striking that Jesus is portrayed as actually eating with toll collectors in Mark 2:15-17 (the only mention of toll collectors in Mark) and in Luke 19:1-10 (the Zacchaeus story may be based on Mark 2:13-17). Thus, if the portrayal of Jesus at table with toll collectors and sinners was not simply created in the development of Jesus traditions as an occasion for the Jesus-saying in Mark 2:17 ("those who are well have no need of a physician, but those who are sick"), then it may reflect the presence of a few toll collectors in certain communities (Capernaum or Jericho?). Although we have actual names in both cases, both the manuscript transmission and the history of the tradition are highly problematic in the case of Matthew/Levi in the "ideal scene" of Mark 2:13-14. The rhetorical question in Matt 21:31b does not appear to indicate anything about actual followers of Jesus (although the sequel in 21:32 and Luke 7:29 suggest that toll collectors and harlots responded to John the Baptist). It is possible that the story about the "sinner" who anointed Jesus' feet attests a prostitute who became a Jesus follower.

Renewed (Local) Social Order

The communities of the Jesus movement thought of themselves as a new social order. This was variously symbolized as "the kingdom of God," or as an alternative new "temple," but one "not made with hands" of which Jesus was the foundational "cornerstone" (Mark 14:58; 12:10), or as the restored "Israel" indicated in the miracle stories or represented by the Twelve (Mark 5-8; 3:14; 6:7; etc.), who would be "liberating" or "saving" the twelve tribes (Matt 19:28/Luke 22:28-30).

It has often been missed that "the kingdom of God" in the Gospel tradition refers not only to the ruling and redeeming activity of God, but to the renewal of society that is the intention or purpose of God's activity. This is clearly indicated in the many sayings that speak of "entering" the kingdom or presuppose that people are or can be "in" the kingdom, which obviously has concrete social "extension."[20] A more concrete sociological approach should make us more sensitive to such concrete dimensions of the "kingdom" than we may have been when it was understood more abstractly as the "rule" of God.

Perhaps most significant in terms of the development of local communities, the Jesus movement was a new "family." Those who had joined the movement, at whatever cost in terms of disruption of their previous pattern of life, received "now in this time houses and brothers and sisters and mothers and children and lands"—even if it also entailed "persecutions" (Mark 10:28–30). In social structural terms, the restoration of the people of Israel, whose life was based in villages, meant the renewal of local communities. The most fundamental social-economic unit in a traditional agrarian society such as Jewish Palestine was the patriarchal family, "the house of the father," villages being composed of several such fathers' houses, with broader patriarchal kinship patterns being important in intra- and inter-village relationships. As we have noted in the previous chapter, the heavy economic pressures on peasant family producers for tithes, taxes, and tribute, were gradually undermining and disintegrating the patriarchal family as well as local community relations generally through indebtedness and loss of land.

It is thus significant that the different strands of the synoptic tradition share a conception of renewed community as familial, but with sharp criticism of the traditional patriarchal forms.[21] Not only does actually doing the will of God count for more than kinship or immediate family relations: "Whoever does the will of God is my brother, and sister, and mother" (Mark 3:35); but the new communities are apparently those of siblings, with no authority figure prevailing among them: "You are not to be called rabbi, for you have one teacher and you are all disciples (brothers). Call no one father, for you have one father (and you are all siblings)" (Matt 23:8).[22] Specifically missing from the statement about doing the will of God is "father," and specifically forbidden in Matt 23:8–9 is calling "any man father on earth." We need not think literalistically that adult males with progeny were not welcome in the Jesus movement, or that actual fathers were either ejected from families or subordinated to some new "matriarchal" authority, or that families were no longer patrilineal. Nor was marriage or the nuclear family rejected or even devalued, as can be seen in the strictures against divorce (particularly by patriarchal prerogative; Mark 10:2–9, 10–12; Luke 16:18; Matt 5:31–32). But, clearly, relations were supposed to be egalitarian in the community, which was conceived of as an extended nonpatriarchal "family" of "siblings." The movement rejected rank, power, and prestige, valuing instead service to the community (e.g., Mark 10:25–45; Luke 11:42, 44, 46).

Instead of patriarchal authority, the tight-knit and disciplined communities had certain procedures for resolving disputes and conflicts between its members. Admonitions such as Luke 6:37–42 and 17:1–2, 3–4 attempted to head off or deal with potential conflicts between community members, but people in the movement had no illusions about conflict. Thus, Luke 12:58–59/Matt 5:25–26 provide instructions on "working things out" between two adversaries. Matt 18:15–20 provides for two further steps to be followed in resolving conflicts. The striking parallel to this passage from the rigorously disciplined community at Qumran (1QS 5:25–6:1; CD 9:2–8) suggests that we have here not some "higher ideal" but rather procedures actually practiced by local communities of the Jesus movement. With whatever foibles and tensions, the Jesus movement embodied renewal of social life in the form of highly (but openly and spontaneously) disciplined egalitarian familial communities.

Renewal of Reciprocity

One of the features of the churches that most impressed later pagan observers, even opponents such as Celsus or Lucian, was the Christians' concrete care of each other.[23] This concrete cooperation with and care of each other apparently stemmed from the earliest phase of the Jesus movement in Palestine. Jesus' own preaching of the kingdom held out the prospect of enough to eat and an end to poverty as well as joy (Luke 6:20–21), and his prayer for the kingdom petitioned for forgiveness of debts. Now there was clearly a certain tendency, discernible in Matthew (e.g., 5:3), to spiritualize somewhat these concrete references to hunger and eating, poverty and sufficiency, debts and release from debts. But there is other material in the sayings tradition that suggests that Jesus and/or his movement were concerned for the concrete alleviation of hunger, debt, and other symptoms of poverty.[24]

For example, once we push out of our consciousness the unwarranted assumption that the "enemies" in the saying about "love your enemies" are foreign political foes—that is, the Romans—then we can discern the concrete social context indicated in the content of that and related sayings in Luke 6:27–36. In fact, those sayings refer clearly to local social-economic relationships and are basically exhortations to take care of each other in local community situations.[25] Borrowing, lending, and cancellation of debts are explicitly mentioned, along with not "standing on one's rights" generally. In this connection Luke 12:22–31/Matt 6:25–33 (a passage that Theissen could understand only in terms of his itinerants) would be highly intelligible as an exhortation to people in local communities to stop being so anxious, in their actual poverty, about food and clothing, but to pursue the broader goal of social renewal, such that sustenance and shelter would be taken care of in the general cooperative well-being. The insistence elsewhere in the synoptic tradition about forgiveness had a concrete as well as a spiritual dimension. The petition in the Lord's Prayer for "forgiveness of debts" is integrally linked with a declaration of forgiving each other's debts. Lest we have any doubts about just how concretely such petitions or declarations were understood, we can observe just how vividly concrete Jesus' parable in Matt 18:23-33 is about passing along the cancellation of debts! This same concern for concrete matters such as hunger, debts, and poverty is reflected in the idealistic summarizing statements in Acts (2:44-46; 4:32). One of the forms that this concern took in Jerusalem and other urban contexts, in which some may have possessed property or things of value while many of the participants in the community probably had few possessions and no productive base, was the sale of the property or goods and the use of the proceeds to feed the whole community (Acts 2:45; 4:32-37). The story of Ananias and Sapphira (Acts 5:1-6) reflects how such sharing and redistribution of resources were integral aspects of the community discipline, sanctioned by God. The clear warning about being attached to one's possessions in certain Jesus traditions (e.g., Mark 10:17-25; Luke 12:13-21) should be understood in this context of mutual sharing and cooperation (e.g., Luke 6:38), and not as exhortation toward asceticism for its own sake. The form that this concern for concrete matters such as hunger and poverty took in (urban) intercommunity relations can be seen in Paul's highly concrete activity to alleviate poverty among "the saints" (2 Corinthians 8-9).

Thus, whether known from the early strata of Jesus teachings such as Luke 6:27-35 or by reflection in what may be late texts such as Acts 5, the Jesus movement was attempting to restore the typical peasant practices of reciprocal generosity between households. Specifically called for were cancellations of debts and mutual sharing, forms of cooperation that had likely been disintegrating under the prevailing conditions of heavy taxation, indebtedness, and even hunger, which left people unable or unwilling to respond to each others' needs and turned "neighbors" into "enemies."

Motivation and Revitalization

In order to understand the motivation of the renewal of village communities or the formation of new communities in certain cities, we must attend to the release or transformation of individual and collective energy taking place in the Jesus movement. We can discern a number of forms that this release or transformation of energy assumed, from a keen sense of fulfillment of hopes to a release from domination by demonic forces. Such an excitement over or anticipation of fulfillment may be operative also in apocalyptic literature, but it would not necessarily have taken apocalyptic form or adopted apocalyptic perspective and language. Such a sense of excitement over revitalization or fulfillment, moreover, could also find adequate expression without any elaborately developed

"Christology" and probably was not what has been conceived of by scholars as "eschatology."

Judging from all strands of the synoptic tradition examined above as sources (Q; miracle chains; pronouncement stories; Mark), the Jesus movement lived out of a keen sense of historical fulfillment or renewal. Apparently the popular tradition (parallel to the official biblical tradition) had kept alive memories of past deliverance or restoration under Moses and Elijah. A new deliverance and revitalization of the people had now been inaugurated by Jesus (see the miracle chains in Mark 5–8; Mark 9:2–8, 9–13; and see Luke 7:18–35; 22:28–30). The people knew of great events in the past; now something greater was here, something that ancient heroes themselves had longed to experience (Luke 11:31–32; 12:54–56; 10:23–24). This sense of fulfillment is perhaps most vividly expressed in the communities' celebrative meals, in which they were both continuing the table fellowship of/with Jesus and (at least some of them) anticipating the completion of the renewal of Israel or the "kingdom" or the people of God (Mark 14:25; Luke 13:28–29; *Didache* 9:3–4; cf. 1 Cor 11:24; Acts 2:46). Thus, in some cases at least, the sense of fulfillment apparently heightened the sense of anticipation of the completion of that fulfillment or renewal.

By means of the preaching of the kingdom, people who had likely been discouraged or in despair about their situation were given "a new lease on life." Especially important, surely, were a sense of hope and an unprecedented sense of their own worth. "Blessed are you poor, for yours is the kingdom!" "Ask and you shall receive!" "Even the hairs of your head are numbered!" "Of how much more value are you than the birds!" "The sabbath was made for people!" (see Luke 6:20; 11:9–13; 12:6–7, 22–31; Mark 2:23–27). Such a message may have been unusually effective when accompanied by condemnation of the rulers and officials who exploited or administered them (Luke 6:24–26; 11:39–52; 14:16–24; Mark 12:1–9).

Beginning with Jesus himself, but continued in the "mission" of his followers, personal energies were being released for creative or productive purposes through healings and exorcisms. Besides whatever release had occurred in whatever actual healings or exorcisms that had taken place, the retelling of the stories served to generate or refocus energies in the hearers. However stereotyped the miracle stories became in the course of transmission, it is clear that healings and exorcisms were prominent phenomena in at least some communities of the movement. In those circles that cultivated the exorcism stories demon-possession provided an understanding of distress and paranormal behavior. For the people who operated out of such a perspective, moreover, the exorcism of demons provided a liberation from distress. Even though such exorcism was operative primarily through a spiritual-psychological dimension, furthermore, it also had effects on the more concrete dimensions of life. "Liberated" from control by alien forces, certain people were freed for renewal of their own personal and community life. In comparison with the more systematically articulated views and calculating analysis of the Qumran community these Jesus communities were operating at a less sophisticated, popular level. Nevertheless, the conviction that the struggle with Satan/the demons was now being won implied that the kingdom of God was replacing the Roman and other instruments of Satan's domination as well as defeating the demonic forces themselves (Mark 1:23–26; 5:1–13; 3:22–27; Luke 11:14–23).

A similar release or transformation of energy for more creative use happened through the forgiveness of debts/sins proclaimed by Jesus and continued in his movement. As is evident from the discussion of indebtedness in ch 5, "debts" are also central in the more spiritual dimension of the social conditions of the Jesus movement. Analogous to concrete economic debts, spiritual or psychological "debts" were a crucial means of social control and, given the situation, of personal and (local) community deterioration. Sickness itself was rooted in both the concrete conditions of poverty and in the corresponding social-psychological conditions of depression and despair. The doctrine of sin, which paralleled demon-possession as one of the principal explanations of sickness and suffering, however, merely compounded the tendency toward personal and social disintegration. When sickness was accepted as due to one's own or one's parents' sin (Mark 2:5–9), then in effect the people were blaming themselves, while the Pharisees, high priests, or other religious authorities were "blaming the victims" of the oppressive circumstances. The link between healings and forgiveness is thus also rooted in, but provides a transformative response to, the prevailing social conditions of poverty and indebtedness. The Jesus movement not only featured as one of its central cries "forgive us our debts," but insisted that the divine forgiveness be passed along to others (Luke 7:36–50; 11:4 par.; Matt 18:21–22, 23–33).

It seems impossible to separate analysis of the Jesus movement's characteristics and activities in Jewish Palestine from that of the conditions of and for its emergence. Many of the features of the Jesus movement are also aspects of how the movement was interacting with and affecting the society which it was apparently attempting to "renew." Thus, in response to illness, self-blame, and possession by alien spiritual forces, for example, the Jesus movement continued the healing, forgiveness of sin, and exorcism initiated by Jesus. In attempting to deal with the heavy indebtedness, poverty, and despair that plagued many of the people, the

Jesus movement advocated mutual forgiveness of debts, social-economic cooperation, and other forms of reciprocity in local communities. In reaction to the disintegration of local village communities and the decline of patriarchal authority, the Jesus movement apparently revitalized local life in terms of egalitarian nonpatriarchal familial communities. In response to despair over declining and disintegrating conditions of life, finally, the Jesus movement appears to have generated a renewal of individual and group spirits, one that could motivate some of the other aspects of the revitalization of social life.

Notes

1. On both the use of Synoptic Gospel materials and the picture of facets of the Jesus movement for which they provide evidence, I must express my debt to three recent works: H. C. Kee, *Community of the New Age* (London: SCM, 1977); W. H. Kelber, *The Oral and the Written Gospel* (Philadelphia: Fortress, 1983); and Burton L. Mack, *A Myth of Innocence* (Philadelphia: Fortress, 1988).

2. Note the utterly vague terms used with reference to those who supposedly supply the link between Jesus and early Christianity: e.g., "the eschatological community," "those gathered around Jesus," or "the band of disciples," e.g., in G. Aulen, *Jesus in Contemporary Historical Research* (London: SPCK, 1976) 87; E. Schweizer, *Church Order in the New Testament* (London: SCM, 1961) 20, 25.

3. Theissen, *Sociology,* 8.

4. Cf. H. Koester, *Introduction to the New Testament* (2 vols.; Philadelphia: Fortress, 1982) 2:86–89; Mack, *Myth of Innocence,* 88–91.

5. See particularly John S. Kloppenborg, *The Formation of Q* (Philadelphia: Fortress, 1987).

6. Done with subtlety by both Burton L. Mack, "The Kingdom that Didn't Come," in *Society of Biblical Literature 1988 Seminar Papers,* ed. D. Lull (Atlanta: Scholars Press, 1988) 608–35; and John S. Kloppenborg, "Redactional Strata and Social History in the Sayings Gospel Q," forthcoming in *Semeia* (1989).

7. Kloppenborg, *Formation of Q,* 166–70. References to Q material are by chapter and verse in Luke.

8. So also Kloppenborg, *Formation of Q,* 119.

9. For more extensive critique of the division of Q into "sapiential" and "apocalyptic" strata, see R. Horsley, "Questions about Redaction Strata and the Social Relations Reflected in Q," *Society of Biblical Literature 1989 Seminar Papers,* ed. D. Lull (Atlanta: Scholars Press, 1989) 186–203; and see Kloppenborg's response (pp. 204–15).

10. See Horsley, *Jesus and the Spiral of Violence,* 200–202, on why the passage should be translated in this way.

11. See further ch 3 above and ch 7 below.

12. See now the discussions in Mack, *Myth of Innocence,* chs 7 and 8. What follows is heavily indebted to Mack's excellent critical summary of recent scholarship on miracle and pronouncement stories.

13. In an imaginative and sophisticated analysis and reconstruction based on just such a projection, Mack traces the social histories of different Jesus movements or communities

that find expression respectively in the pronouncement stories, the miracle stories, and the sayings source; see *Myth of Innocence*, esp. chs 3, 7, and 8.

14. On the prophetic orientation exhibited by scriptural quotations and allusions in Mark (which seldom cites the Torah itself), see Kee, *Community of the New Age*, 45–49.

15. Cf. Mack, *Myth of Innocence*, 198.

16. This has long been the case in German studies of Q such as Theissen's. In 1987 three different dissertations focused specifically on the Q mission passage were completed: Jirair Tashjian, "The Social Setting of the Mission Charge in Q" (Claremont Graduate School); Risto Uro, "Sheep Among the Wolves: A Study on the Mission Instructions of Q" (University of Helsinki); and Leif Vaage, "Q: The Ethos and Ethics of an Itinerant Intelligence" (Claremont Graduate School). (See the convenient summary by Tashjian, "The Social Setting of the Q Mission: Three Dissertations," in *Society of Biblical Literature 1988 Seminar Papers*, ed. D. Lull [Atlanta: Scholars Press, 1988] 636–44). Vaage's dissertation is a veritable compendium of Cynic parallels.

17. Vaage, "Traces of an Itinerant Intelligence," 280.

18. On these points of comparison, respectively, see Vaage, "Traces of an Itinerant Intelligence," 303, 283–84, 287, 288.

19. See W. O. Walker, "Jesus and the Tax Collectors," *Journal of Biblical Literature* 97 (1978) 221–38; and Horsley, *Jesus and the Spiral of Violence*, 212–23.

20. See further S. Aalen, "'Reign' and 'House' in the Kingdom of God in the Gospels," *New Testament Studies* 8 (1961–62) 215–40.

21. Original analysis of this material was made by Elisabeth Schüssler Fiorenza, *In Memory of Her: A Feminist Theological Reconstruction of Christian Origins* (New York: Crossroad, 1983) esp. 140–51.

22. Translation from Schüssler Fiorenza, *In Memory of Her*, 149–50.

23. E. R. Dodds, *Pagan and Christian in an Age of Anxiety* (Cambridge: Cambridge University Press, 1965) 136–38.

24. Some of these Theissen could relate only to the radical ethos of intentional itinerants.

25. See my arguments in "Ethics and Exegesis: 'Love your Enemies' and the Doctrine of Non-violence," *Journal of the American Academy of Religion* 54 (1986) 3–31; or *Jesus and the Spiral of Violence*, 259–75.

7 ◊ Conflicts, Comparisons, and Catalysts _____

Conflicts with the Rulers

It is not surprising that a movement responding to the social malaise of the people came into conflict with the rulers. Insofar as the Jesus movement was alleviating the problems that were rooted in the fundamental social structural conflict in Jewish Palestine, as exacerbated by Roman imperial rule, it might appear that it would have mitigated the basic class conflict. The very opposite was the case, however (precisely contrary to Theissen's claim). It has been pointed out that in traditional agrarian empires, peasant villages or towns receive little or nothing of benefit to their lives in return for the tribute, taxes, or rents that they render up to the rulers – indeed, that they would usually be far better off if allowed to handle their own affairs according to their own traditional ways.[1] We can imagine that ruling groups might have been pleased to have vital and productive local communities. But the autonomy of local communities could also have been a threat to central ruling institutions and rulers, particularly if those increasingly vital and autonomous local communities had developed an awareness of the exploitative relationship to which they were subjected. Whether because of its aggressive criticism of the rulers and their retainers or simply because the rulers were threatened by it, the Jesus movement further exacerbated rather than mitigated the fundamental structural conflicts.

Rejection of Ruling Institutions

Modern biblical scholarship has tended to play down or even to deny that the Jesus movement came into sharp conflict with the ruling institutions of Jewish Palestine. This may be due partly to the modern separation of "religion" from political-economic life, and perhaps it also reflects the modern "concordat" between "religion" and "politics" that they will not interfere in each others' jurisdictions. As long as the Temple and high priesthood are viewed as only religious and Jesus' action in the Temple,

130

for example, understood as a "cleansing" or, at most, an attack on certain "abuses," it is possible to avoid serious implications of substantive social-structural conflict. Arguments for the absence of any serious conflict with the Jewish ruling authorities and institutions are usually based primarily, if not exclusively, on a few passages in the early chapters of Acts. But the texts usually cited do not indicate loyalty to the Temple and its officials even in a supposedly separable religious dimension, much less in general. As has been noted above, Acts 2:46 does not indicate that Jesus' followers were engaged in Temple worship. A careful reading of Lucan portrayals in the early chapters of Acts indicates that when Jesus' followers are praying or "breaking bread" they are not in the Temple at all, and when they are in the Temple area they are there to preach about Jesus, to do healings and exorcisms, and generally to build their movement (Acts 3:1–11; 5:12–16). As the principal public meeting place in Jerusalem, the Temple courtyard was the obvious place for such activities. But the idealizing Lucan summary passages about the piety and solidarity of the earliest Jesus community in Jerusalem (e.g., Acts 2:43–47; 4:32–35; 5:42) provide no evidence whatever that Jesus' followers were devoted adherents of Temple sacrifices, much less loyal and obedient to the high priests. Because of the Davidic monarchy and then the high priesthood centered in the Temple, Jerusalem and the Temple had become the symbolic center of Israel as well as the center of political-economic power. Jesus' climactic confrontation with the authorities and subsequent trial and execution had recently taken place there. And in Luke's own literary-theological scheme it is important to have the movement begin in and then expand from Jerusalem, in which the central building and institution was the Temple. Even if Luke's idealizing summaries do reflect some historical activity, it is understandable that some of Jesus' followers may have centered a continuing "mission" to Israel there. But those standard references from the early chapters of Acts simply do not provide evidence that the Jesus movement recognized the Temple and high priesthood as ruling institutions.

In fact, there is a good deal of evidence to the contrary, that is, that the Jesus movement not only came into conflict with the rulers, but that it rejected them as well, and that the rulers responded with a certain degree of repression. The only question is how that evidence should be interpreted. That is, did the Jesus movement reject just the rulers themselves, or did it also reject the ruling institutions? There is some evidence for the latter as well as the former in Q and pre-Marcan traditions, the primary sources we have been using for the Jesus movement. But that evidence is supplemented by other material from the Synoptic Gospels and by certain information from Acts that indicates or presupposes sharp conflict between the Jesus movement and the ruling institutions. Among the traditions used by Mark there is a considerable amount of material in which Jesus pronounces judgment against either the high priestly rulers (Mark 12:1–9) or the Temple (Mark 11:15–17; 13:2; 14:58; 15:29–30). In Q stands the lament of doom over the ruling city of Jerusalem (Luke 13:34–35/Matt 23:37–38; cf. Luke 19:43–44a). To the degree that these traditions stemmed originally from Jesus, it is significant that the movement transmitted them. To the degree that they originated in the Jesus communities, they become even clearer indicators that the early Jesus movement itself rejected the existing ruling institutions along with the incumbent high priests. In any case, it appears that the Jesus movement clearly anticipated and even proclaimed divine judgment against the established order headed by Temple and high priests.

Jesus' Palestinian followers had apparently also taken seriously the tradition that "the sons are free" from the duty of paying taxes to the Temple, as indicated in the special Matthean tradition behind Matt 17:24–26. The utterly miraculous ad hoc way in which the half-shekel tax is paid in this tradition (in order not to give offense – with a wink) is hardly a paradigm for the early churches to imitate; in the context of the parable in question form, that "the sons are free" clearly states the freedom of Israelites from any claim by the Temple or high priesthood.

Considering that Jesus' crucifixion was action taken by the Jewish and Roman ruling authorities, it should not be surprising that the Jesus movement's very understandings of Jesus are inseparably related to their conflict with the rulers. In contrast with the abstract way in which "Christology" is often discussed, the early articulations of the significance of Jesus must be understood in the concrete social context in which they were embedded. The community behind Q understood Jesus (and John the Baptist) as the latest and climactic prophet in a long history of prophets sent to Israel but rejected, even killed, particularly by the rulers (Luke 7:18–34; 11:47–51; 13:34–35). Precisely because it had killed the prophets, the ruling house itself was doomed. Although there is no corresponding direct prophetic condemnation of the rulers in the Marcan pronouncement stories, the latter do articulate a good deal of direct conflict with the authorities (Mark 9:9–13; 11:27–33; 12:13–17; 12:41–44). Mark itself brings the conflict to the fore explicitly and dramatically, whether in the "plot" of the narrative as a whole, as the conflict escalates toward the arrest, trial, and crucifixion of Jesus, or in particular passages such as the parable told against the rulers, the arrest and trial scenes, and the pronouncement of judgment against Temple and rulers (12:1–9; 14:43–65; esp. 14:58 and 62).

Even the crucifixion-resurrection/exaltation (and return!) Christology that is more standard in scholarly discussions is an expression of this basic conflict with the authorities. Peter's speeches as we have them in Acts are the compositions of Luke, but they contain and/or reflect earlier traditions (as can be seen, e.g., in Acts 3:20, where Jesus is only the "messiah-designate," a tradition that Luke did not bother to conform with the standard understanding of Jesus as the Christ since at least his baptism). These proclamations of the resurrection, exaltation, and return (as "messiah" or "lord" or "savior") of their leader, whom the Jewish rulers (in collaboration with the Romans) had just executed, were tantamount to declarations of God's rejection and imminent judgment of the established order (see, e.g., Acts 2:24–36; 3:15, 21; 4:10–11; 5:30–31).[2] We know from Paul and other early traditions that the resurrection-exaltation of Jesus and his proclamation as the expected messiah were among the earliest Palestinian understandings of Jesus. These have often been reduced in significance to a primarily "religious" dimension. Once they are placed in the context of the fundamental structural conflict that divided Jewish Palestine, however, the political implications could not be clearer. The one who was killed by the authorities has been vindicated by God, even enthroned as God's own regent, who is coming in judgment. Paul presupposes such an understanding of Jesus. And although "(the day of) the son of man" in Q (Luke 17:24, 30, 32) is a reference to judgment but not necessarily to Jesus, "the Son of man" was understood as Jesus returning in judgment in other circles or communities, as indicated in Mark 13:26 and the traditions utilized by Matthew (e.g., Matt 25:31–46).

The "speech" of Stephen (Acts 7), finally, may provide another link between the traditions of Jesus' prophecies against the Temple and high priesthood and the other fragments of evidence that his followers continued that stance. Interpretation of this speech, taking its cue from Luke's description of Stephen as one of the "Hellenists" and from the phrase "houses not made with hands" (Acts 7:48), has often found here a spiritualizing critique of Temple worship as such. But whatever Luke's Hellenistic shaping of the speech, its substance and overall thrust are a dramatic rejection of the Jerusalem Temple and those loyal to it on the basis of an appeal to the paradigmatic events of the liberation from Egyptian bondage led by Moses. "Stephen" here articulates a position that identifies with the Mosaic exodus-covenant(-conquest) tradition, that of the free working of the Holy Spirit and the prophetic challenge to the establishment, over against the Solomonic tradition of the Temple establishment, which is viewed as virtually illegitimate and not really sanctioned by God (7:44–50).

That the Palestinian Jesus movement rejected the ruling institutions, particularly the Temple and high priesthood, is made all the more credible by the high priestly rulers' continued attempts to suppress the movement. Judging from the recurrent theme of persecution in the synoptic tradition, attempts at suppression must have been frequent (Mark 13:9–11; Matt 5:44; 10:23; Luke 6:22; 12:11–12). Stephen was probably not the only preacher to have been executed (Acts 7:54–60). Surely not all of those persecutions and attacks were due to direct action by the high priestly regime. But other evidence, some indirect, some more direct, indicates repressive activity by the priestly rulers in Jerusalem. In Luke's portrayal in Acts, the high priestly rulers understand exactly what Peter and others are pronouncing. Even if Luke makes the movement appear more extensive and more of a threat than it was, surely the high priests and their cohorts recognized the threat posed by the followers of Jesus of Nazareth, just as they recognized the threat posed by the prophecy of Jesus son of Hananiah. Although we cannot rely on the details of Luke's portrayal, it is clear that the high priestly rulers periodically took repressive action against the Jesus movement. Luke's picture of an intense "face-off" between the priestly rulers and Jesus' followers in Jerusalem itself may be overly schematic, but his portrayal of the systematic attempt to pursue and root out Jesus' followers within and outside of Palestine is corroborated by Paul's own testimony (Acts 8:1–3; 9:1–2; Gal 1:13–14). Besides the high priestly rulers, the Roman client king (Herod) Agrippa I (41–44 C.E.) also took action to suppress the movement, executing James the brother of John and very nearly Peter as well (Acts 12:1–9). Later the ruling high priest, Ananus, while momentarily free of the Roman governor's oversight in 62 C.E., took the extraordinary step of bringing James, the brother of Jesus and leader of the "Jerusalem" community, before the Sanhedrin and having him stoned to death (Josephus, *Antiquities* 20.200).[3]

Conflict with the Pharisees

In contrast with its conflict with the rulers, which has been played down, the Jesus movement's conflict with the Pharisees has been readily recognized. It has also been somewhat misrepresented, however, as one involving legalism and/or achievement of righteousness through rigorous observance of the law, or as having to do somehow only with "religious" issues such as "ceremonial law," or as a competition between two *parallel* religious "sects" or "renewal movements." Against the background of a more precisely understood social structure in Jewish Palestine, it is possible to surmise more adequately what the Jesus movement's conflict with the Pharisees (and other retainers) was all about.

The Jesus movement in Palestine may well have come into sharper conflict with the Pharisees than had Jesus himself. As with the Synoptic Gospel traditions of judgment against the Temple and high priests, so with the sharp attacks against the Pharisees or lawyers in Q (Luke 11:39-52): insofar as they stem from Jesus, it is significant that they were preserved and perhaps even elaborated by his followers; insofar as these traditions stem from certain Jesus communities, it is all the clearer evidence that the Jesus movement did not recognize the authority of the established teachers, lawyers, scribes, or other "retainers" of the government. The special Matthean tradition in 23:8-9 indicates that at the very least certain Jesus communities no longer recognized the usual authorities (no "teacher" apart from Jesus himself and no "father" apart from God). But traditions both in Q and in the Marcan pronouncement stories are even sharper, actually declaring judgment against the scribes and/or Pharisees. The Pharisees "make void the word of God" through their "traditions of the elders," in a way that, for example, leads people to neglect the customary economic support of parents, and the scribes themselves "devour" the already meager livelihood of widows (Mark 7:9-13; 12:38-40). The Q people are concerned about the Pharisees' ritual cleanliness not in itself but insofar as it functions as a veil or diversion from their "extortion and rapacity" (Luke 11:39). The Pharisees' concern about the tithes (that is, the taxes) on even minor things such as mint and herbs indicates just how rigorous they were on the more substantive products such as the grain needed for simple subsistence. Hence, they are blind guides who ignore the weightier matters of the Torah such as justice and mercy/love, while laying heavy burdens on the people, including rigorous enforcement of the tithing laws (Luke 11:42, 46). The whole set of sayings in Luke 11:39-48 pronounces woes against the Pharisees and lawyers because of some way in which they are contributing to the exploitation of the people and/or are helping legitimate the established order, including their own positions of privilege.

If communities of the Jesus movement did indeed reject the authority of "the scribes and Pharisees," then it would not be at all surprising that they came into sharp conflict with such "retainers" and that this conflict intensified in the early years of the movement. Scribes and Pharisees would have been the representatives of the government that the local communities actually dealt with. The Jesus movement would have been seriously threatening their very function or role in the social system as well as their "authority." The conflict had serious political-economic and "professional" as well as religious dimensions.

Thus it should not be surprising that, as noted just above, before much time had elapsed after the execution of Jesus, the zealous Pharisee Saul was energetically involved in attempting to suppress the movement then already spreading beyond the borders of Palestine (Gal 1:13–14; Acts 8:1–3). The continuing conflict between the Jesus movement and the Pharisees is reflected in Mark's portrayal of an escalating struggle between Jesus and the authorities in which the Pharisees, apparently as the representatives of the high priestly government on the scene in Galilee, observe, then accuse, and finally test Jesus (Mark 2:6, 16–18, 24; 3:2, 22; 7:1–5; 8:11), then gradually yield to the Jerusalem authorities themselves, the high priests, elders, and scribes, who seek (with the Pharisees' assistance, 12:13) to entrap and destroy Jesus (11:18, 27; 14:1, 43; 15:1).

Once we discern more precisely the concrete social structure of Jewish Palestine, the conflict between the Jesus movement and the Pharisees appears not as a competition between two religious reform movements but as one between local Galilean communities and representatives of the central governing authorities. As spokesperson, Jesus defends the simple "commandment of God" against "the traditions of the elders" (Mark 7:1–13), defends local conservative conventions based in biblical traditions against the "great tradition" (officially established scripture) of the professional scholars, and appeals to "popular tradition" versus the official interpretation of scripture (Mark 12:35–37). The Jesus traditions represent local people's interests (justice and love, and direct appeal to divine authority) against the interests of the central ruling groups (rigorous observance of tithing regulations, timely payment of the Roman tribute, and the established ruling institutions, Luke 11:42, 46, 52; Mark 12:1–17; 11:27–33).

Awareness of the concrete political situation in Roman-ruled Palestine can also help explain why the Hillelite Pharisees were able to establish themselves after the Jewish rebellion, while the Jesus movement was "a failure."[4] Following the Roman reconquest of Jewish Palestine, there was a "socio-political" power vacuum. Rome usually governed provincial societies or cities through the native aristocracies. But the Jewish priestly aristocracy and the Herodian princes were now either dead or not a viable option for Jewish Palestine. Other movements were eliminated during the Roman reconquest. The Pharisees and surely other former "retainers," however, survived; and since they included many trained in interpretation and application of the Jewish Torah, they were able to provide some sort of political infrastructure to govern the largely rural Jewish society. In contrast with the Pharisees, early Palestinian "Christianity" was a popular movement, its leaders not formally trained in application of the traditions (Torah) of the society. The Pharisees "succeeded" because the Romans were convinced that they could be useful in the governing of Jewish Palestine. The Jesus movement may have been doing well in Palestine—we have little evidence to go on—but the Roman reconquest of Jewish Palestine in 67-70 may have weakened it, along with all other movements except for the Pharisees.[5]

Comparisons with Other Movements

Comparisons with other movements in Jewish Palestine may further elucidate certain characteristics of the Jesus movement, particularly its conflict with the ruling institutions.[6] Comparisons with the Qumran community are the easiest because we now have such an abundance of literary sources from Qumran itself and because there are striking similarities in some key features of the two movements. Both movements rejected the established high priestly rulers. The two movements also share particular features such as celebrative common meals and tight community discipline. The Qumran community provides us an earlier movement that was living in eager expectation of imminent fulfillment of longings for a better state of affairs. And the Dead Sea Scrolls provide us with a systematically articulated form of a view of the people as caught in the struggle between the divine and demonic forces, which helps us appreciate the more popular form of an apparently similar view held in at least some of the Jesus communities.

Once such similarities are discerned, however, exploration of the social differences between the two movements may be helpful in reaching a more precise sense of the Jesus movement. Judging from the literature it produced, including some of its central imagery, the Qumran community must have been led by and perhaps been comprised heavily of people from priestly families and men with scribal-scholarly training and orientation. Thus it appears, initially at least, to have been a movement led or strongly influenced by former priestly and scholarly retainers who had rejected the incumbent high priestly rulers, but not the institutions of high priesthood and Temple, which they anticipated restoring at the divinely determined time in the indefinite future. But there appears to be neither priestly nor scribal influence among the earliest followers of Jesus. Moreover, while some among the Jesus movement may have thought of their communities or the people in general as the true "temple," in language similar to that found at Qumran, the Jesus movement had no apparent expectation of a restored Temple and high priesthood.[7] While both movements display a rigorous community discipline, the tone at Qumran was extremely tense, whereas the Jesus movement exhibits a remarkable spontaneity in interpersonal relations, one that appears to be the motive force behind the rigorous intracommunity expectations.

The most striking difference socially, however, was that the communities of the Jesus movement remained within the society, facing all the conflicts that entailed, while the Essenes had simply left the society and its conflicts behind in pursuit of their own utopian life. Theissen labeled the Essenes as "radical" (while the local "sympathizers" of the radical wandering charismatics were "moderate" in their "compromise with the world"). But if radical means strong group discipline, such as the sharing of possessions (not the renouncing) and working out interpersonal disputes, and if "it would have been easier to put the more radical pattern into effect in an oasis in the desert than in the midst of society," then the communities of the Jesus movement were the more radical. They were living not in "compromise with the world," but in openness to and interaction with the world.

The popular "messianic" movements were, like the Jesus movement at the outset, comprised of peasants. Acclaiming one of their number "king," they took direct action to free themselves of domination by the Romans and their client rulers, Herodian kings in 4 B.C.E. and the priestly aristocracy in the case of Simon bar Giora in 68–70 C.E. The Jesus movement was more of what political scientists might call a "social revolution," which, for some, was apparently based on the assumption that God was already taking care of the "political revolution" (overthrow of the established regime in the now victorious struggle against Satan or in the impending judgment).[8] Both the popular messianic movements and the Jesus movement were interested in establishing the people's autonomous life free of domination by the alien and domestic rulers and, presumably, under the direct rule of God (i.e., assuming that the "messianic movements" in 4 B.C.E. and 68–70 C.E. took the form of popular kingship in the tradition of Saul or the early David, not that of elevated and permanently institutionalized monarchy such as was established by the later David and Solomon). The popular messianic movements, especially those of Athronges in Judea in 4 B.C.E. and of Simon bar Giora in 68–70 C.E. (as well as that of Simeon bar Kochba in 132–135) managed to maintain popular control of certain areas for as long as two or three years before the Romans could reconquer them.

This may lead us to speculate concerning the degree to which the local communities in the Jesus movement may have been able to maintain relatively autonomous direction of their efforts at renewal, particularly in Galilee or in the outlying areas of Judea. A movement such as Simon bar Giora's had a relatively free hand (at least for a few years) and could proclaim the release of (debt-)slaves and probably enforce it. The Jesus movement, having only limited local autonomy, could not have enforced such a decree, but it could work out the mutual cancellation of debts locally and attempt to alleviate the worst symptoms of poverty. The popular messianic movements, of course, ended with the death of the popularly acclaimed kings, obviously because the Romans had killed or otherwise suppressed the participants as well. Although it exacerbated conflicts and was persecuted from time to time, the Jesus movement survived in Palestine for a much longer time, since no active rebellion and Roman reconquest were involved (although some members or communities of the Jesus movement may well have been victims of the Roman reconquest in 67–70).

The Zealots proper,[9] who emerged as a coalition of brigand bands in Jerusalem during the winter of 67–68, in the midst of the great revolt, were also peasants, in this case fugitives from the Roman army's advance through northwestern Judea as it reconquered the country. It is difficult and perhaps pointless to make comparisons between a movement that was the product of war and one that emerged in a more normal time, however difficult that time was for the people. The Zealots proper, like the Jesus movement, asserted autonomy from the established rulers (at that point the priestly aristocratic junta conducting a holding-action until they could arrange a settlement with the Romans). But the form that their restoration or renewal of the independence of the people took was very unlike that of the Jesus movement. The Zealots established a popularly elected hierocracy. Apparently accepting the traditional (biblical) forms of governance in Judea, they were attempting to restore the Jewish hierocracy to its proper Zadokite leadership and to its proper popularly elected (by lot) basis.

There is no indication, however, that people in the Jesus movement thought of theocracy in terms of hierocracy, however egalitarian. It is at least conceivable that this difference between the Jesus movement and the Zealots proper can be explained geographically-historically. That is, some Judean peasants may have accepted the traditional form of priestly governance while (for the very reason of that acceptance of the sacred traditions) rejecting both oppressive established priestly rule and rule by illegitimate (esp. non-Zadokite) families. Galilean peasants, from among whom the Jesus movement originated, may have been less accepting even of hierocracy, since they had been subjected to the Jerusalem high priesthood only four generations previously by the expansionist early Hasmonean regime. For them the direct, liberating rule (kingdom) of God was good news. But priestly rule only meant domination and taxation by a relatively distant and semi-alien Temple establishment.

The Catalysts of New Community

The question of how the Jesus movement was spread and led has been left until last because there has been insufficient appreciation of the community form of the movement by Theissen and other individualistically oriented interpreters. Because the evidence for the leadership of the movement is so limited, it is all the more important to set it into as complete a context as possible. Acts provides some idealized portraits, primarily of the apostle Peter preaching in Jerusalem and Paul traveling and preaching in Hellenistic cities of the eastern Mediterranean. Much more relevant to the Jesus movement in Palestine, however, is the commission Jesus gives the disciples in Mark 6:8–11 and Q/Luke 10:(2–)4–11– that is, the principal texts on which Theissen based his sketch of the "wandering charismatics" and on which others now base their hypothesis about Cynic-like itinerants. Both of these alternatives, however, focus on something called *ethos*, without really carrying out an analysis of *roles*, as would be appropriate for any question of leadership (cf. the critique of Theissen in ch 2 above). The question is how the envoys addressed in these texts can be adequately understood sociologically. That is, how can they be understood in the historical social context, taking fully into account both the characterisics of the Jesus movement within the broader setting of the social structure and the historical traditions of the people that might have influenced the particular social form or patterns of action evident in the movement? We can ask the obvious questions that Theissen never asked: in what way those charged in Mark 6:8–11 and Luke 10:3–11 were "charismatic" and why they were itinerant. But we may also want to question the utilization of a concept such as "charismatic" that is so widely used in vague and varied ways.

Apparently not just Jesus himself but a number of his disciples also had powers of exorcism and healing. This is clearly presupposed in Q 10:9 ("heal the sick . . ."–usually deemed an early part of the "mission discourse"),[10] and understood as a commissioning by Jesus for healing activity in towns and villages. The Marcan framing of the parallel mission tradition in 6:7 and the other sending out of disciples in Mark 3:14–15 reflect the same presupposition: the envoys are given "authority over unclean spirits." One aspect of the role of these disciples was thus to be the mediators of healing powers, which brought restoration of personal life and, by implication, renewal of social interaction in those persons' communities. In the case of exorcisms, this also involved the driving out of alien forces that had "possessed" the persons' lives. Closely linked with healing and exorcism was the preaching of these disciples. Besides continuing and extending the "mighty works" of Jesus, they were continuing and extending his preaching of the presence of the kingdom of God. The casual use of the term "charismatic" in an exceedingly vague manner in popular discourse makes its continued sociological usage highly problematic. Weber used the concept for a type of authority or domination and as a way of understanding social change. Even in Weber's usage, however, the concept was overly focused on the individual, such that charisma was "a certain quality of an individual personality by virtue of which he is set apart from ordinary men and treated as endowed with supernatural, superhuman, or at least specifically exceptional powers or qualities."[11]

With specific reference to movements that in some way challenge the established order and lead to social change, movements which bear at least some similarities to the Jesus movement, Peter Worsley has attempted to adapt Weber's concept into a more genuinely sociological one that might be serviceable for historical analysis.[12] Only to an individualistic beholder would charisma appear to be an attribute or quality of an individual personality. Charisma or charismatic leadership rather involves a social relationship. Leader(s) articulate(s) the aspirations of followers in a particular message (and often in a paradigmatic personal transformation as well). Hence, an interactionist concept of charismatic leadership is necessary.[13] Moreover, in order for a movement to develop, certain modes of social action (and even a form of organization) have to emerge from the interaction of leader(s) and followers. The "catalytic function [of the charismatic leader] is to convert latent solidarities into active ritual and political action."[14]

This means, however, that the particular presuppositions, frustrations, and aspirations of the (potential) followers are of fundamental significance, and that the message and modes of action of the leader(s) are culturally conditioned. The social forms that movements take, including leadership roles, are socially conditioned, that is, will depend on social expectations and cultural traditions. Considering how important the traditions of the people were in Jewish Palestine, this consideration should lead us to examine the way in which particular traditions may have influenced or informed the modes of interaction and action led by the preachers and healers of the Jesus movement.

An important clue to the way Jesus' envoys may have been understood and to the tradition-informed roles they may have played, could lie in the portrayal of Jesus in Q and pre-Marcan miracle catenae, as examined in the previous chapter. Q traditions such as Luke 3:7-9, 16-17; 7:18-28; 11:47-51; 13:34-35 clearly represent Jesus (and John the Baptist as well) as the climactic figure in the long line of Israelite prophets who came into sharp conflict with the rulers. Recent analyses of Q suggest that the Q people understood themselves similarly, as indicated perhaps in Luke 6:23b.[15] In the pre-Marcan catenae of miracle stories, the underlying paradigm for the healings and exorcisms appears to be the Elijah-Elisha stories, with Moses and the exodus also in the background. Assuming that the evangelist "Mark" is responsible for the story of the transfiguration, the appearance of Moses and Elijah with Jesus only makes vividly explicit what was already clearly implicit in the pre-Marcan traditions— that Jesus was understood as a prophetic figure restoring the life of the people just as Elijah had done.[16] Our principal sources for the Jesus movement thus point us to traditions of prophetic redemption and challenge to the rulers as the cultural models that informed the understanding of Jesus' social role. Insofar as those same sources portray the disciples as commissioned to continue Jesus' principal activities of preaching and healing, it seems clear that we should attend to that same distinctive Israelite-Jewish cultural tradition.

Mainly from Josephus, but confirmed by the brief references in Acts, we know that the tradition of prophets as leaders of redemption or challenge to the rulers was very much alive during the mid-first century C.E. A generation after Jesus of Nazareth, the "crude peasant" prophet Jesus son of Hananiah pronounced woes of divine judgment against the ruling city of Jerusalem (*War* 6.300–309). Even more striking are the movements headed by Theudas and "the Egyptian," who, like Moses and/or Joshua of old, led their followers out to experience the divine deliverance of the new exodus and/or conquest.[17] We have so little information on these popular prophetic movements themselves, of course, that it is difficult to make precise comparisons with the Jesus movement. For example, we have no idea how much organizing and recruitment went on before the prophets led their followers out to experience God's new acts of deliverance, although there must have been some organizing, considering the numbers involved. Also, these movements were so short-lived that comparison with any continued organizing activity is impossible. However, an exploration of the tradition that informed the popular prophetic movements may be highly suggestive for our understanding of the catalysts of the Jesus movement.

The tradition of prophetic figures leading movements of liberation started with Moses and Joshua, continued through the judges, such as Gideon, Deborah, and Samuel, and then reemerged with prophets such as Ahijah the Shilonite (1 Kings 11), Elijah, and Elisha. Hengel has directed our attention back to this tradition precisely in order to understand distinctive features of the "followers" of Jesus. More particularly, he argues that Jesus' calling of disciples can be understood in terms of the prototype of Elijah's call of Elisha.[18] The "calling" of the disciples, moreover, was a *meaningful task*, again understandable in terms of prophetic prototypes, including Moses' leadership of the exodus and a reference to Elijah's commission to foment revolution in Israel in 1 Kgs 19:15-18, the passage that immediately precedes the calling of Elisha.[19] He does not draw out the connection more explicitly, of course, (a) because he insists that Jesus confined his "call" only to *individuals*, not wanting to stir up the masses, as the popular prophets or messiahs had done,[20] and (b) because he still understands the kingdom of God preached by Jesus as referring to an imminently approaching "eschatological event."[21]

If we were less driven to rescue Jesus from political implications and to make him appear absolutely *sui generis*, then perhaps it would be less threatening to view his movement also in the light of the tradition behind the popular prophetic movements. While the mid-first-century C.E. prophetic movements themselves may appear somewhat fantastic (and less "political") in their pursuit of "the eschatological event," the tradition behind them was explicitly political. The "meaningful task" to which Elijah called Elisha and to which many other "sons of the prophets" were called was a sustained popular struggle against the oppressive (and to a degree alien) regime of Ahab and Jezebel. At one point in the biblical story "the sons of the prophets" had to go into hiding because of the regime's repressive measures (1 Kgs 18:4). It is fairly clear from the narrative in 1 Kings 17-19 and 2 Kings 1-9 that Elijah and Elisha were leading an effort to maintain the traditional (but now threatened) Yahwist or Mosaic covenantal way of life in the village communities of Israel. If we were to suspend modern individualistic concerns and focus less on the individual disciples of Jesus and more on the collective mission or "meaningful task" with which they were charged, then the movement led by Elijah and Elisha provides us with the cultural tradition which could very well have informed Jesus and his movement in some way, perhaps even as a historical prototype for their own mission of restoring or revitalizing the people of Israel. The reference to the roles of "those who followed" Jesus as "liberating" or "effecting justice for the twelve tribes of Israel in the restoration" in the Q text behind Matt 19:28/Luke 22:28-30[22] points precisely in this direction and can be understood as a new manifestation of the tradition of prophetic revitalization of the people.

Perhaps because of its heavy dependence on literature and its transmission, New Testament studies has concentrated on the tradents of Jesus traditions in its reconstruction of the Jesus movement. The latter, however, took the social form of local communities, either as revitalized village communities or as newly formed communities in larger towns or cities. Reconstruction of the Jesus movement as comprised primarily of "wandering charismatics" or Cynic-like itinerant beggars leaves out of consideration the broader dimensions evident in the sources and leaves us unable to account for the renewal or formation of the local communities, that is, for the very process of "group-formation" that is presupposed in the literature produced by this vigorous new movement that emerged in first-century Jewish Palestine. The leadership of this movement can be understood most appropriately not as individualistic itinerants but as prophetic catalysts of the broader movement.

Notes

1. John Kautsky, *The Politics of Aristocratic Empires* (Chapel Hill: University of North Carolina Press, 1982) ch 12.

2. If the author of Acts is politically apologetic, as is often assumed, then how much sharper must have been the Jesus movement's condemnation of those who had refused to hear the prophetic message of Jesus, arrested him, and now persecuted his followers.

3. Thus, what Theissen labels the "scapegoating" of the Jesus movement (112–13), including the persecution under Herod Agrippa I, can more readily be explained as the typical and understandable attempt by the ruling authorities to suppress popular discontent and especially movements representing an alternative to the established government and cultic order. There is, further, simply no evidence that "the Christians belonged to the peace party." It is doubtful in the first place, from a close reading of Josephus, whether there was any "peace party" apart from the Jewish ruling groups, i.e., the high priestly and the Herodian families, both of whom ordinarily collaborated in the Roman imperial order anyhow. Furthermore, there is virtually no evidence on what the Jesus movement did in response to the outbreak of widespread revolt in 66 C.E.

4. Theissen, 113–14. It seems facile for Theissen to speak of success or failure of a movement apart from some attempt to consider its "chances," given not only the inherent conflicts in the situation but also the effect of external "factors," something he does not do.

5. To speculate much on other causes of the "failure" of the Jesus movement is simply that, to speculate.

6. Theissen portrays the Jesus movement as coming into being during a comparatively peaceful period prior to the increase in tensions. His portrayal of Palestinian Jewish society feeling threatened and uncertain at mid-first century then suddenly sets the Jesus movement off by itself over against the whole (rest of) "society." This portrayal, however, focuses narrowly and superficially on the particular, overt conflicts involving the Jesus movement and ignores the more profound underlying conflicts. Contrary to Theissen's statements, *most* of the "renewal movements" we know of (and not only the Jesus movement) *both* reached for traditional patterns *and* criticized the established institutions (or wanted to assert popular control of them). It was not simply a matter of the Jesus movement versus the rest of society, but of the "renewal" groups generally over against the ruling groups, particularly the priestly aristocracy.

7. E. P. Sanders has revived the old hypothesis that Jesus anticipated a rebuilt Temple (*Jesus and Judaism* [Philadelphia: Fortress, 1985] chs 2–3); but the prophetic and apocalyptic texts he adduces do not provide evidence for his claim of such an expectation in "Judaism." See further Horsley, *Jesus and the Spiral of Violence*, 289–91.

8. See the argument in *Jesus and the Spiral of Violence*, esp. the "Conclusion."

9. See the discussion of the modern misconception of the Zealot movement in ch 3 above.

10. J. Kloppenborg, *The Formation of Q* (Philadelphia: Fortress, 1987) 195.

11. M. Weber, *The Theory of Social and Economic Organization* (New York: Free Press, 1947) 358–59; see comments by T. Parsons, "Introduction," to M. Weber, *The Sociology of Religion* (Boston: Beacon, 1963) xxxiii–xxxiv; and more recently Kojiro Miyahara, "Charisma: From Weber to Contemporary Sociology," *Sociological Inquiry* 53 (1983) 368–88.

12. The following is based on Worsley's "Introduction to the Second Edition: Theoretical and Methodological Considerations," to *The Trumpet Shall Sound* (New York: Schocken, 1968) esp. xii–xviii.

13. J. Gager (*Kingdom and Community* [Englewood Cliffs, NJ: Prentice-Hall, 1975] 28–29) has already made this same point, based on Worsley. Bruce Malina ("Jesus as a Charismatic Leader?" *Biblical Theology Bulletin* 14 [1984] 55–62), while sharply rejecting Weber's concept of charisma as inapplicable to Jesus, derives from Durkheim an alternative similar to that offered by Worsley.

14. Worsley, "Introduction," *The Trumpet Shall Sound*, xviii.

15. Kloppenborg, *Formation of Q*, e.g., 167–68.

16. See further Mack, *Myth of Innocence*, 91–93, 217–18, 222–24.

17. See further Horsley, "'Like One of the Prophets of Old': Two Types of Popular Prophets at the Time of Jesus," *Catholic Biblical Quarterly* 47 (1985) 435–63; or *Bandits, Prophets, and Messiahs*, ch 4.

18. Martin Hengel, *The Charismatic Leader and His Followers* (New York: Crossroad, 1981) 16.

19. Ibid., 73.

20. Indeed, Hengel is at pains to avoid any possible misunderstanding of Jesus as having any sort of *political* agenda or implication.

21. Ironically, this leads him to portray the "meaningful task" to which Jesus called his disciples as very similar to the participation in the "eschatological event" to which the popular prophets such as Theudas and the "Egyptian" called their followers.

22. See the discussion of the frequent misreading of this text in Horsley, *Jesus and the Spiral of Violence*, 200–206.

◇ Appendix A
The Conflicting Orientations of Functionalism and the Jesus Movement _____

It is finally being recognized that social science is not "value free." Ironically, however, until very recently the academic ideal of "value free" inquiry may have been an important aspect of the value commitment of established Western social science. When we consider borrowing a particular sociological method, therefore, we must be prepared to recognize that it is both rooted in and tends to perpetuate a particular value orientation and view of the world. That is, not only may a particular social scientific method be problematic, such that its use may distort certain historical materials, but its very value orientation may run counter to that historical material. Indeed, if the Jesus movement is viewed from a non- (or less-)functionalist perspective, then certain fundamental conflicts emerge between this particular modern method and that particular historical movement. The following comparison is heavily dependent on the broad-ranging critique of functionalist sociology articulated twenty to thirty years ago by a number of established sociologists, particularly by Alvin Gouldner in *The Coming Crisis of Western Sociology*.[1] The sketch that follows will be brief and, partly because of that, oversimplified. It is meant to be suggestive, even provocative, in order to pose serious questions of ourselves as we move into ever greater use of the social sciences in study of early Christianity and the New Testament.

In his critical account of the origin and theoretical construction of structural-functionalism, Gouldner finds that with Marx and Comte Western sociology split into two theoretically and institutionally differentiated traditions. Marxian sociology made a fundamental rupture with all previous social theory, which since Plato had addressed and sought the support of the socially dominant strata, and opted for popular self-determination and development. It argued that the internal contradictions of modern society constituted "the seeds of its own destruction"

147

and sought both to understand and to produce that social transformation. Focusing on the historical variability of power and property arrangements, Marxist sociologists criticized modern society in the name of people's potentialities and their possible fulfillment.

The tradition which, beginning with Comte and Durkheim, developed into American academic sociology under the dominant influence of Parsons and his students in the 1950s was the product of and committed to the "middle class" and its popular utilitarianism. As Gouldner explains, Comte, like Saint-Simon before him, had clearly discerned the disintegrating social effects of nascent capitalism and the divisive effects of the industrial division of labor on social cohesion.[2] In order to distance his sociology from socialism, however, Durkheim focused not only on the forced division of labor but on *anomie* and the importance of morality for social order. Following in this tradition, structural-functional sociology has maintained that the problem of social order could be dealt with apart from the problems of technological development, economic institutions, and property arrangements. Functionalism focused instead on moral values and norms as the source for social order, insisting that no basic change in industrialization and its capitalist structure of property and power would be required. For any problems created by the system it sought solutions that would be compatible with the system.

Parsons began constructing the theoretical system of structural-functional sociology during the 1930s, when the modern capitalist economic system had apparently broken down. But, far from calling any aspects of the system into serious question, he looked to religious convictions, moral values, and social norms as the necessary sources of social order. The solution to social conflicts lies in morality and not in structural change.[3]

This critical historical perspective on structural-functionalism suggests that it is in fact not simply an "approach" but in fact embodies a particular worldview, a commitment to and an apology for a particular set of values or a particular orientation toward the world.[4] But favoring any particular view of the world ignores or even blocks other, alternative ways of viewing or understanding reality. As a particular view of the world, functionalism simply misses or cannot comprehend certain data (which, for non-adherents, would make it a poor "hypothesis" about social realities, that is, unable to handle the data). More seriously, its own inherent values may even be opposed to the values inherent in the historical material (the Synoptic Gospel and other biblical traditions) to which Theissen and others have applied it. Thus, interpretations of the Jesus movement in functionalist terms would surely tend to transform the historical realities into something more compatible with the kind of social structure favored by functionalism. The key issue for Theissen's functionalist agenda is how early Christianity met (or did not meet) the needs of society for integration and stability. But as Elliott points out, "the Jesus movement related not so much to the needs of the *system* as to the needs of *people* [emphasis his], particularly . . . those trapped and crushed by the system."[5] It is important, therefore, to discern certain important facets of the functionalist worldview and how those may conflict with values expressed in the Synoptic Gospel tradition and the Jesus movement.

As Gouldner suggests, functionalists appear to believe that the social system is fundamentally good—hence to be integrated and maintained. The social realities or subsystems that make up the whole are also basically good; they are "functional" for the society as a whole, or for the best, whatever their appearance. (The task of the sociologists, of course, is to figure out and explain how this is so—a role that we might have described as "religious" in historical societies.) Besides slighting economic problems, functionalists tend not to raise the possibility that certain political or social arrangements might be "exploitative."[6] Theissen, of course, simply cannot avoid the evidence that the combination of Roman and Jewish taxation in Jewish Palestine was burdensome. Nevertheless, when he comes to a summary of the "social-economic" factor, the "phenomenon" of which is *voluntary* rootlessness anyhow, he focuses on the threat to "the middle classes" and to "traditional values and norms" posed by "the upward and downward trends within society" caused by the basically positive consequences that the *pax Romana* had for Palestine in terms of trade and commerce. But trade and commerce were conducted by the Roman and Jewish ruling elites on the basis of the tithes and tribute taken from the peasant producers. The view that social realities were structured as they should be was highly "functional" for the rulers. But the Jesus movement apparently took a far more critical stance toward those same social realities.

Corresponding to its treatment of social realities as fundamentally good, it is difficult to find any sense of serious evil in functionalist sociology. Historians of Christian thought will be aware of a somewhat similar view. Adapting ancient Platonic thought, Augustine viewed evil as not real itself, but rather as the absence or privation of good. For functionalism, social phenomena are not evil, but merely fail to fulfill their (predetermined) function, or they are dysfunctional—all particular social phenomena being seen from the point of view of the stability or integration of the society as a whole. However much functionalism's lack of value-judgment may be rationalized as "value-free" social scientific objectivity, it is not difficult to discern the underlying commitment to the established order. This can be seen in what Theissen's analysis turns up as dysfunctional. Thus, the effort to *integrate* Jewish Palestinian society into the Roman Empire failed[7] (no mention of how "functional" or "persuasive" the violent Roman methods of conquest, slaughter, and enslavement may have been); and the Jesus movement failed to fulfill its supposed function of controlling aggression in Jewish society (no mention of the Jesus movement's sharply judgmental prophecies against the supposedly integrative institutions of Temple and high priesthood). But there is virtually no historical evidence that either of those hypothetical efforts toward integration and control of conflict was ever undertaken. The functionalist faith in the absence of evil has imposed generalizations that are virtually the opposite of the historical realities.

In stark contrast with the modern functionalist "metaphysics," however, the Jesus movement's own traditions viewed evil as vividly real, symbolized, for example, as demonic forces that distorted or even controlled personal and social life. Perhaps we can explain why Theissen can draw heavily on sayings in the "mission discourse" as evidence for the central "role" of wandering charismatics while totally ignoring the demon-exorcism "function" of those very charismatics in the same sayings by the functionalist assumption of the absence of evil. In this regard as well, functionalism would appear to be sharply at variance with the worldview expressed in certain biblical literature, which takes the realities of evil and sin, both individual and social-institutional, with utmost seriousness.

With functionalism focused on stability and order as its central values, it is not surprising that it is uneasy about change, particularly structural change. The Jesus movement, like the (biblical) prophetic and historical traditions of Israel, advocated and embodied divine judgment on the established order and divinely inspired or effected revolutionary change. Of course, as objective modern social scientists, functionalists could dismiss the Jesus movement's revolutionary prophecies of judgment and renewal as the mere "intentions" (as opposed to the functions or effects) of the wandering charismatics. Apparently "mythological fantasies" were, like demons and evil, quite unreal and valuable only in their "function" of aiding frustrated "outsiders" to work off their alienations so that they did not seriously disrupt or structurally challenge the fundamentally good social order. A reading of Karl Mannheim's *Ideology and Utopia* might have helped the functionalists to appreciate the historical "function" of "utopian" ideas. Even the ancient Jewish rabbis recognized the revolutionary potential of the apocalyptic mentality, which is one reason why they suppressed apocalyptic literature, before it inspired any more disruptive challenges to the established social order and evoked any more devastating reconquests by Roman military might.

As can be seen from the illustrations in the previous paragraph, functionalism provides a basis for criticism of the effectiveness of social institutions and phenomena (in maintaining societal equilibrium, that is); but it is a limited criticism, because the functionalist worldview provides a legitimation of or an apology for the very institutions or phenomena to be criticized. Society, it is assumed, has certain "needs" or "requisites" (and these are universal!), such as order and integration. Thus, criticism focuses not on the Roman or Herodian brutality that caused extensive suffering and hardship but on the failure to integrate a conquered society into the empire. And it is somehow the Jesus movement that failed to head off the Jewish revolt of 66–70, rather than the oppressive policies and practices of the imperial system and the predatory behavior of Roman procurators and Jewish high priests that may have brought Palestinian Jews to such a state of desperation. Functionalism is oriented to an administrated society: the principal political problem in Palestine was that Rome failed to fashion balanced, non-overlapping and non-competitive structures of government. By contrast, the Jesus movement's criticism of the dominant social institutions is radical: God's judgment is proclaimed against them. Indeed, the movement is apparently motivated by the conviction that God is imminently to overthrow the oppressive established order as the kingdom of God is fully realized. Nor did Paul and others in the Hellenistic churches back away from that conviction (e.g., 1 Cor 15:20–28; Rom 8:18–25; 12:14–21; 1 Pet 4:12–19; Rev 17–18).

According to the functionalist worldview, in effect, people's humanity is constituted by society: no society, no humanity. Gouldner compares functionalism to Platonism in this as in other regards. In Platonism, the good and the real lie in the eternal world of forms. Actual people achieve genuine humanity when they copy or approximate the eternal forms or ideas. For functionalism, the good and real lie in society. Actual people become human as they internalize values and norms from society and play out their designated roles in society. In the context of Theissen's functionalist assumptions about humanity, the behavior of the "wandering charismatics" was radical indeed. In abandoning family, home, protection, and particularly traditional norms such as honoring parents, the itinerants were virtually abandoning their humanity. It is understandable that functionalist analysis would discover that a "movement" of such anti-social vagabonds would have no "function" in their society, but would only serve as transmitters of "what was later to take independent form as Christianity."[8] Ironically, the Cynic philosophers, who apparently serve as Theissen's model for the "wandering charismatics," thought that the only way to realize true humanity was to be free of corrupting society and its roles and expectations. The Jesus movement, of course, held that it was necessary (and imminently inevitable) to replace the established order with a new society of justice and love. But for functionalism, society is something *over* people into which they fit or should be made to fit.[9]

In its concern for the order and integration for society as a whole, functionalism makes the mechanisms by which people are made to want what the social system requires seem natural and acceptable. Often expressed in terms of organismic imagery, such mechanisms of social control are understood as fulfillments of universal social requisites of society as such and as basically good. Theissen, to his credit, is more sophisticated than some functionalists insofar as he perceives that in some cases the "intensification of norms" could have a divisive rather than an integrative function within society. Nevertheless, when he comes to the question of the "function" of the Jesus movement, he focuses almost exclusively on how it could serve as a mechanism of social control by containing aggression and overcoming social tensions (ch IX). As noted above (ch 3), critical analysis of expressions of the Jesus movement does not bear out Theissen's claim about the "introjection of aggression." Again functionalist concerns are projected onto ancient historical materials with the effect of making them appear almost the opposite of what they were. The effects of the Jesus movement in Palestine were to avoid or even to challenge the mechanisms of social control, not to supplement them. If the civil rights movement in the United States or conversations with third world churches had not already opened the eyes of biblical scholars, then feminist criticism has surely made the point that the social system's traditional mechanisms of social control can also serve as mechanisms of domination.

Closely related to the last point, as Gouldner explains, functionalism, like Platonism, understands values as "transmissibles rather than emergents." Values are conceived of as coming from outside and above people, on whom they are imprinted by means of certain social mechanisms. One can see how this would work in Palestinian Jewish society via the social position and roles of the scribes who maintained the "official tradition" and in those of the Pharisees and other retainers who interpreted and applied the Torah in the towns and villages. One can also see this mechanism working in the traditional scholarly picture (or caricature) of "the Pharisees" as scrupulously concerned for practice of "the law." But the Jesus movement would appear to have had just the opposite sense of values, that is, as – certainly in effect – emergents (directly from inspiration or instruction by God or Jesus) as opposed to transmissibles (from the social traditions). "Why do your disciples not live according to the tradition of the elders?" "There is nothing outside a man which by going into him can defile him; but the things which come out of a man are what defile him" (Mark 7:5, 15; and compare the motivations in Matt 5:22, 28). The Jesus movement was apparently practicing a spontaneity of social interaction, a directness of interpersonal expression concerned with both motivation and effects, that did not abandon the Torah but understood it at a popular level, which thus threatened or replaced the institutionalized mechanisms of social control, that is, through the Pharisees and other official interpreters.

Its own central concern for social control and integration, including the belief that values are imprinted by society on its members by means of mechanisms of social control, means that functionalism is really at a loss to explain not only how values can change or how alternative values can emerge but also how values develop in the first place. Functionalism is concerned that social tensions and conflicts be controlled, or at least that social conflict have "functions" for the ultimate integration or equilibrium of society.[10] With the benefit of historical perspective and analysis, which (we have seen) is not important in functionalism, it becomes evident that values develop and change historically through conflict. Biblical history is full of just such conflicts, such as the exodus; and the Jesus movement itself is surely an expression of the emergence of new values precisely through intense social conflict. Functionalism would appear simply uninterested in understanding the historically *new*, such as the "breakthrough" that happened in "early Palestinian Christianity" and survived literarily in the Synoptic Gospel tradition.

Functionalism assumes a defensive posture toward reality. The basic problem is *anomie*, for which the solution is to bolster morality. In his functionalist worldview (compounded in this case by his literalist reading of texts), Theissen is thus predisposed to see the Jesus tradition and its itinerant carriers in terms of abandonment or lack of traditional values and norms.[11] Again functionalism tends to transform historical realities into their virtual opposites. It was not the Jesus movement but Herod and the priestly aristocracy who abandoned traditional Jewish-biblical values and norms—and whose oppressive and sometimes even predatory behavior was inducing suffering and disorder. The Jesus movement involved not abandonment or lack but intense commitment to the renewal of traditional values: "Thy kingdom come, thy will be done." The values implicit in the memory of the exodus, for example, were liberation from alien domination and independence of the people under the direct rule of God. God's concern had traditionally been for the oppressed, and that concern was now manifest again in the preaching of the kingdom:

"Blessed are the poor. Blessed are those who hunger." Those whom Theissen views as vagabonds who abandoned the traditional way of life were rather those who believed themselves commissioned to proclaim and manifest (in healings) the presence of God's new liberating and restorative activity (the kingdom). Indeed, the Jesus movement directly addressed *anomie:* the disintegration of social forms at the local community level. But because the revitalization of local communities that constituted "early Palestinian Christianity" was taking place over against the ruling hierarchy, the Jesus movement involved not a lack or abandonment of the integrative values but a deliberate revolt against the dominating central institutions of the Jewish "temple-state" in Roman-ruled Palestine.

At one point in his critique of functionalism, Gouldner offers a capsule summary of how the worldview or value commitments of functionalism determined its approach to the principal problems of modern society:

> Its solution was to say, in effect, that the problem of social order could be solved *apart* from questions of economic institutions and technological levels. The problem could, that is, somehow be solved solely in terms of *morality as such*, and thus would not require basic changes in industrialization or in its capitalist structure.[12]

Now we can almost paraphrase that summary for how Theissen's functionalist assumptions determine his analysis and presentation in *The Sociology of Early Palestinian Christianity:* His solution is to say, in effect, that the problem of rootlessness and social conflicts was solved *apart* from the economic exploitation by means of the political domination of the people by the ruling elites. Even though the Jesus movement in Palestine failed, the problem was solved solely in terms of *morality as such*, such as the "love-patriarchalism" of Hellenistic Christianity, and thus did not require basic changes in the structure and practice of economic exploitation and imperial rule.

But neither in its intention nor in its function did the Jesus movement help solve the problem of social order in the way Theissen conceives of it. The Jesus movement rather both envisioned and, to a degree, realized an independent and revitalized local social order. It emphasized freedom and justice over against hierarchical social order and domination. Its members lived in social spontaneity, instead of according to heteronomously propagated norms, and manifested a creativity that disrupted the established social order. The Jesus movement proclaimed God's overcoming of the old unjust and unfree order and insisted on the possibility of free, just, even creative personal and social life.

Notes

1. Besides the books by Gouldner, Harris, and Turner mentioned in the notes to chs 1 and 2 above, see particularly R. Dahrendorf, "Out of Utopia," *American Journal of Sociology* 64 (1958) 115–27; and A. Giddens, "Functionalism: Après la Lutte," in *Studies in Social and Political Theory* (New York: Basic Books, 1977) 96–134.

2. Gouldner, *Coming Crisis*, 111–13, 141–47, 250.

3. Ibid., 250, 141–47. It should not be surprising that those professionally invested in religion, theology, or morality found functionalism highly attractive, with the central place it has for religion and morality, considering that at least established religion had been consistently under attack and had experienced a steady reduction in its prestige, roles, and function ever since the Enlightenment.

4. This may be rooted in modern utilitarian culture, which both tends to break down traditional "mappings" of the world and yet is highly concerned about situating things contextually in terms of the consequences. "One implicit task of sociology in the modern world is not simply to study society but to conceptualize and *order* it. . . . Much of sociology . . . is engaged in constituting social worlds, rather than simply in researching them" (Gouldner, *Coming Crisis*, 84).

5. John H. Elliott, "Social Scientific Criticism of the New Testament: More on Methods and Models," *Semeia* 35 (1986) 22.

6. "Functionalism dodged the problem of 'exploitation'. . . . Functionalism served to defend existing social arrangements on *nontraditional* grounds, against the criticism that they were based on power or force" (Gouldner, *Coming Crisis*, 124).

7. Theissen, "Legitimation and Subsistence: An Essay on the Sociology of Early Christian Missionaries," in *The Social Setting of Pauline Christianity* (Philadelphia: Fortress, 1982) 29.

8. Theissen, *Sociology*, 8.

9. Gouldner, *Coming Crisis*, 420.

10. Lewis Coser, *The Functions of Social Conflict* (Glencoe: Free Press, 1956).

11. He even uses the language of "socially deviant behavior . . . estranged from society's fundamental norms and necessities" ("Legitimation and Subsistence," 27–30).

12. Gouldner, *Coming Crisis*, 250.

◊ Appendix B
The Limitations and Utility
of Conflict Theory _____

Given the serious problems of functionalist sociology as an approach to the Jesus movement, it is tempting to reach for conflict theory as an alternative. While the recent development of conflict theory has roots in both Marx, who emphasized the divisiveness of conflict, and Georg Simmel, who emphasized the integrative consequences of conflict, its reformulation in the 1950s and 1960s was in direct response to the perceived inadequacies of functionalism.[1] Theissen claims to be using conflict theory at certain points (114), but the description of what he means is simply a repetition of what he explained as functionalist theory in the introduction to Part Three. Moreover, it is clear that Theissen understands conflict theory as a subcategory of functionalism—in a way evoked by the title of Lewis Coser's book, *The Functions of Social Conflict.*[2] Since Theissen gives no evidence of actually having applied conflict theory, it may be useful to explore its potential utility for understanding the Jesus movement. Since Coser is clearly attempting to adjust structural-functionalism itself, to explain how conflict can actually be functional for the integration and order of a social system, we will focus primarily on the work of Dahrendorf, who formulated his theory more directly in opposition to Parsons and other functionalists.[3]

Whereas structural-functionalism assumes that social order rests in a common set of values shared by members of society, Dahrendorf holds that social order is the result of coercion and constraint of some members by others. A few are in positions of "domination"; the rest are in positions of "subjection." A differential distribution of power and authority is the determining factor of systematic social conflicts. "The structural origin of such group conflicts must be sought in the arrangement of social roles endowed with expectations of domination or subjection" (165).

While structural-functionalists such as Parsons deal primarily with the social organizations that comprise the parts of the social whole as "social systems," Dahrendorf finds that the relevant analytical unit is what Weber labeled a *Herrschaftsverband*, or "imperatively coordinated association."[4] This concept of an association can refer to almost any social organization, although the focus is on the state and the industrial enterprise because of their empirical significance (168). Dahrendorf maintains that in the relations of domination and subordination, authority is not generalized control over others. He is thinking, of course, in terms of advanced industrial democratic societies such as the United States or West Germany in which there are separate associations of state, industry, and church. "It is conceivable that the ruling and the subjected groups of each of these associations are largely separate aggregations" (214). In such associations the authority relations involve an understanding of who is subject to control and of the particular area in which control is to be expected.

Dahrendorf conceives of conflict as taking place primarily within imperatively coordinated associations. Since conflict has its structural origin in the differential distributions of power and authority, it is important to understand the dynamics of these arrangements. For his source of understanding power and authority, Dahrendorf draws on Weber once again. Power is the "probability that one actor within a social relationship will be in a position to carry out his own will despite resistance, regardless of the basis on which this probability rests." Authority, on the other hand, is the "probability that a command with a given specific content will be obeyed by given group of persons."[5] The crucial difference is that authority is tied to certain social positions or roles. Power is simply a factual relation, whereas authority involves the legitimacy of the relation of domination and subjection. "Authority can be described as legitimate power" (166). Persons in positions of authority or domination are expected to control those in subordinate positions by such means as commands and warnings. Noncompliance is usually sanctioned, and the legal system usually serves to support effective exercise of domination, i.e., the authority relations that it helps legitimate.

The next step in Dahrendorf's conflict theory is that "the occupants of positions of domination and the occupants of positions of subjection hold, by virtue of these positions, certain interests which are contradictory in substance and direction" (174). This concept of differential and conflicting interests is his way of articulating the necessary assumption that the orientations of the actions of incumbents of defined positions are structurally generated (175). The concept of interests in itself is independent of the question of the consciousness or articulation of those interests. As long as the interests are not conscious, they are simply *latent*. When they become conscious goals, they are *manifest interests* (178). Perhaps because of an obsession with being scientifically "objective,"

Dahrendorf articulates an almost purely formal definition of interests. He insists that the concept implies nothing about the substance of the interests; they are simply "interests in the maintenance or modification of a *status quo*" (176). Those in positions of domination have "an interest in the maintenance of a social structure that for them conveys authority," whereas those in a position of subjection have "an interest in changing a social condition that deprives its incumbents of authority" (176).

Conflict takes social form in groups, which are not just any collectivity but masses of people in regular contact and having a recognizable structure. *Quasi groups* form the recruiting field for *interest groups*, the real agents of conflict, which have identifiable members, specific forms of organization, and programs of goals. Among the great variety of interest groups, including chess clubs or football teams, those whose *interests* are connected to the legitimacy of relations of domination and subjection, such as trade unions and political parties, are directly related to social conflict (180–81). *Conflict groups*, those that actually participate in social conflict, form as interest groups, make their interests manifest, and take action under certain social and political conditions (182–88).

Less Idyllic but Also Problematic

In its fundamental assumption that coercion is the basis of social order, conflict theory would appear to be far more appropriate than functionalism to biblical literature and history. Domination, coercion, and subjection are prominent themes in biblical material, whether in the paradigmatic exodus story or in the classical prophetic harangues against oppressive rulers or in Jesus' conflicts with the Jewish and Roman "authorities." Conflict theory, moreover, would appear to be more appropriate to the multiform social conflicts that Theissen himself found in Palestinian Jewish society than was his own abstract scheme of "factors."[6] In contrast to the idyllic functionalist picture, society is divided between those who dominate and those who are dominated, each group having its own respective and structurally conflicting interests. Groups form to assert their own interests against others who would resist in order to assert their own interests. The Jesus movement, seen in Theissen's "functional outline" to have been working to contain tensions by internalizing aggressions, would be understood in conflict theory as a "conflict group" making the subjected people's latent interests manifest.

Conflict theory, however, may also be problematic as an approach and as social theory.[7] It is unclear just what relation conflict theory may have with actual analysis of societies. Dahrendorf appears to proceed mainly by definition of his assumptions about society and its key components, "imperatively coordinated associations."[8] The principal conceptual components of the theory are defined so broadly and generally that "instances" can be found anywhere and everywhere, which severely limit their value for empirical investigation and certainly for historical analysis. It is difficult to move from such broad conceptual definitions of assumptions to explanation of social realities.

Ironically, "conflict" theory cannot explain the origins of social conflict. It has its source in the institutionalized authority relations of imperatively coordinated associations. Thus, conflict is conceived of as arising from the very thing that provides the integration and coherence of society, institutionalized authority relations. Such a theory has limited explanatory potential.

Perhaps the basic problem is that conflict theory never really separated itself from the functionalism against which it was reacting. Indeed, often Dahrendorf's assertions read like the mirror images (in the sense of reversals) of functionalist assumptions and assertions or appear to be simply the same basic concepts in somewhat variant form. Both are oriented toward social structures and institutions. Society is comprised of institutionalized patterns; Dahrendorf's "imperatively coordinated associations" correspond to the Parsonsian "social systems." Roles in these "associations/systems" are organized according to legitimated normative patterns. Both understand power in terms of the legitimation of some roles in determining the patterns of others' roles. Indeed, Dahrendorf in effect understands conflict as a "functional requisite" of society. Authority is necessary for integration of society; but the conflict that originates in authority relations is also "functional" insofar as it leads to the social change that maintains the vitality of society.

To these general criticisms of conflict theory, many of which are common in sociological circles, must be added more specific criticisms of how limited Dahrendorf's conflict theory is for historical analysis.

(a) That multiple "imperatively coordinated associations" are the relevant unit of analysis is an utter anachronism for ancient Jewish Palestine or any other traditional agrarian society. Dahrendorf developed his theory specifically for "industrial society," as his title indicates. But the social order of most traditional societies was not pluralistic and there were few important associations. As explained above, in the "temple-state" of Judea there was as yet no structural differentiation between religious, political, and economic institutions. Similarly, it is not clear that the people's "roles" were all that differentiated either. This has obvious implications for Dahrendorf's assertion that there is no generalized control in society. In a society such as the ancient Judean temple-state, in which there is no difference between the state, the "church," and the centralized economic organization of the society (in this case, the Temple), then authority relations of domination and subordination do involve generalized control (by the high priestly rulers). It is not difficult to imagine that there could also be implications for the way conflict would be structured in a less differentiated and much less pluralistic society.[9]

(b) In its definition of *power and authority relations*, conflict theory may be as parochial and limited in its perspective as is the functionalism it attempts to complement. Like the structural-functionalists, Dahrendorf is of no help whatever in dealing with conflicts involving other societies. He carefully delimits the scope of social-historical reality he is willing to deal with: "In the present study we are concerned exclusively with relations of authority, for these alone are part of the social structure and therefore permit the systematic derivation of group conflicts from the organization of total societies and associations within them." But some of the most intense and destructive social conflict in modern history has arisen not from authority relations of legitimate domination and subjection, but from the exercise of naked power, whether within a society or between societies.

Perhaps more to the point, Dahrendorf is conveniently leaving out of account imperial or neocolonial relations in which the *power* exercised by the conquering society or regime both overlays and compromises the authority relationships within the conquered society. Historically when one society, or its ruling elite, conquered another, it usually did so by means of military power (including often a superior military technology or technique), carrying out its will despite resistance (to paraphrase Weber). In modern times, of course, equally effective and devastating conquest and domination are carried out by economic means. If the conquering regime (or multinational corporation) then ruled through a puppet or client regime of its own making, it would have been difficult, or would have taken some time, for that regime to attain some degree of "legitimacy" in relationship with the conquered people. According to Dahrendorf's (or Weber's) own definition of power and authority, then, much of the basic conflict in historically colonized and in modern "third world" countries would be rooted in relations of domination based on power, not authority (and Dahrendorf's analysis of authority relations may be largely inapplicable). Even if the imperial society attempted to rule indirectly through the *authorities* of the subjected society, that power relationship seriously strained or compromised the legitimacy of those native authorities. If conflicts emerge from *authority* relations which enjoy legitimacy, how much more are they likely to result from power relationships. Indeed, Weber's concept of power, "one actor . . . carrying out his will despite resistance," is already, by definition, conflict. Any social theory adequate to "all societies under all historical conditions" (Dahrendorf's phrase) must be able to accommodate conflicts resulting from *power* relations as well as the corresponding implications those power relations may have for authority relations on which they impact.

Finally, it obfuscates social relations (in favor of the established powerholders) to pretend that power and authority are all that distinct, as if once legitimate *authority* was present, *power* was no longer operating. Two closely related points that Gouldner makes against Parsons's concept of power are also directly pertinent to Dahrendorf's conflict theory as well. (i) Power and authority are more like dual structures, "both *simultaneously* present, in subtle and continual interaction." The ability of the powerful to withhold at will things that the subordinates want, even though they have no right to do so, influences the servile and dependent attitudes that subordinates often develop toward superiors. "Legitimacy and 'authority' never eliminate power; they merely defocalize it, make it latent. How could 'authority' eliminate power when authority is not merely some unanchored 'legitimacy,' but the legitimacy of *power.*"[10] (ii) Power can shape morality and legitimacy. "In any given case, what is moral is often uncertain, frequently disputed, and invariably resolved in a situation where some have more power than others. Those with more power therefore exert more influence . . . , they define what is moral."[11]

(c) Dahrendorf's *concept of interests* is of limited utility for historical analysis because it is strictly formal. Such a formal concept of interests, moreover, reduces the individual and the collective bodily and psychological aspects of human life to insignificance. Indeed, it would appear that by articulating such a formal concept, Dahrendorf has not only vitiated the potential usefulness of the very concept of interests but obscured the dynamics of social conflict as well. After rejecting the more substantive concept of "pleasure principle" as a way of elucidating "the important notion of socially structured conflicts of interest," he then insists that the respective "objective" interests of the dominant and the subjected are strictly analogous to the objective "role expectations" in functionalist theory (176). Just as persons occupying certain social roles pursue certain "patterned expectations defining the *proper* behavior of persons playing certain roles,"[12] so people find their interests inherent in their positions of either domination or subjection. But Dahrendorf blocks the usefulness of the concept of interests as either latent or manifest and its possible juxtaposition with the concept of legitimacy (of authority relations) by pressing such a formal definition, saying, for example, that a person "behaves in an 'adapted' or 'adjusted' manner if he contributes to the conflict of contradictory interests rather than to the integration of the social system" (178).

(d) Dahrendorf's abstract delineation of types of groups—albeit in sequence of quasi groups, interest groups, and conflict groups—obscures rather than elucidates the process of group formation and the dynamics of developing social conflict. But then this is just the most obvious of the many respects in which Dahrendorf's theory is not designed to accommodate or understand social dynamics. All of the key concepts are abstract and formal, and almost none of the key concepts is understood as variable. With regard to authority in particular, Dahrendorf even explicitly declines to develop a typology—that is, to consider, say, what types of authority with variable degrees of legitimacy and power might lead to what variations in domination and subjection, which in turn might lead to what kinds of opposed interests that might take variable modes of consciousness that in turn might lead to variations of conflict groups and outcomes of social conflict. Indeed, Dahrendorf's conflict theory seems as oblivious to history and historical change as does structural-functionalism, and it is therefore of limited usefulness as it stands for historical social analysis.

Using Some Reformulated Concepts

Despite Dahrendorf's limitations for historical analysis, however, it may be possible to adapt and reformulate some of his key concepts for some limited elucidation of the Jesus movement in its Palestinian Jewish historical context.

While Dahrendorf's discussion of authority relations is limited in its scope to modern industrial societies, the basic concept of legitimacy of power or authority is highly useful for understanding the continuing conflict in a traditional society under foreign domination, such as Jewish Palestine under Roman rule. As explained above, this concept of legitimacy, combined with a critical awareness of the history of relations between the Palestinian Jewish people and their "authorities" under the impact of alien imperial influence or conquest, makes far more understandable a whole series of covert or overt conflicts between the people or various popular movements and their political-economic-religious rulers, whose legitimacy had been increasingly compromised and diminished. This concept helps us *understand how* "the tension between the nominal theocracy and the *de facto* aristocracy became the breeding ground for radical theocratic movements" (Theissen, 59) such as the Jesus movement. To make conflict theory's concept of "authority relations" useful in this connection, however, we would have to do what Dahrendorf (169) declined to do in his static and apparently nonhistorical approach: treat "authority" as a variable and develop a typology of authority. It is likely that the compact traditional authority of the sacred aristocracy of a monistic temple-state would be fairly resilient beneath the impact of compromising conquest by and collaboration with imperial regimes and their client kings. On the other hand, the Jewish biblical tradition, which was known and cultivated among the people as well as by the sacerdotal authorities and their "retainers," included much that was highly critical of established authorities; surely the memories of such biblical traditions would have contributed to the criticism of high priestly authority among those who were supposedly expecting to be subjected.

The only way in which the concept of *interests* can be useful for sociological or historical analysis is if it is *related to the concept of legitimacy* and if both concepts are *variable* in some sort of *substantive* manner.

For example, in the traditional temple-state of Judea under the Hellenistic empires, the high priestly rulers and the peasants (along with the ordinary priests) surely had conflicting interests, the former in maintaining their traditional positions of power and privilege, and the latter in having to produce or render up less in the form of tithes and offerings. The interest of the subjected peasantry and ordinary priests, however, was *latent* insofar as they accepted the power relations as *legitimate*—that is, as established in the Torah and other sacred literature or traditions that articulated that the high priestly authorities were designated by God to receive the tithes, offerings, and other dues owed to God. The peasants and ordinary priests were "adjusted" members of the "imperatively coordinated association" (the temple-state, or Judean society) not insofar as they contributed to the conflict of contradictory interests but rather insofar as they accepted as legitimate the established power relations and brought their offerings and other dues to the Temple, which, of course, was behavior against their (still only latent) interests.

By 175 B.C.E., however, substantial numbers of the high priestly aristocracy, pursuing their cultural and personal interests but against their economic and political interests, abandoned or stepped completely outside of their traditional legitimating apparatus in executing a Hellenizing "reform," transforming the temple-state (themselves as the ruling priestly aristocracy) into a Hellenistic polis (themselves as the dominant citizen body). The result was intense and prolonged "social conflict": the Maccabean Revolt. One obvious way to explain the dynamics of the emergence of the revolt according to the concepts of conflict theory would be that the interests of the people became *manifest* as the power of the high priests became illegitimate. The vision in Daniel 7 of "one like a son of man coming with the clouds of heaven" meaning that God was about to give sovereignty to the people, suggests for some of the people at least that their interests were becoming manifest. As they became more conscious of their own interests they could no longer remain "adjusted" to the expectations of subjection to the previously legitimate power relations. Juxtaposed with the concept of a conflict of interests, the concept of "adjustment" would have to pertain to how subjected people acquiesce in the legitimacy of the established relations of authority (which is also pertinent to why their interests are still latent).

Of course in the case of the Maccabean Revolt, another analysis might provide a better explanation in terms of how Dahrendorf must be adapted to be at all applicable to imperial situations: the interests of the people remained *latent* insofar as they did not question the traditional legitimation of the high priesthood itself and they rebelled because their rulers' domination had become illegitimate, effected by blatant and alien power. This second analysis accounts better for the overall historical situation and subsequent events, especially considering that within twenty-five years of the outbreak of the revolt most of the people had apparently accepted the restoration of the high priesthood itself even with the (traditionally speaking) "illegitimate" non-Zadokite Hasmonean family as incumbents.

The importance of the concept of interests for analysis of the Jesus movement in the context of Palestinian Jewish society is that the multiform social conflict so evident in our sources can be understood not only as rooted in the social structure of domination and subjection but also as rooted in and driven by the "objective" interests of both the rulers and the ruled. The distinction between latent and manifest interest further enables us to discern that people, particularly the subjected, are often (perhaps ordinarily) not conscious of, let alone prepared to act in favor of, their own interests. This provides a highly useful critical analytical tool for literature which, as Theissen recognizes, contains little by way of explicit information about its producers or transmitters. It means that insofar as we can discern aspects of the (legitimate and nonlegitimate) power relations (the social structure of domination and subjection), we must take into account the respective interests of conflicting parties, while allowing for the possibility that they may not have been conscious of their own interests. For biblical scholars and others who are particularly concerned with religious institutions and expressions, which so often embody and articulate the rituals and ideologies of group/social cohesion or unification, the concept of conflicting interests provides a critical perspective completely lacking in the structural-functional approach. That is, insofar as religious expressions or institutions are usually involved in the legitimation of a society's power relations, we may suspect that the ideologies and rituals of legitimacy are expressions of the interests of the rulers, that those who occupy positions of domination also control the "redemptive media" in their own interest. At the very least, it should no longer be *assumed that*, but should be *critically investigated whether*, the extant written sources for the "religion" of a given society, including ancient Jewish society, reflect the understanding and interests of the ordinary people or simply those of the rulers and their governing apparatus.

Notes

1. See the exposition of "The Conflict Heritage" by Jonathan H. Turner, *The Structure of Sociological Theory* (Homewood, IL: Dorsey, 1974, 1978, 1982) ch 5.

2. G. Theissen, "Zur forschungsgeschichtlichen Einordnung der soziologische Frage-stellung," and "Theoretische Probleme religionssoziologischer Forschung und die Analyse des Urchristentums," in *Studien zur Soziologie des Urchristentums* (Tübingen: Mohr, 1979) 3–34, 55–76; Lewis A. Coser, *The Functions of Social Conflict* (Glencoe: Free Press, 1956).

3. Ralf Dahrendorf, *Class and Class-Conflict in Industrial Society* (Stanford, CA: Stanford University Press, 1959), to which references will be given in parentheses in the text. Concise exposition and criticism of both Coser and Dahrendorf can be found in Turner, *Structure*, chs 6–8.

4. Dahrendorf, *Class*, 167; Max Weber, *The Theory of Social and Economic Organization* (New York: Free Press, 1950) 153.

5. Weber, *Theory*, 152.

6. A similar conclusion, from a slightly different understanding of both conflict theory and the historical context, can be found in Bruce J. Malina, "A Conflict Approach to Mark 7," *Forum* 4/3 (1988) 13: "The conflict approach seems far more appropriate to the study of Mark and the rest of the New Testament . . . than the structural functionalist approach, if only because of the agonistic quality of Mediterranean social life."

7. Some of the most incisive criticisms of Dahrendorf are the following: Peter Weingart, "Beyond Parsons? A Critique of Ralf Dahrendorf's Conflict Theory," *Social Forces* 48 (1969) 151–65; Turner, *Structure*, 144–58.

8. Dahrendorf can lay out virtually the whole theory in a mere twenty-five pages (*Class*, 165–89).

9. See chs 4 and 5 above.

10. Gouldner, *Coming Crisis*, 294.

11. Ibid., 297.

12. Talcott Parsons, *Essays in Sociological Theory* (rev. ed.; Glencoe: Free Press, 1954) 61–62.

◊ Appendix C
Aggression and
God's Judgment _____

Theissen's argument that the "functional outline" of the Jesus movement was to control social conflict, besides ignoring the substantial evidence of conflict, is basically psychological: The Jesus movement contained social tensions through the introjection of aggression and the intensification of norms (*Sociology of Early Palestinian Christianity*, ch IX). If we pursue such a social-psychological approach more adequately, however, we arrive at conclusions very different from his. It is particularly important to correct two of the major problems of Theissen's analysis: First, he does not consider the actual symbolization of aggression in the best sources for the Jesus movement and, as a result, confuses the relational sequence between "the grace of God" and "the intensification of norms." Second, partly because he does not appreciate the fundamental social conflict in Palestine, he does not discern that the intensification of norms was part and parcel of a renewal of local community that rejected the established authoritative institutions.

Transference of Aggression and Alleviation of Anxiety

Theissen has not carefully attended to the actual "symbolization of aggression" in materials that are almost certainly good sources for the Jesus movement. This problem is compounded by his treatment of aggression as if it were an abstract general phenomenon and his highly schematic analysis of the ways in which aggression is channeled. An adequate analysis of how the Jesus movement dealt with "aggression" would require not only (a) a theory of the channeling of aggression (which Theissen has) but also (b) close attention to the particular ways in which aggression was symbolized in the sources, (c) some comparison with the ways aggression was symbolized in comparative material (other movements—strangely lacking in ch IX), and (d) understanding of particular forms of channeling of aggression in connection with the particular forms of channeling of aggression in connection with the particular concrete social relationships in which Palestinian Jews or members of the Jesus movement may have been involved.

Analysis of the particular symbolization of aggression according to this more complex procedure leads not only to conclusions different from those Theissen reaches but to different emphases with regard to the forms and channeling of aggression as well. Theissen clearly finds "the reversal of aggression" (introjection in the form of moral reproach and intensification of norms) the key to the "function" of the Jesus movement in its contribution to the overcoming of tensions in society (as noted and criticized in my chs 1 and 3 above). It turns out, however, that the "transference of aggression" in particular ways is more important than the "reversal" and that, although the Jesus movement "contained aggression" in certain ways, it did not contribute to "overcoming social tensions" in Jewish Palestine at all (as Theissen suggests in his conclusion in ch X as opposed to his agenda in ch IX). Although an adequate treatment of the issue would require examination of the texts (regarding symbolization of aggression) that Theissen omits, a few brief examinations of materials he does cite in ch IX may suffice to explore these alternatives to his conclusions.

(i) The "beatitudes" in Luke 6:20–22 (par. Matt 5:3–8) serve to *overcome* the poverty, hunger, depression, and persecution that are the *results of aggression* by others and the sources of resentment and aggression for the poor. Correspondingly, the "woes" (Luke 6:24–26) represent the *transference* of the subjects' own aggression to God's judgment, thus alleviating tension, anxiety, and counteraggression.

(ii) In the Gospel material regarding demon-possession and exorcism, the demons represent the *transference* of others' aggression to another subject, that is, to the demons (from, e.g., the Romans or oppressive Jewish rulers). The exorcism of demons represents the *transference* of an exorcised person's aggression to another subject, that is, to God or his agent Jesus—and it removes the source of others' aggression against the subject and brings about an alleviation of tension and anxiety ("If, by the finger of God, I cast out demons, then the kingdom of God has come upon you!").

What is taking place in these particular symbolizations of the channeling of aggression is the *removal* of the (source of) aggression from others and the alleviation of tensions and anxiety by means of the *transference* of (one's own) aggression. This removal of others' aggression and the transference of one's own counteraggression to God's judgment would appear to be almost the opposite of the introjection of aggression found by Theissen in the Jesus movement. Indeed, closer scrutiny of the reversal of aggression in materials from the Jesus movement throws Theissen's exposition further into doubt.

(iii) Theissen states that it was "introjected aggressiveness" that "turned into self-acceptance." Yet one of the most distinctive features of the Jesus movement was that it placed far less emphasis on the introjection of aggression than did the Pharisees or the Essenes, for example. With regard to the particular symbolization (and understanding) of sin and illness, for example, one receives the impression that Pharisees or others may have been teaching that illness was the result of one's own sin or one's parents' sin, that is, a case of the introjection of aggression. Jesus, by contrast, forgave sins as he healed illness (e.g., Mark 2:1–12), a case of self-acceptance and the opposite of the introjection of aggression. "Introjected aggressiveness" has not turned into anything. Those who were healed and received forgiveness were relieved of introjecting aggression.

(iv) Toward the conclusion of his discussion of the "reversal of aggression," Theissen claims that the Roman crucifixion of Jesus was a revelation not of Roman guilt but of Jesus' followers' own guilt (108). There is little or no evidence that the Jesus movement in Palestine believed that "Jesus had to die for our sins." There is a good deal of evidence, however, that the Jesus movement projected their own resentment or counteraggression against their oppressors or enemies into the judgment of God. That is, the *transference* not the introjection or reversal of aggression would have been the reason why the crucifixion of Jesus "did not call forth any rebelliousness against the Romans within the Jesus movement" (*contra* Theissen, 108).

We are led, therefore, to emphases and conclusions that stand in contrast with Theissen's. Far from the introjection of aggression through the intensification of norms being the key to understanding the function of the Jesus movement, the alleviation of others' aggression, the liberation from anxiety and from the introjection of aggression (sin, guilt), and the transference of their own counteraggression to God's judgment were the key ways of channeling aggression. Theissen himself had a sense of this in the otherwise isolated comment that "what was needed was a new relationship to all norms: putting trust and freedom from anxiety before demands of any kind" (107). However, in the actual symbolization of the channeling of aggression, and particularly through removal and the transference of aggression, the sequence of motivation and movement is virtually the opposite of the way Theissen states it. That is, a new vision of society could lead toward "the overcoming of aggression," or "the grace of God" became the motivation toward "fulfilling the intensified norms" (reversing Theissen's statements on p. 105). Whether in larger blocks of Gospel tradition such as the "Sermon" (on the Mount/Plain) or in particular sayings or actions of Jesus, the sequence is that the grace of God, which removes aggression and anxiety, *precedes and makes possible* the spontaneously accomplished "intensification of norms" and "ethical radicalism."

Intensification of Norms and Intensification of Social Conflict

Second, Theissen does not consider that "intensification of norms" in the Jesus movement would not necessarily have contributed to the alleviation of social conflict. Judging from Q and pre-Marcan materials, the Jesus movement was oriented around the restoration of Israel through the revitalization of local communities. The latter was precisely the purpose of the movement's intensification of norms. Members of the Jesus communities were to restore and/or maintain the fundamental familial and village relationships so that the "commandment of God" would be observed (Mark 7:9–13; 10:2–9, 10–11; cf. Matt 5:27–32). Members of Jesus communities were to take care of each other's essential economic needs and not be taking out their aggressions on each other, however difficult their concrete circumstances (Luke 6:27–36). Such were the fundamental concerns ("weightier matters," Luke 11:42; Matt 23:23) of justice or the Torah.

But such "intensification of norms" was not (or not simply) a matter of love versus "legalism." It apparently also involved a sense that "Israel" consisted fundamentally of local communities that should live under the direct rule of God and not be subject to exploitative centralized ruling institutions. Thus, the scribes, Pharisees, and lawyers, the "retainers" through whom the authorities "ruled," are sharply criticized not simply for their fastidious observance of finite "norms," but for neglecting the more fundamental matters of justice and for loading people with impossible (economic!) burdens (Luke 11:42, 46 par.) Correspondingly, community members are exhorted to work out their own conflicts rather than to resort to the official courts (Luke 12:57–59). In short, "the intensification of norms" in the Jesus movement was part and parcel of the renewal of local communities *and* involved a corresponding rejection of the authority of the established governing institutions. Far from taking the form of an introjection of aggression that resulted in self-blame, acceptance of the situation, and an overcoming of tension through "a vision of love and reconciliation," the Jesus movement sharpened its rejection of the ruling groups and institutions even as it practiced love and reconciliation in its own communities.

Theissen simply assumes that the function of religion is to contribute toward the overcoming of conflicts and the integration of society. It is not surprising therefore that, in a Palestinian Jewish society filled with tensions, he looks for the way in which a renewal movement contributes toward the overcoming of forms of aggression produced by those tensions. Theissen is theoretically correct, moreover, that the containment of aggression primarily through introjection would indeed have contributed toward "social balance" and have lent internal support to the efforts of governing groups to control social pressures. This, however, is clearly not what the Jesus movement did. It did not emphasize containment of aggression by introjection, but alleviation of anxiety by transference of aggression to God's agency. This is clearly indicated in the prominent symbolization of the grace and judgment of God. The Jesus movement proclaimed, and to a degree went about organizing, a new society based in local communities and under the direct and exclusive rule of God. It stood in schismatic tension with other renewal movements (as Theissen himself pointed out in ch VIII) and in direct opposition to the ruling groups of the "society." Indeed, the Jesus movement anticipated (and proclaimed) the termination of its aggressor opposition by means of the imminent judgment of God (or the Son of man). This sort of "religion" would not appear to be able to serve an integrative function for society. It rather persisted in its course of revitalizing or establishing local communities regardless of the consequences (persecution, etc.) for its participants.

Index _____